LASS ONION

BOOKS BY GEOFFREY GIULIANO

The Beatles: A Celebration

John Lennon: My Brother (written with Lennon's sister, Julia Baird)

Dark Horse: The Private Life of George Harrison

Blackbird: The Unauthorized Biography of Paul McCartney

The Beatles Album: Thirty Years of Music and Memorabilia

Rod Stewart: Vagabound Heart

The Rolling Stones Album: Thirty Years of Music and Memorabilia

The Illustrated Series

Paint It Black: The Murder of Brian Jones

The Lost Beatles Interviews

The Lost John Lennon Interviews

Behind Blue Eyes: A Life of Pete Townshend

Things We Said Today: Conversations with the Beatles

Two of Us: John Lennon and Paul McCartney Behind the Myth

Lennon in America 1971-1980

BOOKS BY VRNDA DEVI

Not Fade Away: The Rolling Stones Collection

The Illustrated Series

The Lost Beatles Interviews

The Lost John Lennon Interviews

Things We Said Today: Conversations with the Beatles

Geoffrey Giuliano and Vrnda Devi

THE BEATLES *in their own words*

GLASS ONION

exclusive interviews with

JOHN, PAUL, GEORGE, AND RINGO

and

THEIR INNER CIRCLE

DA CAPO PRESS

LIBRARY OF CONGRESS CATALOGING-IN-PUBLICATION DATA
Giuliano, Geoffrey.
    Glass onion : the Beatles in their own words : exclusive interviews with John, Paul, George, and Ringo and their inner circle / Geoffrey Giuliano and Vrnda Devi. — 1st ed.
        p.   cm.
    ISBN 0–306–80895–1 (pbk.)
    1. Beatles Interviews.   2. Rock musicians Quotations.   I. Devi, Vrnda.   II. Title.
ML421.B4A5   1999
782.42166'2—dc21
    [B]
                                                                                99–42570
                                                                                CIP

First Edition 1999

Published by Da Capo Press
A Member of the Perseus Books Group
http://www.dacapopress.com
1 2 3 4 5 6 7 8 9 10 — 03 02 01 00 99

CONTENTS

PART ONE
THE BEATLES
No One I Think Is in My Tree

PART TWO

JOHN LENNON

Always Smiling and Arriving Late for Tea

PART THREE
PAUL McCARTNEY
Will I Wait a Lonely Lifetime

PART FOUR
GEORGE HARRISON
It's Been a Long, Long, Long Time

PART FIVE
RINGO STARR AND PETE BEST
Dream Sweet Dreams

PART SIX
FAMILY
When You're Listening Late at Night

PART SEVEN
FRIENDS
Only a Northern Song

PART EIGHT

NEWSPAPER REPORTAGE

Though the News Was Rather Sad

Note: All pieces conducted by Geoffrey Giuliano are noted by the use of the author's first name in the interviews. The remainder of this book consists of either press conferences, press releases, or other "fair use" and public domain materials. A complete list of all sources has been kept on file by the authors.

To our Eternal Spiritual Master, His Divine Grace A. C. Bhaktivedanta Swami Prabhupada, who compassionately opened our eyes with the torchlight of knowledge. With love, affection, and deep devotion.

To Sesa Nichole Giuliano (Sri Devi Dasi), your lovely son, Kashi, and your new life.

To Devin Leigh Giuliano for surviving the fire.

To every lost, lonely, and hopeless person everywhere, all the answers are deep inside. Never give up!

To all the untold souls caught in the grip of addiction and madness of alcoholism and drugs, help is only a prayer away.

To the millions of innocent factory farm animals pitiously and need-lessly slaughtered everyday throughout the world. This heartless car-nage must cease before real peace can ever be achieved.

GEOFFREY GIULIANO
(JAGANNATHA DASA)
VRNDA DEVI

September 11, 1999
Jai Sri Sri Gaurunga Jayatah

FOREWORD

Being part of many of the Beatles' initial appearances at the Cavern in 1962, I realized early on just how important the boys had become to Liverpool. Later, of course, they were headline news nationally as well. Frankly, in this country, they all but swept away the tragic remorse many of us suffered in 1963 at the regrettable loss of President Kennedy. In those days the Beatles' incredible charisma enraptured even the older folks, who suddenly all seemed to be talking guitars and strings to one another. Silly as it seems now, you certainly wouldn't have found anything like that before. As far as the Beatles themselves were concerned, all this was still very much small beer in comparison to what might be achieved if only they could spread their wings in America. After all, in England their venues were strictly limited to perhaps a couple of thousand people, but in the States . . . well, just look at Shea Stadium! Invariably, they must have been stunned by the incredible hoopla that surrounded them, but they were driven on by an interminable one-way desire to succeed.

On the road it was George Harrison who was generally the most concerned about peeling off the correct licks in any given number, but, facing off against the absolute barrage of screams they encountered nightly, it was the canny Paul McCartney who advised the justifiably frustrated group to simply, "Go through the motions!" On record

When Giants Walked

surely the Beatles were *a sound,* but in concert mostly just *an image.* A truly fantastic image, though, remember that! Nowadays, I never cease to be amazed at the incredible number of books, records, videos, and the like that are continually issued in their name, and I often wonder how long it might go on. I mean, my God, it's already been more than thirty years since they first exploded on the Universe, and there's only the moon left to conquer, as it were! One group of fans I was addressing recently suggested the Beatles were "forever." Nothing is forever, of course, but some things do last a very, very long time. God speed!

BOB WOOLER*

September 1997

---

*Bob Wooler was the Beatles' original manager, compere, and a lovely man.

INTRODUCTION

"Now I know the only foe is time."
THE MOODY BLUES, "22,000 Days"

Today, the world in which we live is so incredibly boring, bland, and unexciting that one can hardly be blamed for looking back over one's shoulder at the unequaled artistry, affable lunacy, and spiritual poke-in-the-ribs that was the Beatles and company in their time. Like the antiquated "international man of mystery," Austin Powers, sometimes I too wonder where all the good sex, hip talk, and utopian pipe dreams we shared in the sixties have gone. Worse still is this anti-bacterial, republican world of squeaky clean rock stars, politically correct lesbian sitcoms, polite artworks, dirty minds, and over zealous cops and courts which has replaced it. Traveling into the unexplored corners of my brain on numerous occasions, I am always delighted to find such an outrageous cast of characters still lurking in memory. Here is an aging Salvador Dali throwing an anteater at Shelley Winters on the "The Mike Douglas Show" in 1971; the smokey TV image of Abbie Hoffman making David Frost so angry he could hardly speak; Charles Manson's various wide-eyed declarations back in '69 that he was nothing but the inevitable result of the pitiless incarceration he was forced to endure since his early teens and on and on. Now, circa 1998, we don't really talk, we e-mail, and what chat does manage to sneak through the Orwellian technology perched in our living rooms is all finely edited sound bites from smiling young people with neat haircuts and meticulous suits; one just as irreparably name-

Looking Through the Bent Back Tulips

less, faceless, and thoughtless as the other. Somewhere along the line, lawyers and accountants took the place of moviemakers and record producers; televangelists became serious presidential contenders; broken-down actors became world leaders; and airline stewardesses, movie stars. Gone are Lenny Bruce, George Carlin, and Dick Gregory, replaced not nearly as effectively by the questionable wit of Beavis and Butthead, Daisy Fuentes, and Kathie Lee Gifford. It's no accident that Jerry Seinfeld's famous sitcom about "nothing" became the biggest thing on toast. I saw a commercial the other day in which everything was frozen: the people walking down Wall Street, some guy flipping burgers in a greasy spoon, a contagion of yuppies playing tennis, and a couple of executive baby boomers driving along the ocean in their (no longer midsized) luxury car. I can't remember what they were selling, but the point was clear: we've smoothed out the wrinkles in ourselves and our world so effectively that nary a hair is out of place, button undone, zipper unzipped, dream left dangling, or unpopular word uttered. All is predictable, homogenized, government inspected, and of complete equanimity. Thus, American culture at the edge of the millennium beckons back not to the swinging, slightly dangerous 1960s, but rather to the flat-topped, buttoned-down, duck'n'cover, mind-your-p's-and-q's fifties of our goofy parents' generation. As someone said on TV last night, "The fifties have been indefinitely extended." These days Rosemary Clooney is Celine Dion is Tipper Gore is Geraldo Rivera is Katie Couric and so many other squares and pompous airheads too numerous to mention!

Likewise, if you want to burn a pile of leaves in your backyard in the autumn dusk, you risk immediate arrest. Starting a bonfire on the beach is now an environmental crime! Just last week one of Lockport, New York's Finest walked into my home uninvited, for no good reason, started swearing in front of my family, and refused to leave when asked to do so. The eternal madness, it seems, is everywhere.

All of which brings us back to the sanctity, sanity, unpredictability, wit, and courage of John Lennon, Paul McCartney, George Harrison, and Ringo Starr and the bygone days that floated them. Together they spoke of a world in which anything might happen. A place where governments might fall, armies disperse, while four everyday lads from

Liverpool were spinning music that inspired millions to try and un-
cover their own everday genius. I came up in a time when there was an
honest chance of finding a prophet on nearly every street corner. New
ideas were everywhere and people were happy to at least listen. Nowadays nobody's really talking, so I walk the streets without expectation,
chanting my mantra, looking past the golden arches, burned-out
buildings, and seamy technology dives that litter the landscape, remembering a time long before. The Sixties are dead, long live the Fab
Four! Hare Krishna Hare Krishna Krishna Krishna Hare Hare Hare
Rama Hare Rama Rama Rama Hare Hare . . . .

GEOFFREY GIULIANO (JAGANNATHA DASA)

SRI/The Spiritual Realization Institute
Sri Puri Dhama
Western New York
January 1, 1999
http://www.puripada.com
http://www.geoffrey-giuliano.com
e-mail: sri108@webtv.net

THE BEATLES

PART ONE

No One I Think Is in My Tree

THE QUARRYMEN*
(Original Personnel)

Banjo	Rodney Davis
Drums	Colin Hanson
Guitar	Ken Brown
Guitar	Eric Griffiths
Guitar	George Harrison
Guitar	John Lennon
Guitar	Paul McCartney
Guitar	Ivan Vaughan
Guitar and the group's first manager	Nigel Whalley
Tea-chest bass	Len Garry
Washboard	Pete Shotten

A BRIEF HISTORY
OF THE BEATLES DRUMMERS

Tommy Moore	Joined in early 1960 during the band's two-week tour of Scotland with Johnny Gentle.
Pete Best	Joined on August 17, 1960 for a four month gig in Germany. In 1962 Pete made his final appearance with the band at the Cavern. Ringo Starr replaced him the very next night.
Johnny Hutch	Joined in April of 1961 during an audition for promoter Larry Parnes.
Jimmy Nicol	Filled in for Ringo from June 4 to June 15, 1964.
Paul McCartney	Often played drums in the studio during various Beatles sessions.

*The Quarrymen were John Lennon's first schoolboy group.

F.Y.I.
All About Apple Corps Ltd.

Apple was formed in 1967 to manage the Beatles' business affairs. The official subsidiaries were:

Apple Electronics
(Founded by the Beatles way-out friend "Magic" Alex Mardas.)

Apple Films Ltd.
(Producers of the Beatles' *Yellow Submarine* film.)

Apple Management
(Formed in May 1968 to act as agents for various Apple artists.)

Apple Music Publishing
(The first band signed was Grapefruit.)

Apple Overseas
(Formed in 1968 to handle foreign artists. These artists were to record in their home countries for Apple.)

Apple Publicity
(Formed in 1968 to handle both the publicity and advertising for other Apple concerns.)

Apple Records
(The company's biggest success. It still exists today.)

Apple Retail
(Creators of the ill-fated Apple Boutique.)

Apple Tailoring Civil and Theatrical
(Opened in 1968. This venture was run by designer John Crittle, an old school chum of John's.)

Apple Television*

Apple Wholesale*

*Planned divisions of Apple.

THE BEATLES
Press Conference
NORTH AMERICA, 1964

Question: What did you think when your airliner's engine began smoking as you landed today?

Ringo Starr: Beatles, women, and children first!

Paul McCartney: Nothing annoys us, really. Some things make us laugh. Like those "stamp out the Beatles" gags. The other day a photographer asked if he could take two pictures of us: one with our wigs on and one with our wigs off!

Question: Why do teens stand up and scream piercingly and painfully when you appear?

Paul: None of us know. But we've heard that teenagers go to our shows just to scream. A lot of them don't even want to listen because they have our records. We kind of like screaming teenagers. If they want to pay their money and sit out there and shout, that's their business. We aren't going to be like little dictators and say, "You've got to shut up!" The commotion doesn't bother us anymore. It's come to be like working in a bell factory. You don't hear the bells after a while.

Question: What is your personal goal?

George Harrison: To do as well as I can at whatever I attempt and someday die with a peaceful mind.

Question: But you really don't expect that to happen for a long time yet, do you?

George: When your number's up, it's up.

Question: What kind of music do you like?

Paul: Colored American groups.

Question: Do you date much?

Ringo: What are you doing tonight?

Question: Do you fight amongst yourselves?

John Lennon: Only in the mornings.

Question: What do you miss most now that fame prohibits your freedom?

Ringo: Going to the movies.

George: Having nothing to do.

John: School, because you don't have much to do there.

Paul: Going on buses.

Question:s: What impresses you most about America?

John: Bread.

Paul: Going on buses.

THE BEATLES
Press Conference
London, 1965

Question: Well, hello there, Beatles!

Paul McCartney: Hello, it's certainly nice to be here. Certainly is. Certainly is. This is Paul speaking.

Question: Paul, who?

Paul: Paul McCartney!

Ringo Starr: This is Ringo Starr.

George Harrison: George Harrison.

The Beatles: "La, La, La, La!"

Question: What happened to John?

Paul: Well, actually he's gone down to the shipyard to have an estimate for a haircut.

Ringo: I don't know, he's supposed to be here. He's late, isn't he? What's happenin'? I don't know, don't ask me. Please don't ask me!

Question: Well, you're starring in your very first movie!

Beatles: *A Hard Day's Night.* Thank you very much . . . thank you.

Question: Was it a hard day's night, Ringo, making this first one?

Ringo: Well, it was a hard two months. . . . It took two months, actually, to make this film, but the biggest drag was when we were just sitting 'round doing nothing.

George: And getting up early.

Paul: That was one of those things. We had to get up about six o'clock in the morning, which is not good for any one, that. It's very bad for your health!

FORTY-FOUR NEW FACTS ON THE FAB FOUR
1965

1. John flew to Hong Kong wearing his pajamas.

2. John is a great cat lover.

3. Ringo spent much of his childhood in a Cheshire hospital.

4. John used to envy his elder cousin Stanley's Meccano set.

5. Brian Epstein hesitated quite a while before taking on Ringo as a replacement for Pete Best.

6. George is deathly afraid of flying.

7. George has purchased a bow and arrow. Ultimate purpose unknown.

8. Pattie Boyd didn't really like the Beatles before she met them on the set of *A Hard Day's Night.*

9. John's father was a singer on prewar Atlantic liners.

10. Ringo's stepfather, Harry Graves, sings Beatle songs at family parties.

11. The Beatles never visit a barber.

12. Paul washes his hair every day.

13. The Beatles turned down the offer of an appearance on the 1964 Royal Variety Show.

14. Ringo cannot swim, except for a brief doggie-paddle.

15. Brian Epstein made the Beatles have their hair cut after he first signed them in 1962.

16. The Beatles are never photographed with their hair "up".

17. Paul ate corn flakes and bacon and eggs at a champagne and caviar luncheon in London. Music publisher Dick James was the host.

18. The Beatles didn't want to go to Australia without Ringo when he was ill, but manager Epstein persuaded them to change their minds.

19. Paul owns a Mini as well as an Aston Martin DB 4.

20. George's personal Christmas card was a photograph of him scowling at a cameraman.

21. John never saw an audience properly until Dundee in Scotland. He was wearing contact lenses.

22. An American firm wrote to the Beatles asking if they could market their bath water at a dollar a bottle.

23. The Beatles refused the offer.

24. Beatles road manager, Mal Evans, was once a bouncer at the Cavern.

25. Neil Aspinall, their other road manager, was given a Jaguar last Christmas, a present from the Beatles.

26. Paul drinks coffee for breakfast. The other three drink tea. Even in America.

27. Ringo had his new clothes designed by designer Caroline Charles.

28. Jane Asher bought Paul a record player for his Aston Martin.

29. Brian Epstein says, "America discovered Ringo."

30. Paul believes he is not a very good guitarist.

31. None of the Beatles drink Scotch and Coke. They now dilute the occasional spirit with lemonade.

32. John recently told an American journalist that U.S. fashions were five years behind the U.K..

33. The Beatles never really liked jelly babies. They just said they did for a joke.

34. They carry a crate of pop in the trunk of their Austin Princess.

35. Their new chauffeur, Alf Bicknell, used to drive David Niven and Cary Grant.

36. Burt Lancaster sent Ringo a set of pistols. They became friends in Hollywood.

37. Burt let them use his home for a showing of Peter Sellers in *A Shot In The Dark*.

38. Edward G. Robinson and his grandchild twice joined the queue to shake hands with the Beatles at their Hollywood garden party.

39. So did Mrs. Dean Martin and her five children.

40. The Beatles have no pockets in their trousers and only two side pockets in their jackets. Paul designed them.

41. All the Boys carry on them in the way of money is a few bank notes.

42. John bought his mother-in-law a house near his own in Surrey.

43. None of the Beatles wears undershirts.

44. Paul hopes to someday buy a farm.

THE BEATLES
Interview
London, 1969

Question: We were talking earlier. . . .

John Lennon: About the space between us all?

Question: About the gap between us, but also about the documentary* which seems to be grinding to a halt.

John: I think it's taking off! "Here we go loop de loop," as Frankie Hall, the One-Legged Wonder, once said.

Question: Ringo said he thought you ought to just tell it like it is and Mal said . . .

Paul McCartney: I think we are.

Question: So those are the two camps which brings us back to your remarks earlier about "no camp."

John: Well, I do object to all this camp on TV, including Baden-Powell and his foreskin. It's one of the most upsetting things I've ever seen, discouraging young boys from masturbating in case it wets the sheets. Funny you should say that.

Yoko Ono: What?

John: I'm talking about Boy Scouts who aren't allowed to masturbate! It's very tempting when you're wearing shorts. If they only wore short trousers, maybe they'd stand a chance, you know. But I can tell you, you don't go blind, but very shortsighted.

*The film *Let It Be.*

Question: How do you know?

John: From experience. I remember during an English lesson as I came, I suddenly noticed I needed glasses. I thought, "God, they were right!"

FBI MEMO
on John Lennon, George Harrison, and Pattie Harrison

FROM THE DESK OF J. EDGAR HOOVER
WASHINGTON, DC

Date: 23 April 1970
Subject: John Lennon, George Harrison, Patricia Harrison

These individuals are affiliated with the Beatles musical group and Lennon will be traveling under the name of Chambers and the Harrisons are using the name Masters. They will remain in Los Angeles for business discussions with Capitol Records and other enterprises. They will travel to New York for further discussions. Waivers were granted by the Immigration and Naturalization Service in view of the ineligibility of these three individuals to enter the U.S. due to their reputations in England as narcotic users.

While Lennon and the Harrisons have shown no propensity to become involved in violent anti-war demonstrations, each recipient [of this memo] should remain alert for any information of such activity on their part or for information indicating they are using narcotics. Submit any pertinent information obtained for immediate dissemination.

THE BEATLES
Personalities Pictured on the *Sgt. Pepper* Album Cover

Top Row (left to right)

1. Swami Sri Yukteswar Giri

   Indian (1855–1936) Kriya Yoga Master, author of *The Holy Science* and Guru of Paramahansa Yogananda. Read by George.

2. Aleister Crowley

   British author and black magician. Lennon was interested in his work.

3. Mae West

   American actress who was skeptical about being on the cover of the famous LP, but was later convinced by the Beatles via a last-minute missive.

4. Lenny Bruce

   American comedian who died of a heroin overdose in the bathroom of his L.A. home. Harrison was a fan. Played his records to the Hare Krishnas in 1969.

5. Karlheinz Stockhausen

   German composer noted for his experimentation with electronic music. His work greatly influenced the Beatles' later sound.

6. W. C. Fields:

   American comedian born William Claude Dukenfield in 1880. A favorite of all of the Fabs.

7. Carl Gustav Jung:

   Swiss (1875–1961) author and renowned psychologist. Greatly admired by Lennon.

8. Edgar Allan Poe:

   American author/poet who died

of heart problems in 1849. Referred to by John in "I Am the Walrus."

9. Fred Astaire: American actor/dancer who was later friendly with both John and George. He appeared in Lennon's avant-garde *Imagine* film in the seventies.

10. Merkin: American artist/painter.

11. Pretty Girl: Fictional figure, later to end up in a Liverpool museum.

12. Simon Rodia: British artist, sculptor, and designer.

13. Bob Dylan: American musician who became good friends with both John and George. He has collaborated with both.

Second Row Down (left to right)

14. Aubrey Beardsley: British artist who died at age 25. Chosen for the cover by Paul and John.

15. Sir Robert Peel: British (1788–1850) politician and Prime Minister of Great Britain from 1834–1835 and 1841–1846. Included by album cover designer Peter Blake.

16. Aldous Huxley: British philosopher/author who passed away while on LSD in 1963. His works were often read by John and George.

17. Dylan Thomas: Welsh poet/author who died in

New York in 1953. Lennon was a longtime admirer, which was later reflected in his own convoluted, whimsical prose.

18. Terry Southern: American author of *Candy* and *The Magic Christian*, both starring Ringo Starr. A friend of all the Beatles. Deceased.

19. Dion Di Mucci: American musician and teen idol.

20. Tony Curtis: American actor whose distinctive hairstyle had an early influence on the Beatles.

21. Wallace Berman: American artist based in California who often worked in glass. Chosen by Blake.

22. Tommy Handley: British comedian who died in 1949. Picked for the cover by John.

23. Marilyn Monroe: American actress who died of a mysterious drug overdose in her Hollywood Hills home. A secret lover of John F. Kennedy.

24. William S. Burroughs: American author who later became very friendly with John Lennon. They both shared a serious flirtation with heroin. Deceased.

25. Sri Maha Avatar Babaji: Indian Kriya Yoga Avatar still thought to be living high in the Himalayan mountains. Babaji Maharaja is said to be hundreds

of years old. Chosen for the
cover by George Harrison.

26. Stan Laurel: British actor who died in poverty
in California, 1965. Liked by the
Beatles.

27. Richard Lindner: German artist and concert pianist.

28. Oliver Hardy: American actor who died in
1957. Admired by the Beatles.

29. Karl Marx: German (1818–1883) politi-
cian/author. Founder of mod-
ern Communism. A favorite of
John Lennon.

30. H. G. Wells: British (1866–1946) author and
futurist. Born Herbert George.
Read extensively by John.

31. Sri Paramahansa Yogananda: Indian Kriya Yoga Master and
founder of the Self Realization
Fellowship (SRF). One of
George's shiksha (informal) gurus. He died on March 7, 1952
while speaking at an embassy dinner in L.A.. Chosen by Harrison.

32. Wax Girl: Fictional figure.

Third Row Down *(left to right)*

33. Stuart Sutcliffe: British artist/musician who originally played bass in the Beatles.
Very close with John. Deceased.

34. Vargas Girl: Fictional figure.

35. Max Miller: British comedian and music hall
performer.

36. Marlon Brando: American actor whom John once termed his favorite film star.

37. Tom Mix: American actor and stuntman. Included on the cover by Blake.

38. Albert Einstein: German-born (1879–1955) American theoretical physicist.

39. Oscar Wilde: Irish playwright who died in obscurity in Paris in 1900. Often read by Lennon.

40. Tyrone Power: American actor who died of a heart attack while filming in Hollywood. Included by Paul McCartney.

41. Larry Bell: American artist born in Chicago in 1939. Picked by Blake.

42. Dr. David Livingstone: Scottish explorer who passed away in Africa in 1873.

43. Johnny Weissmuller: American athlete/actor most well known for playing Tarzan. Included by Blake.

44. Stephen Crane: American author who expired in 1900 at age 28.

45. Issy Bonn: British actor and popular music hall star.

46. Bette Davis (as Queen Elizabeth I): American actress.

47. George Bernard Shaw: Irish (1856–1950) author/philosopher.

48. Albert Stubbins: British athlete/football player for Liverpool. Chosen by Paul McCartney.

49. Lewis Carroll: British (1832–1898) author and mathematician. Born Charles Lutwidge Dodgson. He inspired John Lennon as a boy and his writing as a Beatle.

50. Sri Lahiri Mahasaya: Indian Kriya Yoga Master who was the guru of Sri Yukteswar and an intimate disciple of Babaja Maharaja. Selected for the cover by Harrison.

51. T. E. Lawrence: British (1888–1935) soldier/writer. Adventurer widely known as Lawrence of Arabia. Born Thomas Edward. He later went by the name T. E. Shaw. Picked by Blake.

Fourth (Front) Row (left to right)

52. Sonny Liston: American boxer whose wax figure still resides in Blake's studio.

53. Vargas Girl: Fictional figure.

54. George (in wax): Courtesy of Madame Tussaud's (though never returned).

55. John (in wax): Courtesy of Madame Tussaud's (though never returned).

56. Unknown Girl: Fictional figure.

57. Ringo (in wax): Courtesy of Madame Tussaud's (though never returned.

58. Paul (in wax): Courtesy of Madame Tussaud's (though never returned).

59. John Lennon: British musician (1940–1980).

60. Ringo Starr:	British musician born to a poor working-class family in central Liverpool.
61. Paul McCartney:	British musician later knighted by Queen Elizabeth. A strict vegetarian.
62. George Harrison:	British musician and nearly life-long student of yogic philosophy and Indology. A dedicated devotee of Sri Kirshna.
63. Bobby Breen:	British musician/singer.
64. Marlene Dietrich:	German actress who appeared on stage with the Beatles in London, 1963.
65. Unknown Ghoul:	Fictional figure.
66. Shirley Temple:	American actress and diplomat.
67. Diana Dors:	British actress and sixties sex symbol.
68. Old Woman:	Fictional figure.
69. Sri Maha Vishnu:	The third incarnation of Sri Krishna, the Supreme personality of Godhead. Statue brought back from India by George.
70. Snow White:	Fictional figure.

Sgt. Pepper Stats

On the famous cover there are:
- 6 women
- 51 men
- 24 Americans
- 24 British subjects
- 4 Indians
- 6 other nationalities
- 7 artists
- 19 actors
- 9 musicians
- 14 writers
- 4 gurus

Left off the cover:

Leo Gotcev*
Adolf Hitler
Sophia Loren
Elvis Presley
Mahatma Gandhi**

Rumored to have been
on the cover:

Binnie Barnes, British actress
Julie Adams, American actress

The Beatles' Best Sellers as of 1970

1. *Abbey Road* (5,000,000)

2. *Meet the Beatles* (4,300,000)

3. *Hey Jude* (3,300,000)

4. *Let It Be* (3,200,000)

*Removed from the finished cover because he reportedly requested a fee.
**Deleted at the insistence of Sir Joseph Lockwood, Chairman of EMI, who feared the Indian market might be offended and therefore adversely affected.

5. *Sgt. Pepper's Lonely Hearts Club Band* (2,700,000)

6. *Rubber Soul* (2,500,000)

7. *A Hard Day's Night* (2,500,000)

8. *The White Album* (2,200,000)

9. *Magical Mystery Tour* (2,000,000)

10. *Revolver* and *Help* (1,500,000 each)

The Beatles' Grammy Awards

1964   Best new artist: *The Beatles*
Best vocal performance by a group: "A Hard Day's Night"
1966   Best contemporary pop vocal performance, male: Paul Mc-Cartney, "Eleanor Rigby"
Best album cover: *Revolver*
Song of the year: "Michelle"
1967   Album of the year: *Sgt. Pepper's Lonely Hearts Club Band*
Best album cover: *Sgt. Pepper's Lonely Hearts Club Band*
Best contemporary rock'n'roll recording: *Sgt. Pepper's Lonely Hearts Club Band*
Best engineered recording: *Sgt. Pepper's Lonely Hearts Club Band*
1969   Best engineered recording: *Abbey Road*
1970   Best original score for movie or television: *Let It Be*
1971   Best arrangement accompanying vocalists: Paul McCartney, "Uncle Albert/Admiral Halsey"
1972   Album of the year: George Harrison and Friends, *The Concert for Bangladesh*
1973   Best arrangement accompanying vocalists: Paul McCartney and Wings, "Live and Let Die"
1974   Best engineered recording: Paul McCartney and Wings, *Band on the Run*

THE BEATLES
Forty Trivia Questions

1. In the song "Maxwell's Silver Hammer," what's Maxwell's last name and what was he majoring in?

2. Which airline do the Beatles use in their trip from Miami back to the USSR?

3. Who was Stu Sutcliffe?

4. What was John's father's first name?

5. What was John's middle name before he changed it to Ono?

6. What was the name of Paul's beloved sheepdog?

7. Besides Linda, who else was engaged to marry Paul?

8. Who instructed George on the sitar?

9. What is Ringo's real name?

10. What was the original title of *Help*?

11. Who played keyboards on the album *Let It Be*?

12. Which pricey American college produced two Beatles wives?

13. Which Conservative Prime Minister is mentioned in the George Harrison song "Taxman"?

14. "Scrambled Egg" was the working title of which classic Beatles hit?

15. Where did John and Paul meet?

16. Who was Dr. Winston O'Boogie?

17. How many times has Ringo been married?

18. What was Starr's first wife's name?

19. Which Beatle has the most children?

20. Who was George's first wife?

21. How many Beatle children have followed in their father's musical footsteps?

22. Name all of the Beatles' movies.

23. What is the name of George's luxury English estate in Henley?

24. What is the name of the estate John owned and Ringo later bought?

25. Who is Paul's talented younger brother?

26. Which Beatle is an only child?

27. How old was George when he got booted from Germany during the Hamburg days?

28. What was the name of Stuart Sutcliffe's photographer girlfriend?

29. What was the name of the Beatles' fatherly producer?

30. Who managed the Beatles after Brian Epstein died?

31. What was John Lennon's famous politically incorrect comment on womanhood?

32. What was John Lennon studying to be before forming the Beatles?

33. For what project did the Beatles win an Academy Award?

34. Which two exotic brands of cigarettes did John Lennon prefer?

35. What was the name of Paul McCartney's band after the Beatles?

36. What is the name of George Harrison's son?

37. What is the name of Paul McCartney's music publishing corporation?

38. In the song "Sgt. Pepper's Lonely Hearts Club," how long was it since Sgt. Pepper taught the band to play?

39. Who was the first Beatle to officially quit the group?

40. What is the name of Ringo Starr's movie star wife?

1. Maxwell Edison, majoring in medicine.
2. B.O.A.C.
3. The Beatles' original bass player.
4. Fred.
5. Winston.
6. Martha.
7. Actress Jane Asher.
8. Ravi Shankar.
9. Richard Starkey.
10. *Eight Arms to Hold You.*
11. Billy Preston.
12. Sarah Lawrence.
13. Edward Heath.
14. "Yesterday."
15. Woolton Village Fête.
16. One of John Lennon's many humorous aliases.
17. Twice.
18. Maureen.
19. Paul McCartney (four).
20. Model Pattie Boyd.
21. Three: Zak Starkey, Julian Lennon, and Sean Lennon.
22. *Hard Day's Night, Help, Magical Mystery Tour,* and *Let It Be.*
23. Friar Park.
24. Tittenhurst Park.
25. Mike McGear of the popular Liverpool group the Scaffold.
26. Ringo.
27. Eighteen.
28. Astrid Kirsher.
29. George Martin.
30. Allen Klein.
31. "Women should be obscene and not heard."
32. Artist and illustrator.
33. The soundtrack to *Let It Be.*
34. Gauloises and Gitanes.
35. Paul McCartney and Wings.
36. Dhani.
37. MPL (McCartney Publishing Limited).
38. Twenty years ago today.
39. Paul McCartney.
40. Barbara Bach.

Apple Corps Press Releases
London, 1968–1996

FROM GEORGE HARRISON TO ALL APPLE STAFF

The Hell's Angels will be in London within the next week on the way to straighten out Czechoslovakia. There will be twelve in number, complete with black leather jackets and motorcycles. They will undoubtedly arrive at Apple and I have heard they may try to make full use of Apple's facilities. They may look as though they are going to do you in, but they are very straight and do good things, so don't fear them or uptight them. Try to assist them without neglecting your Apple business and without letting them take control of Savile Row.   December 4, 1968

PRESS OFFICE RELEASE TO UPI, AP, REUTERS

Apple's world sales since August 1968 now total some 16,192,126 records.

Press Office Release to UPI, AP, Reuters

On behalf of Apple Corps and associated companies, Apple spokesman Derek Taylor today said, "Allen Klein, who one month ago signed a business contract with the Beatles and their company, Apple Corps, Ltd., is not, as was reported in *Variety*, July 2, in any way terminating his relationship with the Beatles or with their associated companies. It is not true, as suggested in *Variety*, that his representation of the Rolling Stones and Donovan has impaired his relationship with the Beatles. The New York firm of Eastman and Eastman, is said by *Variety* to be taking a more active role in managing the Beatles' business affairs, in fact acts solely as representatives of Beatle Paul McCartney as an individual. Eastman and Eastman does not act as general counsel for the Beatles or any of their companies. Apple, the Beatles, Eastman, and Klein have over the past few months established a warm, workable relationship which is to their benefit."

Press Office Release to UPI, AP, Reuters

Apple announced today, September 30th, that John and Yoko are resting comfortably at Tittenhurst Park after their completion of mixing and recording with the Plastic Ono Band the single, "Cold Turkey."

Press Office Release to UPI, AP, Reuters

Yoko Ono Lennon lost the baby she was expecting today at King's College Hospital, Denmark Hill, London. Mrs. Lennon is resting comfortably.

Press Office Release to UPI, AP, Reuters

On behalf of the Beatles and their company, Apple Corps, their business manager Allen Klein of ABKCO Industries, after discussion with the Beatles, announced in New York today that all negotiations between the Beatles, Associated Television, and Northern Songs have been terminated by the Beatles. All of the Beatles and their companies intend to sell all their shares in Northern Songs to Associated Television at a price in accordance with the terms laid down by the takeover panel. John Lennon and Paul McCartney have no intention of involving themselves in any further relationship with Northern Songs or Associated Television beyond the fulfillment of their songwriting contract to February 1973. The Beatles intend to keep all their rights within their own company, Apple, which has divisions in records, music publishing, motion pictures, and television. After discussions with the Beatles' solicitors and after taking advice of counsel, the writ served upon Northern Songs by the Beatles-owned Maclen Company will not be withdrawn and a statement of claim will be served within the next few days.

ATTENTION PRESS OFFICE FROM CAPITOL RECORDS

Russ Gibbs, a Program Coordinator for WKNR Radio (Detroit, Michigan), plans a broadcast, possibly this Sunday, suggesting that Paul is either dead or under a "death spell." He bases this on various symbols from the Beatles' albums, including *Abbey Road* on which Paul is barefoot, which signifies a corpse in Eastern religion. Previous broadcasts by this station have resulted in mass hysteria and panic by Beatle fans and certain radio stations and newspapers suggest you communicate with him to stop this outrage. *Urgent.*

PRESS RELEASE BY YOKO ONO TO UPI, AP, REUTERS

Every cent John earns goes into Apple at the moment. All that he means by saying he would like to free his money is that he would like some pocket money, some spending money, for some of our joint endeavors. It would be wrong to think that John is going to leave Apple because he, like the other Beatles, is a quarter of Apple, but like everyone else he could do with some loose change which is entirely his own. He needs some freedom.

PRESS OFFICE TO UPI, AP, REUTERS

John and Yoko Lennon today announced from their Apple Headquarters, 3 Savile Row, London W1, that they plan to make a film about James Hanratty, the convicted A6 murderer. After discussion with Hanratty's parents, the Lennons, convinced that James Hanratty was innocent of the crime for which he was hung [sic], said they are going to make a film that will insist a new public inquiry be held, and they themselves plan to reveal startling new facts about the case.

PRESS OFFICE RELEASE TO UPI, AP, REUTERS

Beatle Ringo Starr spent the whole day shooting a promotional film of his forthcoming solo album, *Sentimental Journey*. Dressed in a dark blue suit, a blue-and-pink-striped shirt, and a maxi-sized, shocking-pink bow tie, Ringo sang and danced through the title track in front of a specially invited audience of friends and friends of friends. The film, produced by Neil Aspinall and directed by John Gilbert, will be primarily for American promotion. The Talk of the Town Orchestra was under the direction of George Martin. The dancers, dressed in white, and the three backing singers were Apple's Doris Troy with Marsha Hunt and Madeleine Bell. A projected backdrop showed the album cover, a pub at the end of the street where Ringo lived in Liverpool.

PRESS OFFICE RELEASE TO UPI, AP, REUTERS

We in the Press Office, as undersigned, are paying for an advertisement ourselves because we believe the record *Govinda* by the devotees of the Radha Krishna Temple, produced by George, to be the best record ever made! You too?

AUGUST 1971

Dear People:

The time has come for me to withdraw from the Beatles Fan Club. As you may know, the band split up over a year ago and has not played together since. Each of us is getting together his own career, and for this reason, I don't want to be involved [sic] with anything that continues the illusion that there is such a thing as the Beatles.

Those days are over. In the past, you have been great superstars, and the idea of this letter is to let you know how I want it to be in the future, in case you wanted to know. Now I'm not a Beatle any longer, and want to get back to where I once belonged—living my own life, having my own family, my privacy, and getting on with my own music.

Thanks for everything . . .

Paul, Child-Bride Linda, Boy Prodigy Heather, and Baby Mary

THE BEATLES
Press Release
LONDON, FEBRUARY 5, 1996

NEW BEATLES LOVE SONG IS THEIR LAST

There was never a more romantic band than the Beatles. Throughout their career they only really said one four-letter word: l-o-v-e.

Love is the theme in almost every song they wrote. Although the actual word only appears in the titles of ten of the 213 Beatles' compositions ("All My Loving," "All You Need Is Love," "And I Love Her," "Can't Buy Me Love," "It's Only Love," "Love Me Do," "Love You To," "P.S. I Love You," "She Loves You," and "You've Got to Hide Your Love Away"), the loving feeling hallmarks the Beatles' musical history.

Love is all around in Paul's "Here There and Everywhere." There's the lust for constant love in "Ooh I need your love, babe . . . eight days a week." There's the idolized love of George's "Something in the way she moves, attracts me like no other lover." There's the desperate cry for love in John's "Help!" There's the happiness of being in love in John's "I'm in love with her and I feel fine." And, of course, there's Paul's classic lost-love lament: "Yesterday, love was such an easy game to play."

Even the last song they ever recorded together—the aptly-titled, "The End," at the very end of *Abbey Road*, their last album—highlighted the importance of love to the Beatles when they sang their very last lines: "And in the end, the love you take is equal to the love you make."

For the Beatles, all you ever really did need was love. And now they are releasing their very last love song as their absolutely final word. Aptly it's called "Real Love."

"Real Love" is the final track from the Beatles' "Reunion Sessions" that were the talk of last year after Paul, George, and Ringo came together in the studio for the first time in 25 years to re-record unreleased songs penned by the late John Lennon.

Unlike "Free as a Bird," which basically Paul, George, and Ringo had to piece together and write extra parts for around an unfinished demo of John's, "Real Love" was completed as a song by John before he died. However, to make it a Beatles song, Paul, George, and Ringo spent hours in Paul's Sussex studio layering over drums, bass, electric guitar, acoustic guitars, and instantly recognizable Beatles harmonies.

The results is a more catchy song than "Free as a Bird" and is many people's favorite of the two for being the more "poppy." In essence it passes the record industry's "whistle test," one listen and you can whistle along with it.

"Real Love" was different from "Free as a Bird" in that it had all the words and the music and so it was a bit more like being sidemen to John. "But that was very joyful and good fun and I think we did a good job," said Paul. "I think "Real Love" is slightly deceptive. It's one of those songs that the more you hear it the more you go 'ooo'."

Sessions for "Real Love" began at Macca's studio in February 1995 and lasted for a week. In June, Paul and George came together again to make the final edit. It is probably the last time that the Beatles will record together as Beatles. As Paul admits, that day is probably done.

"I think it may be a nonstarter, just the three of us. You know, maybe we've done enough. If you look at our career, hell, it wasn't a bad one. And now we've done the *Anthology*, had great success with that, and I think the only thing that might excite me and George and Ringo now would be some crazy idea someone might have or finding another crazy John track that we've all got to work on. But the three of us working on our own, I just can't see it myself. But you never know."

If this really is, as it seems, the end, then it is fitting that the world's most celebrated band is ending it all with a love song. For Paul, leaving love as the Beatles' last message is very important. As it is, the Beatles led the Love Generation and influenced the spread of peace and kindness throughout the Sixties. But, Paul warned, the world could have gone a worse way had they used their influence to tell their millions of fans to riot and violently rebel.

"The one thing that I'm really proud of with the Beatles is that I'm glad of the content of the songs, of what we said in them," said Paul. "Because if you listen to Beatles' songs, we're saying good things, we're saying love and peace, let it be, there will be an answer. Hey Jude, don't make it bad— looking back on it, none of it says go and screw your brother. I thought spreading love was important then and I still do now. I really do think that's all there is. I don't think you need much else and a lot of the problems in society that you're getting now is because there isn't enough love, es- pecially between families. Kids are just not getting it.

"But I think the overall impression that the Beatles left people with was an affectionate feeling. Most people I talk to say, 'Aah, great days.' They've got lovely memories of it. And if there is any residue of love for the Beatles, I think it's because we had that very honest, loving attitude and our message still remains a very positive, loving message."

As he sang long ago, "In the end, the love you take is equal to the love you make."

THE BEATLES
Anthology Press Release
LONDON, MARCH 4, 1996

The Beatles' newest single "Real Love" is appropriately set for its first play on American radio this Wednesday, February 14th, Valentine's Day. It will be released Monday, March 4th on CD, cassette, and vinyl formats. Featured with "Real Love" on the CD single are "Baby's in Black," "Yellow Submarine," and "Here, There and Everywhere." Vinyl and cassette for- mats are backed with "Baby's in Black." All three extra tracks are previ- ously unreleased versions and are unavailable elsewhere. This greatly affecting song, "Here, There and Everywhere," is considered by some to be McCartney's best. Superimposed near the end, there is a remix of the fa- mous Beatles harmonies, remixed in 1995 by George Martin.

"Real Love" is the second new Beatles single in three months. The first new Beatles song in 25 years, "Free as a Bird," was released on December 4, 1995. Both were written by John Lennon, sung by him with his own piano accompaniment, and passed to the three surviving Beatles, Paul McCartney, George Harrison, and Ringo Starr by John's widow Yoko Ono Lennon.

The tracks were in cassette from demos recorded by John in the late Seventies and, with Yoko's blessing, the three surviving Beatles, with their producer Jeff Lynne, transformed the songs into high quality Beatles recordings with harmonies, instrumentation, and, in the case of "Free as a Bird," additional words. Of "Real Love," Jeff Lynne says, "It is much simpler than "Free as a Bird," sort of a love song, and bouncier. It's a beautiful tune as well and they all do great harmonies with John." Both songs were recorded at Paul McCartney's studio in the South of England, "Free as a Bird" in 1994, and "Real Love" last year.

While the actual recording of "Real Love" took several days (February 1994) with engineers Geoff Emerick and Jon Jacobs, Mr. Emerick's association with the Beatles dates back to the heyday of their recording career. He received a Grammy for his work on *Sgt. Pepper.*

The surviving Beatles decided to use as little state-of-the-art equipment as possible to give a timeless Beatles feel to the single. To enhance this effect, Paul McCartney used a stand-up double bass originally owned by Elvis Presley's bassist, the late Bill Black. Both Paul and George used six string acoustic guitars to augment the electric instruments and Ringo used his famous Ludwig drum kit. The result is a bona fide organic Beatles single with an ageless appeal.

Of the song, Paul says, "It was fun doing it. Unlike 'Free as a Bird,' it had all the words and music and we were more like 'sidemen' to John, which was joyful, and I think we did a good job."

The "Real Love" video was directed by Kevin Godley and filmed both in Liverpool and in London. The song is featured as the first track on the new Beatles album *Anthology 2,* to be released on March 19th. The album features 45 Beatles tracks recorded between February 1965 and February 1968. It is the second of three volumes in the *Anthology* series. *Anthology 1,* released in November, is already chalking-up sales approaching ten million worldwide.

THE BEATLES
Anthology, Volume 2 Press Release
NEW YORK, 1996

THE BEATLES ANTHOLOGY, VOLUME 2: YEAH! YEAH! YEAH!

March 21, 1996: *The Beatles Anthology, Volume 2,* released this past Tuesday, sold nearly 225,000 copies in its initial 24-hour sale period, according to Capitol Records. The figure was derived from eight of the top ten reporting retailers—including Best Buy, Musicland, and Target—which represent nearly 65 percent of the marketplace.

"Sales are certainly faster than we had anticipated," said Bruce Kirkland, executive vice president, Capitol Records. "No network television series. No Christmas season. Limited radio airplay. But the consumer knows what they want. Imagine what sales would be if radio programmers played what their listeners wanted to hear."

Volume 2, which has received glowing reviews from publications across the country, was not expected to match initial sales of *Volume 1,* which sold 255,000 units overnight and 855,000 its first week.

"The Beatles have another Number 1 album," said Phil Sandhaus, vice president of strategic marketing, Capitol Records. "It's a true reading of fan loyalty and certainly a tribute to the music of the Beatles."

The Beatles Anthology, Volume 2 is expected to debut at Number 1 on *Billboard*'s "Album Chart."

THE BEATLES
Emmy Nominations, *Anthology* Press Release
LONDON, JULY 19, 1996

The Beatles Anthology TV series has been nominated for the top prize in factual television, an Emmy award for the best documentary series. The five-hour series that caught the imagination of the world when it was screened in 94 countries last November was nominated in Los Angeles last night.

The Beatles Anthology has been nominated for three additional Emmy awards: Outstanding Informational Series, Outstanding Picture Editing, and Outstanding Sound Editing.

Five years in the planning and the making, *The Beatles Anthology* made TV history as, for the first time, the Beatles' story was told personally by John Lennon, Paul McCartney, George Harrison, and Ringo Starr. It is estimated that the series was watched by an audience of 420 million worldwide.

Neil Aspinall, head of Apple Corps and executive producer of the TV series, said today: "This nomination is a great honor and it reflects the enduring worldwide interest in the Beatles."

Anthology producer Chips Chipperfield added: "It is a great accolade for a British-made documentary series to be nominated in this, the biggest TV market in the world."

This September will see the release of *The Beatles Anthology* video collection, a double-length, ten-hour version of the TV series, which tells the Beatles' story in even greater detail. This autumn will also mark the release of *The Beatles Anthology Volume 3*, the final album in the trilogy of the Beatles' unreleased recordings that has to date sold the equivalent of 25 million albums around the world.

For further information, please contact:

DEREK TAYLOR

GEOFF BAKER

The Beatles Anthology Press Office

THE BEATLES WITH GEORGE MARTIN AND JEFF LYNNE
Press Release Interview on the Beatles' *Anthology*
LONDON, 1996

George Harrison: The gist is to find the most ancient Beatles music possible. It comes in chronological order through the various records we'd made and brings it up to date. We want to put as many songs on the CDs as possible, to make it of greater value. So, we include like sixty or seventy minutes, or like 25 songs on a CD. We're talking really about an historical thing.

George Martin: I'm trying to tell the story of the Beatles' lives in music. It traces their lives from the moment they met to the moment they split in 1970. My job is to try and give people an idea of that by means of CDs. The way I'm doing that is to draw upon any source I think is viable. That includes live performances, broadcasts, television shows, all the stuff we did together at EMI, all recordings prior to that, their auditions, private recordings, all sorts of things. It's been a kind of voyage back in time.

Ringo Starr: It kicks! It's so great, you know. We go into the records themselves and we get into sort of cross-fading, take one to take four. On some of them we were just working the song out, running through it because we'd always run through the song. The attitude was like from the beginning to seven takes later, like a mile. It's not like, oh, we've changed a note. . . . So there's some of that cross-fading on the CDs, which is really exciting.

George Martin: Some of the very early takes of most numbers are interesting, seeing how the song developed and how it changed. In some instances they started quite differently to the masters that everybody knows, so we're kind of lifting the lid a bit on the Beatles. We're eavesdropping on the way they made their records.

Ringo: It was really great to hear all the live shows on the CDs, to hear the Beatles as a live band again. Because we'd all got so involved in the records, people forgot we were a live band. I love that stuff of us playing live.

George Harrison: Now, as it gets into the mid-to-late sixties, we found different outtakes or maybe a version of something that had some vocals that were different to the vocals that ended up on the master, so what we've done is present the alternate version. We've tried to create a lot of the most famous songs but totally different versions of them.

Paul McCartney: We've used alternative takes, so if you look down the track list, you'll think, oh, I know that song, I know "Roll Over Beethoven," I know "And Your Bird Can Sing," I've heard "Yesterday" before, but they are all different takes of them. We don't actually ever use the released take the public knows. For instance, we've included the first take of "Yesterday," because we did two takes and the second take was the one with the string quartet on it, which we eventually released. The first take is kind of more acoustic. There is no string quartet on it, and the intro is a little bit more folksy, but listening to that and sort of thinking, "Wow, here's my most successful song in the making," and I was twenty-two!

George Martin: I couldn't imagine telling the life story of the Beatles without having "Yesterday." It so happens there is a take one of "Yesterday" that is charming and exquisite and, of course, it doesn't have any string quartet on it, and we're putting that out. I think people will like that.

George Harrison: There are some funny songs and some songs we didn't even remember. I heard this song that Ringo's singing, I still don't know the title of it, but it's got the most amazing lyrics and it's quite a good production. . . . I don't recall what it was, but the words are ridiculous. There's a song of mine they've found, on some small reel in a cupboard, or in a drawer somewhere. People have written about this song, but I have no recollection of ever doing it. It must have been something where I had a song, got to the studio, and, by the sound of it, sounds just like me playing electric guitar and Ringo on the tambourine. So, the only thing I can imagine was that I played the song and the engineer was recording it, and this I wouldn't even have said was a demo, it hadn't even got to the demo stage, it has nothing else on it. But because it's kind of thirty-odd years old, it now has some importance.

Paul: One of my favorites is "And Your Bird Can Sing," which is a nice song, but this take was the one previous to the one we actually used. We couldn't use this one at the time because John and I get a fit of giggles while we are doing the double track.

George Martin: You hear them off-guard. There's one version of "And Your Bird Can Sing" when they were overdubbing a final track and they started giggling and they went through the song and they completed it, but it was just giggles all the way through and you can't help laughing with them. It's so funny.

Paul: You couldn't release that at that time. But now you can. Sounds good just hearing us lose it on a take. And there's lots of things like that, rarities on it, and so it traces our career. You can also see our development, you can see it happening on the CDs. The good thing about the *Anthology* and the CDs is that it's the four of us. Even though John's not here, he's here. He's represented; his point of view comes over. And, on the single, he's singing lead.

Ringo: It was always down to the music. *The music is the Beatles.*

On the Beatles' Single "Real Love"

Ringo Starr: It came about because we were going to do some incidental music and just get in there and play the instruments and see what happened. That seemed like an okay idea and then we thought, well, why don't we do some new music? And then we always hit the wall, and okay, Paul had a song, or George had a song, or I had a song, well that's the three of us, why don't the three of us go in and do this? And we kept hitting that wall because this is the Beatles. It's not Paul, George, and Ringo. So Paul asked Yoko if there was anything of John's that never came out. Maybe we could work with it. And so she sent us these tapes and that's how it came about.

George Harrison: Different ideas had been talked about, that we could do the background music or even write a new song or something, but this became the perfect vehicle because we always had a thing between the four of us that if any one of us wasn't in it, we weren't going to get kind of Roger Waters and go out as the Beatles, so therefore the only other person who could be in it was John.

Paul McCartney: It was actually a very joyous experience. It was a lot of fun seeing the guys and working with them. Little things, nice little things, you know. I was sitting down trying to work out the piano part and Ringo would happen to just come on the drums so that we'd have a tiny little jam. And I'd think, "My God, it's twenty years since we did that." And, of course, you just fell in. It was like it was yesterday. We just read each other so easily, that it was a lot of fun.

George: It was interesting to actually get back together. For Ringo, Paul, and I, we've had the opportunity to let all the past turbulent times go down the river and under the bridge and get together again in a new light. I think that has been a good thing, it's like going full circle, and I feel sorry John wasn't able to do that, because I know he would have really enjoyed that opportunity to be with us again.

Paul: It was very good fun for me to have John in the headphones when I was working. It was like the old days and it was a privilege.

Jeff Lynne: When you hear George and Paul sing along with John, you go, "God, it's the Beatles." Absolutely the greatest group ever.

Ringo: And for me being away from it for so long, I listened to it and I thought, "It sounds just like them." I'd taken myself away from it for so long, it was like listening to it like an outsider.

Paul: When George and I were doing the harmonies that was what Ringo said when we got back in the control room. He said, "Sounds just like the Beatles."

Ringo: I was shocked. It just blew me away. I don't know why I didn't think it is us anyway, but I just had a moment of being far enough away from it to look at it like a real thing. And it's just like them. It was a mind blower.

George: It's gonna sound like them if it is them. It sounds like them *now,* that's what I think. It doesn't, when you say, it sounds like the Beatles, people may expect it sound like, you know, '65 or '68 or '69 or *Abbey Road.* But the whole technical thing that has taken place between 1969 and 1996 is we are now in 1996, so technically it sounds more like now.

Paul: And there was a kind of crazy moment, thinking, "Oh yeah," because of not having done it for so long, you become an ex-Beatle. But, of course, getting back in the band and working on this *Anthology,* you're in the band again. There's no two ways about it. It was good, it was good being them again for a little while. We work well together, that's the truth of it. We just work well together. And that's a very special thing. When you find someone you can talk to, it's a special thing. But if you find someone you can play music with, it's really something.

Ringo: When we are all together, there's no separation. It really works.

Jeff: When they played, it was really tight playing. Just like they'd always been playing together.

George: We've had so much of the same background, our musical background and where we came from. What we listened to in common and all those years we played together, somehow it's made a very deep groove in our memories, and it doesn't take much to lock in. It just shows that there is a certain harmony. We do lock in together very easily and it kind of sounds like the Beatles without much effort.

Jeff: "Real Love" is a great song again. A much simpler song than "Free as a Bird," sort of a love song. And it's a bouncier song, a beautiful tune as well, and they all do harmonies with John. They all join in and have a great time.

Ringo: Well, "Real Love"'s poppy, it's more of a poppy song.

Paul: I think George actually liked "Real Love" a little better. It's just a matter of opinion. They are both good songs. "Real Love" had all the words and the music. It was more like we were sidemen to John, which was joyful and it was good fun and I think we did a good job. I think it is slightly deceptive, "Real Love," because it's one of those the more you hear it, the more you go, "Ohh, ohh"!

Ringo: I think John will love it when he hears it!

Beatles, Etc.

Paul McCartney: It was a cool thing, the Beatles. One thing I'm very proud of, looking back on the Beatles, I'm glad about the content of what we said. Our songs were, you know, "Let It Be," peaceful, and "All You Need Is Love." They weren't anthems of rebelliousness and "come on, kids, hate your parents," but the thing was we had that power. And had we chosen to use that power it would have gone a very different way, the whole thing. So I think if there is any sort of residue of love for the Beatles, I think it was because we were on a very loving vibe that was genuine. I still feel that way, I think that's all there is. I really don't think there is much else between families and people. I think a lot of the problems you're getting now is because there isn't enough of it. It's really good that our message still remains a very positive, loving message. I'm pleased with that. I mean we could have just gone off on the psychedelic thing and really majored in that and forgot the love thing, but it was important to us.

Ringo Starr: Oh, yes, because everything we did we did for good, and that still relates to today. "All You Need Is Love," so that's what it's about. We tried to do it with peace and love.

George Harrison: I think we have to remember that in the end it's the stress. People gave, fans gave, record companies gave, the media gave, but we gave our nervous systems. The Beatles were so stressed out, just the travel, the intensity, the noise, people yelling at us all the time, and being confined to a little room, or a plane, or a car. To get back to that thing of love, we all had each other to dilute the stress. And, being born in Liverpool, we had the sense of humor. It was very important, so we always had a laugh as well.

Ringo: We were lucky there were four of us to take that pressure. We all said this about Elvis, that he was on his own. But the four of us held each other together.

George: The love people feel for us, we don't understand that. That's the mystical side to it, and that's the thing that we should cherish, that aspect of it, to realize that.

Ringo: I think people still love us because we were kind and loving. But seriously, oh yeah, we loved each other. We put a lot of love out. We loved that audience and they loved us back.

Paul: At the end of the *Anthology*, Ringo says, "We were just four guys who loved each other." There's a lot to that.

George Martin: One of the strengths of the Beatles was the fact that they had eternal curiosity. They were on an eternal quest for something new.

George Harrison: Well, it's amazing. As it was happening, you don't think about it. I just got out of school and all I wanted to do was be in a band. I didn't want a proper job, and I had no idea what I would have done had I not done this. But at the age of seventeen I was in Hamburg, in St. Pauli, and by the time I was 23 we had done *Sgt. Pepper* and I was in the Himalayas. Basically that's how much my life went from a school boy in Liverpool to the Himalayas just in five years. But every experience was great. It was speeded up. We put in maybe twenty years in every year. And the music was always there in the background, reflecting our feelings and our desires and all the various things we'd experienced.

Paul: So I think we were kind of conscious of trying not to repeat ourselves. We'd been in Hamburg and sometimes we'd been working over a kind of eight-hour period, and one of the little aims became to try and not repeat a song. Because when we first went there, there were ten songs we just repeated endlessly, and we used excuses like, "We've had a request for 'Dancin' in the Streets,'" and we'd do it and then five minutes later, "We've just had another request for 'Dancin' in the Streets.'" So we'd try to stretch that material. Eventually we got a lot of stuff in our repertoire and I think that then kind of carried through this idea of not wanting to repeat. People are going to get bored or we are going to get bored, maybe more importantly. So it was important to us to be different and not to make the same record twice. I think that is a factor in the Beatles' thing, you never hear that kind of thing where there are three records in a row that sound a bit similar. They are always vastly different. You will get a "Yesterday" and then a "Strawberry Fields" or something. I'm not necessarily in the right order there, but you'd get jumps of that magnitude. I think that was attractive. It certainly was attractive to us, and I think it made people think, oh, well, they are not just one-hit wonders.

Ringo: That's two-fold, that's mainly because of the writers, John and

Paul writing all these great songs, and we were becoming better musicians. So it was all a growth. It's not like we were born and then we did that. We'd all struggled in Liverpool, we'd been trying to learn, we'd all be crazed in Germany, and then we started playing, and the songwriting got better, and our playing got better. So it just all grew.

Paul: There was the growth within us. For instance, I noticed I came on later with some of my songs. There was a kind of period where John and I were just writing together, "I Want To Hold Your Hand," "She Loves You," that kind of thing, where we were just very equal, and the two of us were just putting equal input into the songs. As you go through the story, you start to find things like me doing "Yesterday," "Let It Be," or "Hey Jude," which was very me. John doing "Strawberry Fields," "Walrus," which are very him. We were able to discover our own identities within this chemistry as well, which is a good thing. So that became the growth factor and then you could actually hear us growing. Part of that, I think was because we just complemented each other. So I think the chemistry of the combination of these four people was obviously something special. We felt it.

George Martin: The Beatles were so unique. They were a unique combination of talents. And spearheaded by two of our greatest songwriters ever. But the two of them weren't just the Beatles. There were four of them and the four of them, united, became much more important than the individual people. So that the sum was greater than the individual parts. I think the Beatles were an extraordinary phenomenon of our time.

Jeff Lynne: Whenever I think about music like pop music or rock music, whatever you want to call it, there were all these groups and then there were the Beatles, they just sat on the top, and everybody else was sort of good and great, but the Beatles were the Beatles.

Paul: We were a good little band. I always used to feel that if we ever sat down and had a little jam, it always used to work.

George Harrison: It's just some little magic that when you get certain people together it produces—it makes fire or it makes more dynamite—and plus we had excellent songs. We were consistent, we were honest, had a sense of humor, and kind of looked quite good at the time, which always helps.

Ringo: We knew we were the best band in the land. And at that time the biggest band. We opened up stadiums, they hadn't done that before, and we were just playing to more and more people, selling more records than anybody, so that was a hidden clue! Well, the best was musically, of course. The best was friendship. I still meet a hundred people a day, saying, "Thanks for the music."

George Harrison: I have a balanced view of it. Like John says in the documentary, "All we were was a little rock'n'roll band," and that's all it was. The way it was blown into this huge big thing and it became that, I don't know how or why, but really all we were was just a little rock'n'roll band.

JOHN LENNON

PART TWO

Always Smiling and Arriving Late for Tea

JOHN LENNON
Questionnaire

LIVERPOOL, 1963

Date of Birth: 9th October 1940.

Weight: 11 ½ stone.

Height: 5 feet 11 inches.

Color of Eyes: Brown.

Color of Hair: Brown.

First Professional Performance: Club in Liverpool.

Likes: Music, books, painting, television.

Hates: Thick heads and trad jazz.

Favorite Food: Steak and chips, curries and jelly.

Favorite Clothes: Dark colored in suede and leather.

Favorite Color: Black.

Favorite Games: Ball games.

Favorite Singers: Carl Perkins, Chuck Berry, Kay Starr.

Favorite Actors: Marlon Brando, Peter Sellers.

Favorite Actress: Brigitte Bardot.

Favorite Companions: Blonde, intelligent girls.

Ambition: Money and everything.

Instruments Played: Rhythm guitar, harmonica.

Educated: Quarry Bank Grammar and Liverpool College of Art.

Hobbies: Writing songs, poems and plays, girls, painting, TV,
   meeting people.

Favorite Drinks: Whiskey and tea.

Favorite Band: Quincy Jones.

Taste in music: R&B, gospels.

Personal Ambition: To write a musical.

Favorite Instrumentalist: Sonny Terry.

Favorite Composer: Luther Dixon.

Former Occupation: Art student.

Brothers/Sisters: None.*

*Actually, John has three half sisters on his mother's side—Julia, Jacqui, Victoria—and two half brothers, David and Robin, on his father's.

JOHN LENNON
Questionnaire
LONDON, JULY 2, 1963

Favorite Food: Jelly
Favorite Drink: Tea
Favorite Day of the Week: Saturday (my day)
Favorite Season of the Year: Summer
Favorite Foreign Country: France
Favorite Color: Black
Favorite Actor: Brando
Favorite Actress: Greco
Favorite Male Singer: Elvis
Favorite Female Singer: Mary Wells

Do You Like . . .
Tea: Yes
Coffee: Yes
Milk: Yes
Beer: Yes
Whiskey: Yes
Water: Yes
Beans on Toast: Yes
Spaghetti: Yes
Fried Egg: Yes
Boiled Egg: Yes
Cheese: Yes
Jam: Yes
Cream: Yes
Blondes: Yes
Brunettes: Yes
Redheads: Yes
With Glasses: Yes
Girls Without Glasses: Yes
Riding in Cars: Yes
Riding in Buses: No

Riding on Motorbikes: No
Are you married or unmarried: Yes
If unmarried, do you ever have time to date girls: No
Do you like life in general: YEAH!

JOHN LENNON
Questionnaire
1966

Marriage: Just a name.
In Crowds: Do me a favor!
War: Terrible! No excuse for it.
Power: I haven't used mine fully yet.
Clothes: Useful for taking off.
Television: Love it. Sometimes great, sometimes a joke, but I like it.
Death: The end, daddy-o.
Paul McCartney: Just our Paul . . .
Animals: I love.
Swimming: Keeps you clean.
Sky: That's where I belong, baby.
Journalists: Fruitcakes.
Fans: Harmless.
Cigarettes: Cancer.
Vegetarianism: I've not come across it. If people want to eat nuts, that's
    okay with me. I wish I could do it, the way I feel about animals.
The Bomb: Should be bombed.
Jagger: A good nut.
America: Great possibilities.
Life & Death: Time I was on stage.

JOHN LENNON
Questionnaire
London, 1969

Surname:	Lennon
First or Christian Names:	John Ono
Title/Academic Degrees:	Gold Discs
Date of Birth:	9/10/40
Place of Birth:	Liverpool
Nationality:	British
Parentage:	Alfred Lennon
	Julia Stanley
Marriage (Year and Names):	20th March 1969
Number of Sons/Daughters:	Julian, 2
Profession/Occupation:	Artist
Education:	Schools
Short Biographical Note (State year you assumed and relinquished principal position):	Born 1940
	Lived
	Met Yoko and married
Present Position(s) (State year(s) appointed):	Kyoko
Honors, Awards, Prizes:	Yes
Publications/Major Works:	*In His Own Write*
	A Spaniard in the Works
	You Are Here
Full Addresses and Telephone Number(s):	3 Savile Row
	London, W1
Leisure Interests:	Working for Peace

JOHN LENNON
Disc and Music Echo
Valentine Awards Nomination

LONDON, 1969

Best British Boy Singer: John Lennon

Best British Girl Singer: Mary Hopkin

Best British Group: Beatles

Top Disc Jockey: John Peel

Mr. Valentine 1969:   John Lennon

Miss Valentine 1969:   Yoko Ono

Best 1969 British Single: "Revolution"

Best 1969 British LP: *The Beatles*

Top TV Show: *Magical Mystery Tour*

Best Dressed Boy Star: John Lennon

Top Radio Show: "Life With the Lyons"

Best Dressed Girl Star: Yoko Ono

Top Film: *No. 5.* by Yoko Ono

1969 Hope (Britain):   John Lennon

Best British Musician: John Lennon

Top TV Artist (Boy):   Kenny Evertt

Top TV Artist (Girl)::   Yoko Ono

Best Boy Singer (World):   John Lennon

Top Girl Singer (World):   Yoko Ono

Top World Group: Beatles

Best 1969 Single (World):   "Hey Jude"

Best 1969 Album World: *The Beatles*

World's Top Musician: John Lennon

1969 Hope (World):   Berenice Kinn

Name: John Lennon

Age: 28

Address: 3 Savile Row, W1, London

JOHN LENNON
Questionnaire
MAY 9, 1972

Full Name (surname first):   Lennon, John Winston Ono
Place of Birth: Liverpool, England
Date of Birth: 9/10/40
Profession: Gentleman
Married on: 3/20/68
Wife's name: Yoko Ono
Children (date of birth):   Sons: Julian Lennon, Sean Taro Ono
    Lennon; Daughters: Kyoko
Details of Education (please give dates, degrees, diplomas, etc.):   Life, etc.
Professional Employment (in chronological order with precise details and
    dates):   Self Employed
Creative Works (books, compositions, paintings, etc.):   Many

JOHN LENNON
Japanese Immigration Card
1975

Name: Blow Job
Nationality: Weird
Date of Birth: *Day:*   Yes, *Month:*   Yes, *Year:*   Yes
Permanent Address: Aronville Belaway
Home Address: Aronville Bullock
Occupation: Hazardo Us
Passport No.:   Thank You
Date of Issue: Regularly
Place of Issue: Crutch
Issuing Authority: God of Air
Destination: Simultaneous Discharge
Purpose of Visit: For Sightseeing/On Business
Visa No.:   Time
Ticket No. & Date of Issue: Won't Tell

JOHN LENNON
Every Day Telephone Numbers
New York, 1979

	Name	Number
Butcher:	Yoko	1
Baker:	Yoko	1
Baby Sitter:	Yoko	1
Store:	Yoko	1
Dressmaker:	Yoko	1
Grocer:	Yoko	1
Haberdasher:	Yoko	1
Laundry:	Yoko	1
Shoe Repair:	Yoko	1
Tailor:	Yoko	1
Doctor:	Yoko	1
Dentist:	Yoko	1
Police:	Yoko	1
Fire Department:	Yoko	1

JOHN LENNON
Selected Quotations on Politics
London, April 2, 1966

"The trouble with government as it is, is that it doesn't represent the people. It *controls* them. All they seem to want, the people who run the country, is to keep themselves in power and stop us from knowing what's going on. The motto seems to be: 'Keep the people happy with a few cigarettes and beer and they won't ask any questions.' I always wondered what it was about politics and government what was wrong. Now, since reading Aldous Huxley, I've suddenly found out what it's all about.

"I'm not saying politicians are all terrible men. It's just the system of government I don't like. It's been going on for hundreds of years and it'll be hard to change. I'm not an anarchist and I don't want to appear to be one. But it would be good if more people started realizing the difference between political propaganda and truth. The only possible reason they have had so many TV election broadcasts is because they've got to *force* the public to watch them. Otherwise, people couldn't care less, because in the back of their minds most thinking people know there's something wrong with the present form of government.

"We're being conned into thinking everything's okay, but all these bloody politicians seem the same to me. All they can talk about is the economy, but what about people and freedom? These things that matter more don't seem to worry them. Politicians wrongly thought that if they provided everyone with a TV set, a bed, a car, and enough money for smokes and drinks, 'they'll keep quiet.' What can you do about it? There's nothing you can do about it—it's too big. What I would really like to see is people generally getting more say in what goes on. From what you hear, none of the politicians has any intention of giving ordinary people complete freedom. Just keep them down, that's all they really want. I'm not suggesting I know what the answer is. I just know there's something wrong with the present way of governing the country, and the more people like us realize it, at least we are on the way to changing it. Politicians are not politicians because they genuinely want to do the people good. They're politicians because they want power!

"What we need to change things is a bloody revolution. I'm bored by politics because the three of them, Harold, Ted, and Joe, all seem the same to me. They know all the tricks. It's a drag, but I can't see the way out."

JOHN LENNON AND YOKO ONO
on the Film *Rape*
LONDON, 1969

Question: What are you projecting on the wall?

John Lennon: It's a film Yoko is making and directing.

Yoko Ono: It's going to be about rape.

Question: What a nice happy subject.

John: Are you going to tell him what it is really?

Yoko: It's rape with a camera. You just go on following somebody with a camera. At first they might be very happy, but you keep following them and really try to expose them until they get upset. They don't have to get upset, I just want to see how it goes.

John: You might call it an experiment.

Yoko: They don't know what it's for. I was thinking I had to make a movie where shots look like they came from a newsreel. I was thinking about the Beatles and Prime Minister Yoshamp, who is well known in Japan as someone who does not like to be photographed. Pop stars and celebrities say, "Just a quick shot," while there are those people who, when you try to get their photos, cover their face.

JOHN LENNON AND YOKO ONO
"Acorn for Peace" Press Conference
APPLE CORPS, LONDON, 1969

John Lennon: This is our next big move for peace. Yoko and I plan to send one of these envelopes containing two acorns to the head of state of every country in the world. We want them to plant them for peace.

Yoko Ono: If they want us to, we will go to the countries and plant them ourselves.

John: We are not laughing at you any more than you are laughing at us. Our Bed-Ins were simply our protest against violence. Everyone has their bag and this is ours. In Paris, the Vietnam peace talks have got only as far as sorting out the shape of the table they are going to sit around. Those talks have been going on for months. In one week of our honeymoon, we achieved a lot more. What? A little old lady from Wigan wrote to the *Daily Mirror* asking if they could put Yoko and myself on the front page more often. She said she hadn't laughed so much for ages. That's exactly what we want! I mean, it's a funny old world when two people going to bed on their honeymoon can make the front pages in all the papers for a week.

Question: Are you tired after a week-long Bed-In for peace?

John: Mentally we were both still very alert, but physically we were exhausted. In fact, we had to go to bed for a week to recover!

JOHN LENNON AND YOKO ONO
Bed-In Press Conference
QUEEN ELIZABETH HOTEL, MONTREAL, 1969

John Lennon: The press is like a post box, they can reach the people wandering around the streets.

Yoko Ono: We worked for three months figuring out the most functional approach to boosting peace before we got married, and then spent our honeymoon talking to the press in bed in Amsterdam. For us, it was the only way. We can't go out in Trafalgar Square and join in because it would create a riot. We can't lead a march because of the autograph hunters.

John: We're all responsible for war. We *all* must do something, no matter what, by growing our hair, standing on one leg, talking to the press, or staging Bed-Ins to change the attitudes. People must be aware that it's up to *them*. The effect of our Bed-Ins has made people talk about peace. But it must be done by nonviolent means, otherwise there can only be chaos. We're looking to the young people (and they have always been the hippest ones), we're telling them to get the message across to the squares. A lot of kids have been ignoring the squares when they should be helping them. The whole scene has become far too serious and intellectual.

Question: Why aren't you trying to talk directly with the world political leaders?

John: Talk about what? It doesn't happen like that. The U.S. government is too busy talking about how to keep me out! If I'm a joke, as they say, and not very important, why don't they just let me in? Bed-Ins are something everybody can do, as they're so simple. We're more than willing to be the world's clowns to make people realize it. If everybody stayed in bed for a week, there'd be no more killing. Right now we want to stir everybody, the entire world. Leaders can't exist without a following. We hope we can inspire people to do something about the leaders. I guess I'm a bit of an antinationalist, but I also fancy myself a bit of an Irishman. Still, I think antinationalism will eventually have to come if we really want peace.

Question: What about your Jesus Christ statement?

John: I think I said the Beatles have more influence on young people than Jesus. Yes, I still think it. Kids are influenced more by us than Jesus! Christ, some ministers even stood up and agreed with it. It was another piece of truth that the fascist Christians picked on. I'm all for Christ, I'm very big on Christ. I've always fancied him. He was right. As he said in his book, "You'll get knocked if you don't follow my way." He was so right about that. We got knocked. But I'm all for him. I'm always saying his name, I use it in songs, and I talk about him. "The Ballad of John and Yoko" was a fairly journalistic account of each step of our drive for peace.

Question: How did you come up with the concept of the Plastic Ono Band?

Yoko: I had an idea for a band which would never actually exist, a group made of transparent boxes with tape recorders and record players in their stomachs. It was admittedly a cynical attitude about bands, intimating that a tape recorder and a record player could do just as well. But it led me to the idea of a conceptual group, an imaginary band without actual people in it. I conceived of the idea of a group that didn't have a set number of members, a band which could accommodate anyone who wanted to play with it. Everybody in the audience and everybody who wanted to play would all be a part of the band. John made a beautiful sculpture piece for me in which we glued transparent boxes with hands to a little stand. We actually made a few transparent stands and we were going to send them all over the world and let people play any music they wanted to. John gave it the name the Plastic Ono Band. Every time we record, it comes to life. But we don't have a fixed number of members. Anyone who happens to be in the room can join. Sometimes, people who do not even play an instrument get up with us. They shout! They scream! It's marvelous.

JOHN LENNON AND YOKO ONO
Press Conference
LONDON, MARCH 1969

Question: Where did you meet?

Yoko Ono: It was the Indica Gallery. I was having a very important show there. It was damn successful. John came the night before the opening.

John Lennon: I knew the guy who ran the gallery, y'see, and he'd tell me when something was worth seeing.

Yoko: John asked if he could hammer one of the nails of the *Hammer a Nail In* piece. It's so symbolic, you see, the virginal board, for a man to hammer a nail in. I decided people should pay five shillings to hammer each nail. But when the gallery owner told John he had to pay, he stopped a moment and asked if he could just hammer an imaginary nail! It was fantastic! That is what my art is about. It was my game! The two of us were playing the same game. I didn't know who he was and when I found out, I didn't care. I mean, in the art world, a Beatle is, well, you know. Also, he was in a suit. He looked so ordinary.

John: I was not! I was in a highly unshaved and tatty state. I was up three nights. I was always up in those days, trippin'. I was stoned. I wasn't in a suit! That was my psychedelic period. It's disgusting, taking me for a clean-cut lad.

Yoko: Okay, I take it back.

John: I don't remember her at all at the gallery. I was stoned. Then she called up. She wanted scores of my songs for John Cage for some book.

Yoko: You're always changing the story.

John: But I didn't have any scores, y'know.

Yoko: I'm getting uptight.

John: What are you getting uptight about? Because I didn't remember you from the Indica Gallery? Serves you right. After saying I look like a bank clerk. We were friends. I used to bring her out to the house when my wife was here. I mean, we were just friends. I respected her work and she was having trouble with her husband. I tried to teach her how to meditate.

Yoko: I was getting very famous. My career was going well, but my husband and I were fighting about who would answer the phone. He wanted always to answer the phone so that he would be into everything. I always thought of him as my assistant. He wanted it to be both of us. All I wanted was someone who would be interested in my work. I needed a producer. The only thing about being in love is that it takes so much time. The work suffers. I am not working enough now.

John: What do you mean? It's never been easier for you to work. Because if no one else will produce what you do, I will. Whenever I'm not doing my Beatle work, I'll do her stuff completely. There's not much Beatle stuff now anyway. We both think alike and we've both been alone. We both had these dreams, the same kind of dreams. I had a dream of this woman coming. I knew it wouldn't be someone buying the Beatle records. The way it was with Cyn was she got pregnant and we got married. We never had much to say to each other. But the vibrations didn't upset me because she was quiet and I was away all the time. I'd get fed up every now and then and I'd start thinking this "Where is she?" bit. I'd hope that the "one" would come. Then I'd get past it. I mean, everybody's thinking of the one. I suppose I was hoping for a woman who would give me what I got from a man intellectually. I wanted someone I could be meself with. Of course, I'm a coward. I wasn't going to go off and leave Cyn and be by meself. Now Cyn keeps saying in the papers she didn't know anything was wrong. I don't understand that. At the beginning I was just enjoying Yoko's company. I didn't know what was really happening. Pretty soon after we knew one another, I had given up about the one-woman thing. It was gonna be the holy thing. I went to see the Maharishi and Yoko stayed here. I kept telling her to meditate, but I still had no idea about us. Then, in India, she wrote me these letters, "I'm a cloud. Watch for me in the sky." I'd get so excited about her letters. There was nothing in them wives or mother-in-laws could've understood, and from India I started thinking of her as a woman, not just an intellectual woman. I wasn't gonna write back or anything like that, though. Being a Beatle, anything you write goes right to *Confidential* in America. Then, when I got back, well, that's when it began. At first, I didn't want to get married. Yoko and me, we got such a kick out of just being in love, changing the food in the larder like young married kids. But then when we thought the baby was coming, we thought it over. Okay, so we're swinging pop stars, but he'd have enough of a freaky time just being our child, now, wouldn't he?

Question: Tell me about your nude album cover.

John: I just thought it would be a nice cover for her to be naked, alone. Then, after we got friendly, it seemed natural for it to be us both. I took the photograph meself. I didn't think there'd be such a fuss. I guess the world thinks we're an ugly couple.

JOHN LENNON
Press Conference
HEATHROW AIRPORT, LONDON, NOVEMBER 1969

Question: Couldn't you find a white belt?

John Lennon: I'm not looking for one.

Question: Is that belt leather?

John: Yes, but you've got it wrong. I'm not a vegetarian. I eat microbiotic food.

Question: Where will you and Yoko live?

John: In England, where the hell do you think we'll live? It's easier to live in the country in which you were born. You can speak the same language for a start.

Question: Are you and Yoko tired of lying in bed for the last seven days?

John: Mentally we are both still very alert. But physically we are exhausted. In fact, we're going to bed for a week to recover. These are our next moves for peace. Yoko and I plan to send one of these envelopes containing two acorns to the head of every state of every country in the world. We want them to plant them for peace.

Yoko Ono: And if they want, we would go to the countries and plant them ourselves.

Question: How can we help?

John: What we need are the addresses of the various big heads.

Question: Will they go by four-penny or five-penny post?

Question: Was the Amsterdam Bed-In just a big put-on?

John: We are not laughing at you any more than you're laughing at us. It was just our protest against violence. Everybody has their bag and this is ours. The way we look at it is this: in Paris, the Vietnam peace talks have got only as far as sorting out the shape of the table they are going to sit around. Those talks have been going on for months. In one week of our honeymoon we achieved a lot more. What? A little old lady from Wigan or Hull wrote to the *Daily Mirror* asking if they could put Yoko and myself on the front page more often. She said she hadn't laughed so much for ages. That's great, that's what we wanted. I mean, it's a funny world when two people going to bed on their honeymoon can make the front pages in all the papers for a week.

Yoko: Everything we do now is for peace. It is so important to us.

Question: But don't you think people are laughing at you?

John: I wouldn't mind dying as the world's clown. I'm not looking for epitaphs.

Question: Is your film *No. 6* a condemnation of the press?

John: No, just a reflection. It happens and you learn to accept it. If I felt that way about the press, I wouldn't have invited them to our hotel in Amsterdam. And you can tell Donald Zec we've finished with turning the other cheek. A film was being made in the room which will show exactly what Zec was saying at the time and how it differed from what he wrote afterwards.

Question: What about Northern Songs?

John: I can't make any comment about Paul or myself selling our shares. Dick James said the deal he made had to be concluded in a hurry and if that's what he said, I believe him. It won't make any difference to my songwriting, that's my main concern!

Question: Is it back to work after your "working honeymoon"?

John: I need the money. I'm not down to selling the jewelry or the Rolls, but I haven't got nearly as much as you think I have. In fact, we never did. I'm back, Paul's back, George isn't in prison, and as soon as we can drag Ringo away from the film set, we'll get down to the next album.

Question: Will you go back on the road?

John: Back on the road? It's a possibility, but it would have to be where the money is, and that's America.

JOHN LENNON
on Ronnie Hawkins
Toronto, 1969

"On our last trip to Canada somehow it was arranged that we stay at his house. I had a great time and of course I knew him from way back from his records. He turned out to be a great guy and it happened, as it were, that he had just made an album. He's about the only person that doesn't try and grease you, you know, as they say. And he played us this album, but he didn't want to play it, he's shy like most musicians. I mean I don't like playing my new record for people. I have to do it because you have that need. Anyway, I was signing these twenty-million lithographs while this album was going on, and I was just listening and signing until this track came on, 'Down in the Alley,' and it really sort of buzzed me. It sounded like now and then, and I like that."

JOHN LENNON
Open Letter to Paul McCartney
NEW YORK, 1970s

Dear Paul, Linda *et all* the wee McCartneys,

Thanks for your letter.

1. We give *you money* for your bits of Apple.

2. We give *you more money* in the form of royalties that legally belong to Apple (I know we're Apple, but on the other hand we're not). Maybe there's an answer there somewhere . . . but for the millionth time in these past few years I repeat: *What about the TAX?* It's all very well, playing "simple, honest old Paul" in the *Melody Maker,* but you know damn well we can't just sign a bit of paper!

You say, "John won't do it." I will if you'll indemnify us against the tax man! Anyway, you know that after we have our meeting, the fucking lawyers will have to implement whatever we agree on—right?

If they have some form of agreement between *them* before *we* meet, it might make it even easier. It's up to you; as we've said many times, we'll meet you whenever you like. Just make up your mind! E.g., two weeks ago I asked you on the phone, "Please let's meet without advisers, etc. and decide what we want," and I emphasized especially Maclen, which is mainly our concern, but you refused, right?

You said under *no condition* would you sell to us and if we didn't do what you wanted, you'd sue us again and that Ringo and George are going to break you, John, etc. etc.

Now I was quite straight with you that day and you tried to shoot me down with your emotional "logic." If *you're not* the aggressor (as you claim), who the hell took us to court and shat all over us in public?

As I've said before, have you ever thought that you might *possibly* be wrong about something? Your conceit about us and Klein is incredible. You say you "made the mistake of trying to advise them against him [Klein] and that pissed them off" and we secretly feel that you're right. Good God! You must *know we're right about Eastman* . . .

One other little lie in your "It's only Paul" bit: *Let It Be* is not the "first bit of hype" on a Beatle album. Remember Tony Barrow? And his wonderful writing on "Please Please Me," etc. The early Beatle Xmas records!

And you gotta admit it was a "new-phase Beatle album," incidentally written in the style of the great Barrow himself! By the way, what happened to my idea of putting the parody of our first album cover on the *Let It Be* cover?

Also, we were intending to parody Barrow originally, so it was hype. But what was your *Life* article? Tony Barrow couldn't have done it better. (And your writing inside of the album isn't exactly the realist, is it?) Anyway, enough petty bourgeois fun.

You were right about New York! I do love it; it's the *only place to be.* (Apart from anything else, they leave you alone, too.) I see you prefer Scotland . . . I'll bet you *your* piece of Apple you'll be living in New York by 1974 (two years is the usual time it takes you, right?).

Another thing, whadya mean *big* thing in Toronto? It was completely spontaneous. They rang on the *Friday*—we flew there and we played on the *Saturday*. I was sick because I was pissed. Listen to the album, with no rehearsal, too. Come on, Macka! Own up! (We'd never played together before!) Half a dozen live shows—with no big fuss—in fact, we've been *doing* what you've said the Beatles should do. Yoko and I have been doing it for three years! (I said it was daft for the Beatles to do it. I still think it's daft.) So go on and do it! Do it! Do it! E.g., *Cambridge, '69*, completely unadvertised! (A *very* small hall.) *Lyceum* Ballroom (1969, no fuss, great show, thirty-piece rock band! "Live Jam" out soon!). *Fillmore East* (1971), unannounced. (Another good time had by all—out soon!!) We even played the streets here in the Village (our spiritual home!?) with the great David Peel! We were moved on by the cops even!! It's best just to DO IT.

I know you'll dig it, and they don't even expect the Beatles now anyway!

So *you* think "Imagine" ain't political. It's "Working Class Hero" with sugar on it for conservatives like yourself! You obviously don't *dig the words*. Imagine! You took "How Do You Sleep?" so literally (read my own review of the album in *Crawdaddy*). *Your* politics are very similar to Mary Whitehouse's, saying *nothing* is as loud as saying *something*.

Listen, my obsessive old pal, it was George's press conference not dat old debbil Klein! *He* said what you said, "I'd love to come but . . ." Anyway, we did it for basically the same reasons, the Beatles bit. They still called it a Beatles show, with just two of them!

Join the Rock Liberation Front before it gets you!

Wanna put your photo on the label like uncool John and Yoko, do ya? (Ain't ya got no shame!) If we're *not* cool, *what does that make you?*

No hard feelings to you either. I know basically we want the same, and as I said on the phone and in this letter, whenever you want to meet, all you have to do is call.

All you need is love
Power to the people
Free all prisoners
Jail the judges
Love and peace
Get it on and rip 'em off

JOHN LENNON

P.S. The bit that really puzzled us was asking to meet *without Linda and Yoko*. I thought you'd have understood *by now* that *I'm JohnandYoko*.
P.P.S. Even *your own* lawyers know you can't "just sign a bit of paper" (or don't they tell you?).

JOHN LENNON
Press Release

DECEMBER 13, 1971

Apple was/is a capitalist concern. We brought in a capitalist to prevent it from sinking (with the Beatles on board). The whole problem the ex-Beatles have is concerned with their commitment [sic] to Apple. I referred to tax in answer to Paul's article in M.M.* and other British weeklies, i.e., "let's just sign a bit of paper." *You* may not worry about our tax-scene, but if we don't, your Fab Four will end up like Mickey Rooney, Joe Lois [sic], etc., performing, for the rest of their lives to pay back the tax man.

We, John and Yoko, have asked them, Apple, to reduce the cost of Yoko's album *Fly*, and they told us they had.

I personally have had enough of Apple/Ascot and all other properties which tie me down, mentally and physically. I intend to cash in my chips as soon as I can, and be *free*.

John/Yoko intend to do all performances around the world *free* and/or whatever we've earned will go, e.g., to prisons to release people who can't afford bail, etc., and many other ways of getting money back to the people.

This is one way of paying the people back.

Until we find an alternative, the Pete Bennetes and the Apples, EMIs, etc., are the only way of getting our product to the people. (Not to mention the contractual angle). If you know of any other way don't keep it a secret!

Power to the People

JOHN AND YOKO

*M.M. refers to the British music magazine *Melody Maker*.

JOHN LENNON
FBI Memo

New York, May 1972

TO: Acting Director, FBI (100-469901)

FROM: SAC, New York (100-175319) (P)

SUBJECT: John Winston Lennon

SM-REVACT

MIREP

Re: NY airtel, dated 5/25/72, and Miami airtel, dated 6/5/72.

Attached are 5 copies for the Bureau, and 7 copies for Miami, of an LHM dated and captioned as above. Miami should note that Lennon is reportedly a "heavy user of narcotics" known as "downers." This information should be emphasized to local Law Enforcement Agencies covering MIREP, with regards to subject being arrested if at all possible on possession of narcotics charge.

Local INS has a very loose case in NY for deporting subject on narcotics charge involving a 1968 arrest in England.

INS has stressed to the Bureau that if Lennon were to be arrested in the U.S. for possession of narcotics he would become more likely immediately deportable.

2 - Bureau (Encls. 5)

2 - Miami (Encls. 7)

1 - New York

CONFIDENTIAL

John Winston Lennon

Source advised that Lennon appears to be radically orientated, however he does not give the impression he is a true revolutionist since he is constantly under the influence of narcotics.

Jerry Rubin, is a convicted defendant of the so-called Conspiracy Seven Trial, Chicago, Illinois, in the period September, 1969 through

February, 1970, involving those persons earlier indicted for violation of the Federal Anti-Riot Status.

On March 14, 1972, Mr. Vincent Schiano, Chief Trial Attorney, INS, New York City, admitted that Lennon and his wife Yoko Ono, on March 6, 1972, were served with an INS order to show cause as to why they should not be deported from the United States as over-stayed visitors. Mr. Schiano advised that Lennon and his wife are scheduled at INS, New York City on March 16, 1972 to answer the show cause order.

JOHN LENNON AND YOKO ONO
Press Release
NEW YORK, 1973

NEWSWECANALLDOWITHOUT

Although John and Yoko and George, and George and Ringo, had played together often, it was the first time the three ex-Beatles had played together since the band broke up. As usual, an awful lot of rumors, if not downright lies, were going on, including the possibility of impresario Allen De Klein or grABCKO playing bass for the other three in an as-yet-untitled album called, *I Was a Teenage Fat Cat*. Producer Richard Perry, who planned to take the tapes along to sell them to Paul McCartney, told a friend: "I'll take the tapes to Paul McCartney."

The extreme humility that existed between John and Paul seems to have evaporated. "They've spoken to each other on the telephone, and in English, that's a change," said a McCartney associate. "If only everything were as simple and unaffected as McCartney's new single, 'My Love,' then maybe Dean Martin and Jerry Lewis would be reunited with the Marx Bros and *Newsweek* could get a job,' said an East African official.

Yours Up To The Teeth,
John Lennon and Yoko Ono.

JOHN LENNON AND SAMUEL BECKETT
Interview
New York, 1970s

Samuel Beckett: I wanted also to ask you about the eggman from "I Am the Walrus."

John Lennon: Jerry.

Sam: What? Who?

John: Jerry Furman, he was our eggman. Every Saturday Jerry would come round and Mum would give him a bob for a dozen eggs. Once, while he was inside the house, I peeked into the back of his van. So many eggs! I'd never seen anything like it! God, I wanted his job!

Sam: So the eggman was Jerry! Why didn't you put that in the lyric of "Glass Onion" as well, like "and here's some good advice for the way/the eggman was Jerry."

John: No, no! I couldn't have done that!

Sam: Why not?

John: Furman was a very private bloke! I mean, shit, Paul was fair game. He'd already adjusted to the public. Furman's gig was eggs, just eggs. People would have fucking hounded him to death! Anyway, he left after a time. We got a new, nastier eggman when I was about twelve. Jerry moved to Pennsylvania, Maryland, or someplace like that. Just one of the many fascinating commodity "men" I watched when I was small.

Sam: Lord, yes! There was a man for everything, wasn't there?

John: Now that you mention it, Christ, there was a milkman, a bread-man, a fruitman, garbageman, rag-and-bone man.

Sam: Neighborhood life was a parade! There was the postman, police-man, fireman, telephone man, insurance man, Fuller Brush man, the Culligan man, the Maytag repairman.

John: Right! And always they'd identify themselves as such, like they didn't have a name or something. I mean, you'd hear this rap-rap-rap on the door followed by a muffled "milkman", or "eggman", or whatever!

Sam: Thank heaven that's all stopped. Can you imagine the cacophony in this age of overspecialized marketing?

John: And what on earth would "I Am the Walrus" have sounded like? Ha, ha, ha!

Sam: What?

John: Rap-rap-rap! Hemorrhoid Reeferman! Kemorrhoidman! Need anything up yours today?

Sam: Rap-rap-rap! Tweezerman!

John: Rap-rap-rap! Hola! Yardstickman here! Yardstickman!

Sam: Or in the rural areas: Rap-rap-rap! Pitchforkman! Pitchforkman!

John: Or for the Pinteresque machinists: Rap-rap-rap! High speed, tapered shank, spiral flube reamerman! Any high-speed, tapered shank, spiral flube reamers today?

Sam: Rap-rap-rap! Astronaut! Rap-rap-rap! Paperclipman!

John: Door-to-door Einstein Rap-rap-rap! Cosmologyman! Theoretical physicsman! Fresh picked photoelectric effects! Nice pipe unified field theories!

Sam: Rap-rap-rap! Beanman!

John: What? Beanman? You mean like navy beans and kidney beans, like that?

Sam: Yes! That's it!

John: That's what I could have said. "I am the beanman, they are the beanman, I am the bovus! Toot, toot, toot, toot!"

Sam: Rap-rap-rap! Fartman! Fartman!

RE: John Lennon and Yoko Ono
Immigration and Naturalization
Service Memo

WASHINGTON, D.C., OCTOBER 10, 1974

FROM: Supervisor, Intelligence Division, Unit 2.

TO: Regional Director, Group 3.

SUBJECT: The Supervision of the Activities of Both John and Yoko Lennon

It has come to the further attention of this office that John Ono Lennon, formerly of the Beatles, and Yoko Ono Lennon, wife of John Lennon, have intentions of remaining in this country and seeking permanent residence therein. This has been judged to be inadvisable and it was recommended that all applications are to be denied.

Their relationships with one (6521) Jerry Rubin, and one John Sinclair (4536), also their many commitments which are judged to be highly political and unfavorable to the present administration . . . Your office is to maintain a constant servaillence [sic] on their residence and a periodic report is to be sent to this office. All cooperation is to [be] given to the INS and all reports are to be directed by this office.

JOHN LENNON
Selected Quotations

LONDON AND NEW YORK, DATES UNKNOWN

"I always was a rebel, but on the other hand I wanna be loved and accepted by all facets of society and not be this 'loud mouth lunatic, poet, musician,' but I cannot be what I'm not."

"When I was sixteen, I re-established a relationship with my mother Julia for about four years, she taught me music. And then unfortunately she was run over by an off-duty policeman who was drunk at the time. That was really a hard time for me. And it just absolutely made me very, very bitter."

"You know, you went to see those movies with Elvis or somebody in it when we were still in Liverpool, and you see everybody waiting to see him. And I'd be waiting there, too. And they'd all scream when he came on the screen. So I thought, 'That's a good job!'"

"When the Beatles were depressed, thinking the group is going nowhere, I'd say, 'Where are we going, fellas?' And they'd go, 'To the top, Johnny!' And I'd say, 'What's that, fellas?,' and they'd say, 'To the toppermost of the poppermost!' and I'd say, 'Right!'"

"When I was a Beatle, I thought we were the best group in the god-damn world! And believing that was what made us what we were."

"Beatlemania was like being in the eye of a hurricane. You thought, 'What's going on? How did I get here? The last thing I remember was playing music in a club, and the next minute . . . this!'"

"Don't you think the Beatles gave every sodding thing they got? That took our whole life, a whole section of our youth. When everybody else was just goofing off we were working twenty-four hours a day."

"The whole Beatle thing was just beyond comprehension, and I was eating and drinking like a pig, and subconsciously I was crying for help."

"Don't confuse my songs with your own life. I mean they might have relevance to your life, but a lot of things do. I'm just a guy who writes songs. We can only say hello and what else is there? . . . Are you hungry?"

"Shea Stadium was happening. You couldn't hear any music at all. And sometimes things'd break down and nobody'd know."

"Women should be obscene and not heard."

"A woman's place is on the floor."

CLOCKWISE FROM TOP LEFT:

George (center) as a tidy little Liverpool lad.

Mimi Smith, who raised John as a boy.

*Relaxing in the Grapes on Matthews Street
after an early gig with original
drummer Pete Best, 1960.*

TOP TO BOTTOM:

A very early gig with Pete on drums.

Soaked to the bone following a very rainy welcome in the mid-sixties.

Mr. and Mrs. Starkey at the initial height of the Beatles' success. February 10, 1964.

TOP TO BOTTOM:

The Boys meet the press in Boston. September 12, 1964.

On the road somewhere in America, 1965.

The Fabs.

THIS PAGE, TOP TO BOTTOM:

Meeting the press in Manila following a particularly dreadful concert tour.

(Left to right) Beatles road manager Mal Evans, Lennon, Apple promo man Derek Taylor, McCartney, and best bud "Magic" Alex Mardas, 1967.

FACING PAGE, TOP TO BOTTOM:

Hari with mentor pundit Ravi Shankar. India, 1966.

The Fab Four as we remember them: happy, productive, and very together. May 20, 1967.

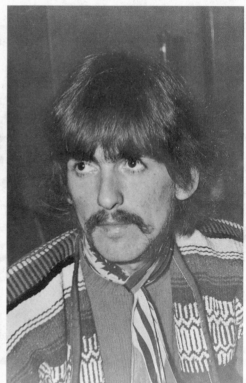

TOP TO BOTTOM:

*The Magical Mystery Tour is waylaid
at a particularly tiny British bridge.
September 13, 1967.*

*Frolicking during a break in shooting
for the Mystery Tour.*

*A break in editing for the ill-fated film.
London, November 27, 1967.*

*The wonderful Bonzo Dog Do Dah
Band in a vintage sixties shot, 1968.*

JOHN LENNON
Press Release
New York, 1975

*And opened lettuce to Sodd Runtlestuntle** (from Dr. Winston O'boogic)

Couldn't resist adding a few "islands of truth" of my own, in answer to Turd Runtgreen's howl of hate (paine.)

Dear Todd,

I like you, and some of your work, including "I Saw the Light," which is not unlike "There's a Place" (Beatles), melody wise.

1. I have never claimed to be a revolutionary. But I am allowed to sing about anything I want! Right?

2. I never hit a waitress in the Troubadour. I did act like an ass, I was drunk. So shoot me!

3. I guess we're all looking for attention Rod, do you really think I don't know how to get it, without "revolution"? I could dye my hair green and pink for a start!

4. I don't represent anyone but my *self*. It sounds like I represented something to you, or you wouldn't be so violent towards me. (Your dad perhaps?)

5. Yes Dodd, violence comes in mysterious ways, it's wonders to perform, including, verbal. But you'd know that kind of mind game, wouldn't you? Of course you would.

6. So the Nazz use to do "like heavy rock" then *suddenly* a "light pretty ballad." How original!

7. Which gets me to the Beatles, 'who had no other style than being the Beatles'!! That covers a lot of style man, including your own, to date. . . .

Yes Godd, the one thing those Beatles did was to affect *peoples' minds.* Maybe you need another fix?

*Todd Rundgren.

Somebody played me your rock'n'roll pussy song, but I never noticed anything. I think the real reason you're mad at me is 'cause I didn't know who you were at the Rainbow (L.A.) Remember that time you came in with Wolfman Jack? When I found out later, I was cursing, because I wanted to tell you how good you were. (I'd heard you on the radio.)

Anyway,

However much you hurt me darling,

I'll always love you,

J. L.

JOHN LENNON
Interview
New York, June 5, 1975

Question: There's still a good feeling among the guys?

John Lennon: Yeah, yeah. I talked to Ringo and George yesterday. I didn't talk to Paul because he was asleep. George and Paul are talking to each other in L.A. now. There's nothing going down between us. It's all in people's heads.

Question: You went to one of George's concerts; what are your thoughts on his tour?

John: It wasn't the greatest thing in history. The guy went through some kind of mill. It was probably his turn to get smacked. When we were all together there was periods when the Beatles were in, the Beatles were out, no matter what we were doing. Now it's always the Beatles were great or the Beatles weren't great, whatever opinion people hold. There's a sort of illusion about it. But the actual fact was the Beatles were in for eight months, the Beatles were out for eight months. The public, including the media, are sometimes a bit sheeplike and if the ball starts rolling, well, it's just that somebody's in, somebody's out. George is out for the moment. And I think it didn't matter what he did on tour.

Question: George told *Rolling Stone* that if you wanted the Beatles, go listen to Wings. It seemed a bit of a putdown.

John: I didn't see what George said, so I really don't have any comment. *Band On The Run* is a great album. Wings is almost as conceptual a group as Plastic Ono Band. Plastic Ono was a conceptual group, meaning that whoever was playing was the band. And Wings keeps changing all the time. It's conceptual. I mean, they're backup men for Paul. It doesn't matter who's playing. You can call them Wings, but it's Paul McCartney music. And it's good stuff. It's good Paul music and I don't really see the connection.

Question: What do you think of Richard Perry's work with Ringo?

John: I think it's great. Perry's great, Ringo's great, I think the combination was great and look how well they did together. There's no complaints if you're Number One.

Question: George said at his press conference that he could play with you again, but not with Paul. How do you feel?

John: I could play with all of them. George is entitled to say that, and he'll probably change his mind by Friday. You know, we're all human. We can all change our minds. So I don't take any of my statements or any of their statements as the last word on whether we will. And if we do, the newspapers will learn about it after the fact. If we're gonna play, we're just gonna play.

JOHN LENNON
Interview
New York, 1977

Question: Will you tour in 1977?

John Lennon: No.

Question: Is Dallas (or Texas) on the agenda?

John: No.

Question: Will you have a new album out prior to the tour?

John: Sometime or other.

Question: Have you read Allan Williams' *The Man Who Gave the Beatles Away?*

John: Yes.

Question: Is it completely true or has the story been fictionalized somewhat?

John: Mostly true.

Question: How do you look back upon your early years in Liverpool and Hamburg?

John: From a distance.

JOHN WINSTON ONO LENNON
Last Will and Testament
NEW YORK, NOVEMBER 12, 1979

I, JOHN WINSTON ONO LENNON, a resident of the County of New York, State of New York which I declare to be my domicile, do hereby make, publish, and declare this to be my Last Will and Testament, hereby revoking all other Wills, Codicils and Testamentary dispositions by me at any time heretofore made.

FIRST: The expenses of my funeral and the administration of my estate, and all inheritance, estate or succession taxes, including interest and penalties, payable by reason of my death, shall be paid out of and charged generally against the principal of my residuary estate without apportionment or proration. My Executor shall not seek contribution or reimbursement for any such payments.

SECOND: Should my wife survive me, I give, devise, and bequeath to her absolutely, an amount equal to that portion of my residuary estate, the numerator and denominator of which shall be determined as follows:

1. The numerator shall be an amount equal to one-half (½) of my adjusted gross estate, less the value of all other property included in my gross estate for Federal Estate Tax purpose, and which pass or shall have passed to my wife, either under any other provision of this will or in any manner outside of this will in such manner as to qualify for and be allowed as a marital deduction. The words "pass", "have passed", "marital deduction", and "adjusted gross estate" shall have the same meaning as said words have under those provisions of the United States Internal Revenue Code applicable to my estate.

2. The denominator shall be an amount representing the value of my residuary estate.

THIRD: I give, devise, and bequeath all the rest, residue, and remainder of my estate, wheresoever situate, to the Trustees under a Trust Agreement and any amendments made pursuant to its terms before my death.

FOURTH: In the event that my wife and I die under such circumstances that there is not sufficient evidence to determine which of us has predeceased, that I shall have predeceased her and that this, my will, and any and all of its provisions, shall be construed based upon that assumption.

FIFTH: I hereby nominate, constitute, and appoint my beloved wife, Yoko Ono, to act as the executor of this, my Last Will and Testament. In the event that my beloved wife Yoko Ono shall predecease me or chooses not to act for any reason, I nominate and appoint Eli Garber, David Warmflash, and Charles Pettit, in the order named, to act in her place and stead.

SIXTH: I nominate, constitute, and appoint my wife Yoko Ono, as the Guardian of the person and property of any children of the marriage who may survive me. In the events that she predeceases me, or for any reason she chooses not to act in that capacity, I nominate, constitute, and appoint Sam Green to act in her place and stead.

SEVENTH: No person named herein to serve in any fiduciary capacity shall be required to file or post any bond for the faithful performance of his or her duties, in that capacity, in this or in any other jurisdiction, any law to the contrary notwithstanding.

EIGHTH: If any legatee or beneficiary under this Will or the Trust agreement between myself as Grantor and Yoko Ono Lennon and Eli Barber as Trustees, dated November 12, 1979, shall interpose objections to the probate of this Will, or institute or prosecute or be in any way interested or instrumental in the institution or prosecution of any action or proceeding for the purpose of setting aside of invalidating this Will, then and in each such case, I direct that such legatee or beneficiary shall receive nothing whatsoever under this Will or the aforementioned Trust.

THE FOREGOING INSTRUMENT consisting of four (4) typewritten pages, including this page, was on the 12th day of November, 1979, signed, sealed, published, and declared by John Winston Ono Lennon, the Testator therein named, as and for his last Will and Testament, and in the presence of each other, have hereunto set our names as witnesses.

IN WITNESS WHEREOF, I have subscribed and sealed and do publish and declare these presents as and for my Last Will and Testament this 12th day of November, 1979.

John Winston Ono Lennon

YOKO ONO
Press Release
DECEMBER 10, 1980

I told Sean what happened. I showed him the picture of his father on the cover of the paper and explained the situation. I took Sean to the spot where John lay after he was shot. Sean wanted to know why the person shot John if he liked John. I explained that he was probably a confused person. Sean said that we should find out if he was confused or if he really had meant to kill John. I said that was up to the court. He asked what court, a tennis court or a basketball court? That's how Sean used to talk with his father. They were buddies. John would have been proud of Sean if he had heard this. Sean cried later. He also said, "Now Daddy is part of God. I guess when you die you become much more bigger because you're part of everything."

I don't have much more to add to Sean's statement. The silent vigil will take place December 14th at 2 p.m. for ten minutes.
Our thoughts will be with you.

LOVE, YOKO AND SEAN

YOKO ONO
Press Release
DECEMBER 14, 1980

Bless you for your tears and prayers.
I saw John smiling in the sky.
I saw sorrow changing into clarity.
I saw all of us becoming one mind.
Thank you.

LOVE,

Yoko
December 14, 1980
NYC

YOKO ONO
Interview
NEW YORK, 1981

Yoko Ono: I thought about writing happy songs [on this album] because I had gone through such a sad period in my life. My last LP, *Season of Glass,* was, I suppose, a primal scream, therapeutic, more than anything else. Songs I wrote during that period, "Walking on Thin

Ice," "Dogtown," were beautiful, but sad and have haunted me. Rather than relive those feelings, I wanted to try and write songs like "Dream Love" or "It's Alright" to inspire people to feel happier. That's the way *I'm* starting to feel. I think we all could use some energy, encouragement, and positive thinking.

When I wrote "It's Alright" I was going through a very difficult time just coping with being a widow. I was shaky inside, and to combat the fear one day I began to compose a list of things I had to be thankful for. I wasn't really in the mood to be saying, "It's alright," but as soon as I started banging it out on the piano, I began to feel better.

When I was younger, I used to write a lot of melancholic songs, "to be or not to be," that sort of thing. I've since learned it's a luxury to be melancholic. When you're really up against a wall, you can't afford to ponder, "to be or not to be." You just say, "I'm going to survive!"

In the past when I was making music, I thought, "Let's do something really funky, be musically experimental." This time I thought only about creating something beautiful that would comfort people. I was trying to bring out the healing power of music more than anything else. In the old days, I suppose music was my security blanket, a way of cutting myself off from the pain. But when I met John, it just clicked in me, why, it's the heartbeat, of course. And then, suddenly, rock made sense.

Speaking about my avant-garde days is like talking about an old boyfriend; it doesn't interest me. On my early albums, I did some pretty daring things, making songs with only my voice in place of guitar, bass and drums. But I don't really want to repeat the things I did before. In avant-garde you can also be experimental to the point of self-indulgence. And then there's the chance your work won't be appreciated for twenty years! I want to communicate *now*! So whenever the "arty" side of me would start to show, I would say, "No!" Try to imagine someone on roller skates in Central Park listening to my record with headphones. That doesn't mean I've sold out. Pop is the language of the people I'm interested in reaching. It communicates directly and with simplicity, cutting through the garbage to express true feelings.

I've been criticized for making my songs "too personal." But I'd like to think my experiences are not so unique. After all, the emotion that inspired "Loneliness" is something we all share. I thought that expressing my vulnerability was important at this time because a lot of people see me as a superstrong woman. Which I'm not. Somebody said to me, "What a price you've paid to write these songs!" Which is true. I'm proud that both John and I were genuine and honest in our efforts to communicate. What else is there to give but your soul?

This album covers not only the range of emotions but the spectrum of music in my life. You can hear the classical influence in the layers of harmonies. The avant-garde influence in the introduction to "Never Say Goodbye." There's a gospel flavor to "Let the Tears Dry." And the rock beat, well, it's a part of my life now. I can't really think of music without it.

Our world is getting smaller, so I've tried to make this an international album. I've used Third-World percussion, rock, on top of that, classical harmonies, and above everything the sound of the future, synthesizers and space guns. We are together, the whole world is sharing, that's the concept of "I See Rainbows."

When I wrote that song, I was feeling the scarcity of love and warmth in my life. In fact, I was thinking of leaving New York, escaping, just Sean and me. Forgetting all about political commitment and our efforts for peace. I thought, "We've done enough in that direction. Now we have to be selfish and worry about our own survival." I looked at the map, trying to find a safe place to go, and I just had to laugh because, of course, there was none! So I had to own up. We can't just save ourselves. We're all in this together. So let's really try to make this a better world.

As John and I used to say, "A dream becomes a reality when two people dream together." Little by little, things *can* change. First be good parents. Improve your city. Create a better country, and then, finally, a better world.

Now, John is up there. It's not the two of us dreaming anymore. So I have to ask the world to dream with me. Start in your mind. Visualize a rainbow and then send it out.

People may ask, "Why put John on this album? This album can stand on its own. It's your life, a new life. Isn't it better you don't include the past?"

I really had to think about that, yet I decided to take the chance and put John on this album because I knew he would have wanted to be on it. I put his voice on "Never Say Goodbye," along with Sean's and my own. On the cover collage, John is standing beside Sean and myself, as if telling the world, "Look at these two, how beautiful they are. And they're mine!"

To you, well, John belongs to the world. But to me, he is my husband. Even if his name had been Joe Smith when he died, I would still like a little something of him to be with me for my first real debut album. It's a sweet gesture to him. My single, "My Man," is a gesture, too. John always used to say, "Yoko, how come you never write a love song for me? I'm *always* telling the world how I feel about you!" Well, John, here is your love song. And I know wherever you are, you're hearing it.

YOKO ONO
Selected Quotations
New York, 1983

"John and I were part of the huge crowd of world youth who grew up believing in American idealism and its claim for human rights. We lived in societies under lingering Victorian influence while sharing the American dream in our hearts. America was us: The Navigator to the future world. John held this belief to the end."

"Oh yes, I remember this. It was just something John did back in London around the Apple time. Just his usual madness and funny sense of humor, you know. Don't bend it or anything. They're selling it for over two hundred dollars now. Can you imagine?"
    Yoko Ono on John's little-known third book, *John Lennon's London Diary 1969*

"There should be a place to keep everything."
    Yoko Ono on the creation of a John Lennon museum

PAUL McCARTNEY

PART THREE

Will I Wait a Lonely Lifetime

PAUL McCARTNEY
Interview

Question: Have you finished with the Maharishi?

Paul McCartney: Not finished with, but we're over that phase. It was a bit of a phase. He's still a nice fellow and everybody's fine. But we don't go out with him anymore.

PAUL McCARTNEY
Self Interview, Press Release
LONDON, 1970

Question: Why did you decide to make a solo album?

Paul McCartney: Because I got a Studer four-track machine at home, practiced on it, playing all the instruments, liked the results, and decided to make it into an album.

Question: Were you influenced by John's adventures with the Plastic Ono Band and Ringo's solo LP?

Paul: Sort of, but not really.

Question: Are all the songs by Paul McCartney alone?

Paul: Yes, sir.

Question: Will they be so credited?

Paul: It's a bit daft for them to be Lennon/McCartney credited, so "McCartney" it is.

Question: Did you enjoy working as a solo?

Paul: Very much. I only had me to ask for a decision and I generally agreed with me. Remember, Linda's on it too, so it's really a double act.

Question: What is Linda's contribution?

Paul: Strictly speaking, she harmonizes, but of course, it's more than that, because she is a shoulder to lean on, a second opinion, and a photographer of renown. More than all this, she believes in me, constantly.

Question: Where was the album recorded?

Paul: At home, at EMI number two studio, and at Morgan Studios Willesden.

Question: What is your home equipment, in some detail?

Paul: One Studer four-track machine. I only had, however, one mike, and as Mr. Pender, Mr. Sweatenham, and others only managed to take six months or so, slight delay. I worked without VU meters or a mixer, which meant that everything had to be listened to first for distortion, etc., then recorded. So the answer, a Studer, one mike, and nerve.

Question: Why did you work in the studios you chose?

Paul: They were available. EMI is technically good and Morgan is cozy.

Question: The album was not known about until it was nearly completed. Was this deliberate?

Paul: Yes, because normally an album is old before it comes out. Witness *Get Back*.

Question: Why?

Paul: I've always wanted to buy a Beatles album like "people" do and be as surprised as they must be. So this was the next best thing. Linda and I are the only two who will be sick of it by the release date. We love it, really.

Question: Are you able to describe the texture or feel of the album in a few words?

Paul: Home, family, love.

Question: How long did it take to complete, from when to when?

Paul: From just before, I think, Christmas, until now. "The Lovely

Linda" was the first thing I recorded at home and was originally to test the equipment. That was around Christmas.

Question: Assuming all the songs are new to the public, how new are they to you? Are they recent?

Paul: One was from 1959, "Hot as Sun," two from India, "Junk," "Teddy Boy," and the rest are pretty recent. "Valentine Day," "Momma Miss America," and "Oo You" were ad-libbed on the spot.

Question: Which instruments have you played on the album?

Paul: Bass, drums, acoustic guitar, lead guitar, piano and organ, Mellotron, toy xylophone, bow and arrow.

Question: Have you played all these instruments on earlier recordings?

Paul: Yes, drums being the one I wouldn't normally do.

Question: Why did you do all the instruments yourself?

Paul: I think I'm pretty good.

Question: Will Linda be heard on all future records?

Paul: Could be, we love singing together and have plenty of opportunity for practice.

Question: Will Paul and Linda become a John and Yoko?

Paul: No, they will become Paul and Linda.

Question: Are you pleased with your work?

Paul: Yes.

Question: Will the other Beatles receive the first copies?

Paul: Wait and see.

Question: What has recording alone taught you?

Paul: That to make your own decisions about what you do is easy and playing with yourself is difficult, but satisfying.

Question: Who had done the artwork?

Paul: Linda has taken all the photos and she and I designed the package.

Question: Is it true that neither Allen Klein nor ABKCO have been, nor will be, in any way involved with the productions, manufacturing, distribution, or promotion of this new album?

Paul: Not if I can help it.

Question: Did you miss the other Beatles and George Martin? Was there a moment, e.g., when you thought: "I wish Ringo was here for this break?"

Paul: No.

Question: Assuming this is a very big hit album, will you do another?

Paul: Even if it isn't, I will continue to do what I want when I want.

Question: Are you planning a new album or single with the Beatles?

Paul: No.

Question: Is this album a rest away from the Beatles or the start of a solo career?

Paul: Time will tell. Being a solo means it's "the start of a solo career . . ." and not being done with the Beatles means it's a rest. So it's both.

Question: Have you any plans for live appearances?

Paul: No.

Question: Is your break with the Beatles temporary or permanent, due to personal differences or musical ones?

Paul: Personal differences, business differences, musical differences, but most of all because I have a better tie with my family. Temporary or permanent? I don't know.

Question: Do you foresee a time when Lennon/McCartney becomes an active songwriting partnership again?

Paul: No.

Question: What do you feel about John's peace efforts? The Plastic Ono Band? Giving back the MBE? Yoko's influence? Yoko?

Paul: I love John and respect what he does, but it doesn't give me any pleasure.

Question: Have you plans to produce any other artists?

Paul: No.

Question: Were any of the songs on the album originally written with the Beatles in mind?

Paul: The older ones were. "Junk" was intended for *Abbey Road,* but something happened. "Teddy Boy" was for *Get Back,* but something happened.

Question: Were you pleased with *Abbey Road?* Was it musically restricting?

Paul: It was a good album. Number one for a long time.

Question: What is your relationship with Klein?

Paul: It isn't. I am not in contact with him and he does not represent me in *any* way.

Question: What is your relationship with Apple?

Paul: It is the office of a company which I part own with the other three Beatles. I don't go there because I don't like offices or businesses, especially when I am on holiday.

Question: Have you any plans to set up an independent production company?

Paul: McCartney Productions.

Question: What sort of music has influenced you on this album?

Paul: Light and loose.

Question: Are you writing more prolifically now? Or less so?

Paul: About the same. I have a queue waiting to be recorded.

Question: What are your plans now? A holiday? A musical? A movie? Retirement?

Paul: My only plan is to grow up.

PAUL McCARTNEY AND WINGS
Press Release
LONDON, 1972

New Double "A" Side from Paul McCartney and Wings

Welcome to the new single from Paul McCartney and Wings. It's a double "A" side to be released on Friday. December 1st, coupling two Paul and Linda McCartney compositions, "Hi Hi Hi" and "C Moon."

Both songs were recorded in early November at EMI's Abbey Road recording studios and feature Paul and Linda McCartney, Denny Laine, Henry McCulloch, and Denny Seiwell. The sessions were produced by Paul.

"Hi Hi Hi" was played for the first time on the band's recent European tour. So good was the reception the song received that Paul McCartney and Wings were left with little choice—"Hi Hi Hi" just *had* to be the band's third single. (It's strictly a single release and won't be on the album which the band is currently recording for release in the early New Year.)

"C Moon"? It's simply a very beautiful and subtle song. As all of you remember, Sam the Sham in "Woolly Bully" sings: "Let's not be L7", meaning: "Let's not be square". "C Moon" is the opposite of "L7", so it's obvious that "C Moon" means "Cool".

So here's the new single—"Hi Hi Hi" and "C Moon."

All the best,

Paul McCartney and Wings.

"Hi Hi Hi"—Paul McCartney (Bass, Lead Vocals), Linda McCartney (Piano, Vocals), Denny Laine & Henry McCulloch (Guitars, Vocals), Denny Seiwell (Drums).

"C Moon"—Paul McCartney (Piano, Lead Vocals), Linda McCartney (Tambourine, Vocals), Denny Laine (Bass, Vocals), Henry McCulloch (Drums, Vocals), Denny Seiwell (Trumpet).

PAUL AND LINDA McCARTNEY
in Conversation
New York, 1980s

Paul: Thorn EMI. They don't want to damage their image sufficiently to say "we cheated the Beatles. We shan't be the company that goes down in history for that . . ." I explained to the Beatles what the deal was. . . . So in the end I said, "We're very happy about the override situation and sue us. If you've got a problem, you better sue us." They said, "We'd better talk," seeing I was sticking to it. They feel I'm so desperate [Harrison, Starr, and Ono] to settle the Apple thing I will go along with all their other stuff.

Linda: Paul's desperate like a hole in the head. It's just that [Harrison] doesn't want his kids to be hung up with Apple . . . Paul is willing to blow up Apple.

Paul: I was ready to blow up Apple, had my finger on the plunger, I said to them, "I'm so fed up with this company, if it all has to go to Maggie [Thatcher] and her tax man, fine.

Linda: [Paul] still is ready, by the way, so don't be threatening us!

Paul: I threatened that and Ringo says, "Oh, come on, don't be silly." George said, "I can't understand how you'd want to do that. It would all go to the tax man." I said, "Yeah, I know, you don't think I want to send it to the tax man, but I'm getting on quite nicely with my own affairs and I want a bit of quality of life, so I'm ready to blow it up. To do that I will withhold promotion fees and then it'll be seen as a nontrading company . . . and that's it, gone! I'm prepared to do that . . . So I said to Ringo, "No," to promotion fees. He said, "I'm asking for one set of pocket money, I need it, I'm your buddy, here's why." He pleaded personally with me. I said, "Okay, here's the deal; I'll give you one more set of promotion fees, but you must understand, I only have one lever in this entire situation, the rest of the time I'm at your mercy," (which I knew was my veto) and maybe I'm not going to pay anything, and he said, "One more set please, just be a buddy." I said, "Right, but if you come to me after for anymore . . . you're definitely not getting them." So he said, "It's a deal, if anyone asks you for more . . . after this I'll be on your side with the plunger. We'll both push it together. One more set of fees, okay?" "You've got it. You're my friend, I hate to see you begging and stuff so lets just do it. [You and] your missus, I like you a lot." And, of course, I don't want this adversarial position anyway, to I'm happy to do that. So we met December first, gave one more set of promotion fees and tried to get some sense out of everyone. Ringo convened that meeting and he did rather well to get everyone at the same place at once. We then went through the whole thing. I said, "Stick it!" And they blame me for the override. [I said] "We're perfectly clean . . . If you want to fight us, fine, we're ready for you, let's do it." At which point they got a little more sensible and said, "Well then, let us work something out . . ." I'd come to that meeting wanting one thing, certainly not Capitol because I've got it. I wanted Apple to be closed down that day and I capitulated, I said, "All right then, I'll do you all a deal seeing as you're my friends, let's all go to Capitol, and let's try and get you equalized, or better . . . If you get equalized, I'll be compensated for my six albums by three million, a snip, but it's the price of peace, I'll do it." That was the agreement, and then the second point was . . . as soon after as possible, finish Apple up. As point one was impossible (as we sort of thought it might [be]), we [should] move to point two. They're arrogant, pigheaded, and they're dopes. They really are arrogant. They really think they're something, especially someone like Ringo . . .

Linda: Don't say that on tape, honey.

Paul: I don't care. That's how I feel. I wouldn't say that if I didn't understand them . . . It's insane . . .

Linda: I don't talk anymore, it's such madness.

Paul: They would rather spend double to achieve less than that. "Good thinking boys!" This is very similar to the preemption thing. Ringo, who was holding us all up on that, did not understand it. I'm telling you, I sat down with him and he said, "You don't want me to sell this thing [Ringo's share of the Beatles]." And I said, "No, no, no. If you sell it you must offer it to George and I." He said, "Oh, you know, I'd do that." I said, "Could you say that into this tape? . . ." I said, "Barbara, I want you to get this straight, he just said he would offer it absolutely unequivocally to me and George." Ringo said, "Yeah, but that's not what you're after. You just don't want me to sell, do you?" I said, "You can sell to anybody, Arab or not, but before you do, allow George and I to match his offer." He said, "You know I'd do that." Ringo, I'm going to ring right now and tell him [George] just what you said. Barbara, did he say this?" And I got it checked out the very next day . . . The point I'm making is Ringo did not have half a finger on grasping that issue. You just said in a nutshell, that they're willing to spend double that $600,000 to get less back each year. This is another heavy set of long fees . . . You're talking about a woman [Yoko] who thinks she can get Northern Songs for $5,000,000, talking of a woman who said ATV stunk and now agrees £4,000,000 later (each, by the way)—that's £4,000,000 (each) we lost on this. She now agrees we were right. This is the arrogance of the whole thing.

Linda: They're fools, if you ask me. Fooling themselves.

PAUL McCARTNEY
Selected Quotations
1980s

"I don't visit Liverpool as regularly as I used to because my dad is no longer alive. But I still go up to see my brother and other relatives. I'm there at least once a year, usually a lot more than that. The last time I was there I met up with an actor friend, Victor Spinetti. We were going out for a drink. We went driving around the Dingle. I showed him where Ringo lived, where my mother used to work and then we went on to the Brow and 'zap' it had gone . . . I love the city, but I don't like what they've done to the inner precinct, because I remember St. John's Market when it was the old "Get yer loy apples." They were all *real* people there . . . If I was brought up here now I'm sure I would be in a gang, just roaming the streets . . ."

"I used to live in Speke, me and George, and the Garston lads used to get the bus down to Speke and duff us up. They've changed the city a lot, but for me it was only ever about the people and they're still great! I've never really met anyone better and you look for it, because you leave your home town and you're looking for 'it' in the world."

"Generally, there aren't many things I would have changed in my life, but yes, there are some specifics. If I had known John was going to die I would not have been as typically human and stand-offish as I was. You know how people are in relationships. If someone tells you to 'piss off' you say, 'well piss off yourself!' You don't realize there may be pain, and it's very hard to do the Jesus thing of turning the other cheek. If I knew John was going to die I would have made more of an effort to try and get behind his mask and have a better relationship with him. As it was, we did have a pretty good relationship, but when he started slagging me off, I was not prepared to say, 'Well, you're quite right,' because I'm human . . ."

"It was only after John was killed I realized his dad had left him when he was only three. John's life was very tough in a way. He was not the big 'Working-Class Hero' he liked to make out. He was the least working-class of the Beatles actually. He was the poshest because his family almost owned Woolton at one time. His mum used to live with a fella he was not that wild on, then she got knocked down outside his house, and before that his Uncle George died. John had a lot of personal tragedies, then he got married, that ended in divorce and he did not know a lot about how to relate to his son."

"George and I had a barney the last time we talked. It's incredible after all we've gone through together. It's madness really. I find it weird, but that's life. All the other stuff, what we did musically and the fame I don't regret. It has its advantages. It has its disadvantages."

"Since the Beatles came down from Liverpool I've met so many people in high places who are not that smart—it's terrifying actually—Prime Ministers and stuff. They're not how you think they are. We used to have an image that the President of America was a wonderful man. That was around the time of JFK. Then Nixon comes in and blows the whole thing sky-high. And no one can believe Reagan. They'll have Frankie Avalon in there next!"

"I've seen recording go from four-track to forty-eight-track and more and it isn't as much fun. I don't mean that it's hell on wheels or lousy. I just mean it's not as much fun as four lads travelling down from Liverpool to shake up the world . . . I don't think you could recapture four lads from Liverpool, seeing the music scene, having a bit of success, then more success, and doing well. I pick up papers now and it's like everyone's thinking very deeply about music. We weren't. We were just having fun and I don't see music as that serious."

"I'm very lucky with my relatives. I have a good bunch actually, a very salt of the earth mob, not a lot of posers. It's a big warm family and my dad's mob were originally from Everton so they're just working class people and I still have a good laugh with them whenever we go up. I'm nearly always up there at New Year. I do wish I could get up there more often. I could go up there right now, just take a train or a bus, I could get up there every day if I wanted. But I work here and I live here because of work, so my kids go to school down here, so that means I can't just dash up there everyday."

PAUL McCARTNEY
Broadstreet Press Conference
CHICAGO, OCTOBER 1984

Question: How do you feel about all the security that has to surround you wherever you go?

Paul McCartney: I only get this kind of security in these high-profile situations. But I don't do this often. I normally live quite a normal life. On these occasions it's okay. It comes with the job. I try not to notice, really. In fact, where are they?

Question: Did you think about asking George to be in the film?

Paul: No. But because Ringo's in it and I'm in it, it implies that maybe George ought to have been in it, too. The truth is, he's not a ham. I don't think he's got any ambitions in front of the camera. He was the least keen to be acting in *A Hard Day's Night* and *Help*. Before *The Complete Beatles* we were going to put our own version together. The definitive story of the Beatles, and George was the least keen to even be involved. He's more interested in being behind the camera. And he happened to be out of the country anyway.

Question: What did you think about *The Complete Beatles*?

Paul: I haven't seen it.

Question: Do you plan any collaboration with George?

Paul: I don't rule it out, but it's nothing that would normally come up. Maybe.

Question: What prompted you to get back into films after such a long absence?

Paul: I like being in movies, the entire ambience, the lifestyle. Even getting up earlier in the morning, it's just different than how I usually do it. I like being pampered. Some people don't like getting their hair brushed and don't like to be touched, but I'm the opposite. Most importantly, I get to be on a creative team, something I really like. The whole idea of everybody pulling together to make something is an exciting thing to be involved in.

Question: The movie is not serious, but are you, in fact, serious about movie making? Is this something you want to do continually, or do you just want to see how this one goes?

Paul: I will probably see how this one goes, but it won't affect me much if it doesn't. I'm interested in the whole game of making movies, so I should think I'd still stay interested.

Question: I was surprised by the inclusion of a lot of Beatles songs.

Paul: Either we were going to create a new musical with a whole new score or we were going to think of it as a live show. In which case, you go to see [Mick] Jagger or you want to hear "Satisfaction," you don't go to hear an entire evening of new numbers. We chose to take that direction, so most of the songs you've heard before. Some of them I haven't performed anywhere except on record—songs like "For No One"—I thought that was a good enough reason to sing them again.

Question: How possible is it that one of your master tapes could be stolen?

Paul: Actually it almost happened during the filming. I didn't think it was that plausible. Six guys broke into Abbey Road, where the tapes were stored, overpowered the guard, and spent the whole night looking for my master tape of this picture. They couldn't find it because it was badly filed.

Question: Where did you find that charming drummer for the film?

Paul: It's just some bum off the street! Actually, he's a friend of mine from way back.

Question: I had heard Rupert, your cartoon character bear, would share the bill with *Broadstreet*.

Paul: In the theaters. Rupert's a cartoon character from England who's about sixty years old. He's a little white bear, he's about eleven.

Question: What do you consider your finest work?

Paul: There's this little chicken coop I just built. I find it very difficult to chose from what I've done. I can give you an answer but it won't be very real. "Here There and Everywhere," "Yesterday," "Michelle," "Eleanor Rigby," "The Long and Winding Road," "Hey Jude." I consider a lot of them equally. Those are amongst the best, probably.

Question: Was "Hey Jude" written for Julian Lennon?

Paul: Yes. I happened to be driving out to see Cynthia Lennon and Julian after the divorce. It's an hour's drive and cars are good places to get ideas. I just thought, "Hey Jude." It was originally, "Hey Jules, take a sad song and make it better, take this divorce situation you find yourself in young man and try to stick it out." Then I changed it to "Hey Jude" and found out it meant "Jew" and some guy got really mad at me because he thought it was anti-Semitic.

Question: Are your children musically inclined?

Paul: Yes, but I don't really push them. A couple of them take piano lessons. They've got great rhythm and sing in tune. When they're older and want to go into music, I'll encourage them, but I wouldn't yet. They're too young to cope with any fame that might come their way.

Question: When you do go out, do you have to take precautions like disguising yourself?

Paul: No, I never do. There was this guy on MTV the other day who was saying, "You know, you and I, Paul, we just can't walk down the street." I said, "I don't know about you, but I can." It's true, I've always done that. It's something I've always demanded. I don't like the quality of life the other way, it's not living. I may have to do an autograph occasionally, but it's all right. I was a fan once, myself. I used to wait at stage doors.

Question: For who?

Paul: The Crewcuts. Remember them?

Question: "Shaboom"?

Paul: "Shaboom," yeah.

Question: Do you think what your songs would have sounded like if you had the technology of the eighties in the sixties?

Paul: More bass drum, probably. I'm not sure there would be any major differences. Probably just the sound would be stereo, plus.

Question: Given that you are so well known and the amount of money you're said to be worth, why is it you haven't gotten more involved in more social and political causes, at least visibly involved?

Paul: That's the key word, *"visibly."* I don't believe in charity if it's, "Hey, look at me! I've just given money to him." It really embarrasses me. I couldn't do that but I do get involved. I'm not really a political animal. If our paratroopers shoot some people in Ireland, I'll write a song called "Give Ireland Back to the Irish" which will get banned in England but be number one in Ireland and Spain. I do my bit, but it's not very visible because I'm not that kind of person.

Question: For instance, gun control comes to mind. After John Lennon was shot, a lot of people lent their name and image as well as money to the cause—is that something you've thought about doing?

Paul: I did it! The Harry Nilsson thing, I was involved with that.

Question: How far back does your relationship with Michael Jackson go?

Paul: A couple of Christmases ago he rang me and I didn't believe it was him. I thought it was a girl fan because his voice is so high.

Question: What artists or albums, if any, can you sit down, put their album on, and like it?

Paul: These days I like Michael's music, the Thompson Twins, the Police, and a lot of reggae. I like Stevie Wonder and Howard Jones. It tends to be the good musicians. I like Prince's music.

Question: Have you heard Julian Lennon's album?

Paul: I've heard one track. I think it's great. At first I heard it sounded very much like his dad and tended to think that it might be a cop-out. But when I heard it I was very surprised by the qualities of his voice. He's got a really good voice. He sounded amazing. His voice was going all sorts of places I didn't expect it to. The kid's good!

Question: What effect did Little Richard have on your development in the Beatles?

Paul: Quite a lot. He was one of my first idols. The high-pitched wailing that I did, and do, on records was based on him. It came from the last day of school. At the end of the term we used to take a guitar, stand on the desks, and entertain each other, and I used to do little Richard.

Question: Ringo said that when he was on stage with the Beatles he often wanted to be out in the audience to experience the group.

Paul: It's always been a fantasy ambition, but it would be nice to have a clone or something to put up there. You're giving them this great pleasure and they're going crazy, but you're not watching it. You're the only one missing out.

Question: How do you feel about the film now that you've seen the final product? Are you happy with it?

Paul: Yeah. It was a big deal for me to write the thing, and I'm rather nervous that most of the people that are going to have a critical opinion on it are writers. That's a bit intimidating. For what the film is, and it ain't Shakespeare, being a gentle, light-hearted English picture, I believe we accomplished that. So I'm proud of it to that extent.

Question: What was the most difficult thing for you in making the movie?

Paul: Getting up at 5:00.

Question: I sensed a little note of melancholy in the film, in you particularly.

Paul: You may be right. You may see things I don't.

Question: A lot of the old Beatle songs you sang in the film you had to license. How much did you have to pay?

Paul: Well, in actual fact, I pointed out it was a bit zany for me to actually ask to sing "Yesterday" in a film after all the money I made them. So they charged a token fee. It was a pound or something.

Question: Are you still trying to buy your songs back?

Paul: If the man who owns them is willing to sell them, I'm willing to buy them, but I'm not holding me breath.

Question: Have you, George, and Ringo succeeded in dissolving Apple?

Paul: No, not quite. It's looking hopeful, but I believe I said that ten years ago. I think it should be done by the end of this year. It's about time.

Question: Since you seem to feel so bad about having lost the royalties to some of those songs, why do you retain the royalties to so many other people's songs?

Paul: Who said I feel bad about losing the royalties? I lost my babies, not my royalties. I wrote those little things and it was decided by business managers to sell it all. It was a bad mistake. This is not quite modest, but it's like Picasso selling all his pictures and not having any left. It's not the money, it's just the fact that they're mine and emotionally they belong to me. If you tell any one on the street I don't own "Yesterday," I don't think they'd see that as logical. It's not that I think publishing is a bad business. The reason I'm in the business is because it's music. I've learned that to make money you have to invest it. I used to say to our advisors, "Well, I don't want to do anything with it. We can just leave it in the bank, can't we?" It was put to me that I was going to either invest in computers, brush factories, clotheslines, or whatever, and I said, "Couldn't it be music?" It just happened to work out well. The publishing company I bought has been very successful.

Question: Do you still own the rights to "On Wisconsin"?

Paul: Yes.

Question: Do you make them pay every time the University of Wisconsin plays it?

Paul: Well, that's the rules of publishing. It's not this wicked old me walking up saying, "You'll pay!"

Question: If you made a token payment to play "Yesterday," then would you give a token payment to the University of Wisconsin?

Paul: Yeah. Are you their agent?

Question: Do you still keep in touch and jam with the musicians from Wings, like, Denny Laine?

Paul: No, Denny's living in Spain these days and Joe English has got a gospel group.

Question: Now that John Lennon is dead, do you ever regret you never got together with him again after you split?

Paul: Yes, sure. It's the same when anyone dies, you wish you could have told them everything you wanted. People just don't open up. I would have liked to have told him I thought he was okay and straighten things out. The one consolation was that the last phone call we had was a really good, warm call. We didn't talk about business at all, that was always the problem. Once we began to talk about business we began to suspect each other's motives. We learned eventually not to talk about business. It became a taboo subject. He was talking about his kids and his cats, it was very nice. So I take that as some kind of consolation.

Question: After five of the nine days you were incarcerated in Japan, did you think, "Wait a minute, this is a lot more serious than I thought it could be?"

Paul: After one minute I thought that! I was looking at seven years' hard labor, understand?

Question: Was that the most frightening moment of your life?

Paul: One of them. I was more annoyed at myself for being so dumb and involving my family in it. I'm quite an upstanding father normally, it's just unfortunate that on this issue, I disagree with the law. I'm not sure what the majority view is on all of this. My view is if someone came up to me and asked what drugs I should get involved in, I'd tell them,

"None." But our society is very involved with drugs and happens to think that particular one [marijuana] is one of the less harmful. I believe there is a mistake in the fact that you'd be perfectly all right to take three scotches, three martinis, or a six-pack of beer. I believe it's more debilitating, all of which is very legal. I don't want to come out as a preacher for pot, but I'm not sure they're right when they come out and say, "Seven years' hard labor." I have a feeling that's a bit heavy.

Question: What would you like to say to potential viewers of the film?

Paul: Don't go in there expecting some kind of huge sci-fi blockbuster or something with incredibly deep meaning. Just go for a pleasant evening out, and I hope you come out of it with a warm glow.

PAUL McCARTNEY
Broadstreet Press Conference
OCTOBER 28, 1984

Question: Do you think you have a bad-guy image?

Paul McCartney: Well, like anyone I wouldn't mind being understood rather than misunderstood. I know it was very tempting when John was slagging me off in the press. There was a period there when he was really going for me. I was very tempted to answer back. But I'm glad I didn't now. I just thought, "Well, the hell with it. He's just going over the top like he does." John was a great fellow, but he had that about him. He would suddenly throw the table over and go on to a new thing. And I was the table. I think a lot of it was just talk. John loved the group, but he had to clear the decks for his new life. That was my feeling at the time. There's nothing really you could say to him. I don't think I was the bad guy or the good guy. Originally what happened . . . my theory, anyway, is that I'm from a very close, warm family in Liverpool. If they hand you a baby, you don't treat it like a piece of ice. You just go "doo-de-doop." It comes naturally with certain families, Italians, Greeks, whatever and the same with the North of England.

I was very lucky to come from that kind of family and John wasn't.

John was kind of an only child. His father left home when he was three. His mother got killed when he was sixteen. Mine moved out when I was fourteen. That was what we had in common. But when it came to meet the press, when I saw a guy in the outer office, I'd go out and say, "D'ya wanna cuppa tea?" Because I didn't like being around that nervousness. So it fell to me to chat with the guy and put him at ease, which then looked like PR. So I became known as sort of the PR man of the group. I probably was. They'd say, "I'm not doin' that bloody interview. You do it." So I tended to look a bit like the good guy in the media's eyes, too. Because that was who disseminated all the information. That was who I was being nice to. I suppose the others may have resented that a little. I've now got this "wild, ruthlessly ambitious" kind of image. If you do well, you get a bit of that. I don't think it's really true. I think everyone was just as ruthless and as ambitious as I was, really.

Question: What do you think about Julian Lennon's singing?

Paul: I think it's great. I tell you what surprised me is he's got a very good voice. I'd heard that he sounds like his dad and I guessed that producer Phil Ramone was doing a sort of Lennon sound-alike record, but I find it surprising that his voice goes to some very pleasant places. Okay, it's like his dad, but that's on purpose. But it shows a musicality I didn't know he had. Mind you, I haven't met him in about ten years.

Question: Do the McCartneys still sing together?

Paul: Yeah, we do bits and pieces, but never very formal. Normally it's just sitting around, screaming and making a lot of noise at dinner. "Just for once couldn't we have a quiet dinner!"

Question: Are you still a prisoner of your great fame?

Paul: I can actually move around a lot better than in the old days. I was talking to an MTV guy yesterday and it was, well, not an argument, but it was weird because he wouldn't believe me. He said, "You and I couldn't walk down Madison Avenue, could we, Paul?" And I said, "I don't know about you, but I certainly could." Seriously, 'cuz I can and particularly in New York. I really do walk the streets here. Madison, I'm always up and down there. Ask anyone. This is the kind of town where you can do it. And you see people and they say, "Hey Paul, all right. Wooo!" They do a bit of that and maybe I sign an autograph, but it's never hectic. When everyone knows you're going to be at a premiere, they come to scream or to look. But if you're actually just in the street, most of them don't think it could be you. They think, *"No!"* That's my character. I don't like to be closeted away. I like to just get out.

Question: Were your songs with the Beatles your best work?

Paul: I would have to admit for myself, looking at all the songs I've written, probably there's a period in there that was my hottest, "Yesterday," "Here, There and Everywhere." There's a bunch of stuff that all came during a few years and I suppose it was because we were at our height and the novelty of it was a very important factor. We'd never actually written number ones before. What's happened in the last ten years it that I tend to just assume the critics are right, "Yeah, you're right, I'm not as good as I used to be," but in actual fact, I've started to think, "Let's check this fact out! Is this fact really true?" There's a song called "Mull of Kintyre" which sold more than any other record since the invention of the gramophone in England. Now that's since all of that. That's my *bad* period! A song called "My Love." That's also from my bad period. There's a song called "Band on the Run." That's in my bad period as well. I think they're right, you know. I think what happens is that after a success like the Beatles, everyone, including me, thinks there's no way you can follow that. So you just tend to assume it's not.

I think as a body of work I would say that my ten years with the Beatles was probably better than this stuff. But I'm starting to doubt it. I do tend to be a bit gullible and go along with whoever's criticizing me and say, "Yeah, you're right, I'm a jerk." The truth is I read a lot of criticism myself of people I admire and a lot of them really get slagged off. Like Bowie's new album. Someone like Picasso and I'm not comparing myself with him, there's an artist who kept going a long time and went through several periods. And the critics said, "Well, his Blue Period was the best." All of this is absolute rubbish. I don't really agree with that. I think someone like Picasso, some of the stuff that doesn't immediately seem like his best work can later be among his greatest stuff. And even when Picasso's banal, I'd rather have him than some of the others. Nobody's perfect. You've got to get it wrong sometimes! With the amount of songs I've written they can't all be good.

Question: Who do you have dreams of collaborating with?

Paul: Cole Porter, or Gershwin, or somebody like that. Those are my greats.

Question: How did you pick the old songs for *Broadstreet*?

Paul: I took about fifty songs, I'm not sure how many I was looking at. I think there's around three hundred. I've never actually counted them. I narrowed it down to about fifty I fancied singing and I gave a list of those to the director and said, "Let's just choose." Some of them got chosen purely for story reasons. "Yesterday" was included at his request, because he wanted to set up the thing that happens towards the end of the movie where I become a busker. Something like "For No One" was simply because I love that song. And I realized I haven't sung it since twenty years ago. I never ever did it in public. I did it only once on the record and it just vanished up my trouser leg. I thought, "It's a pity that song could just come and go so quickly." So I wanted that one in, for my own pleasure.

Question: How do you feel about not actually owning many of your early songs?

Paul: It seems natural I should be allowed to own my own songs at some point. I figured whoever's been publishing them has made a lot of money out of them. But if you sing them away, you sing them away. That's the law of the land. So I really can't blame the fellows who bought them. But yeah, I'd like to get them back. They're John's and my babies. And something like "Yesterday," if you say to the man in the street, "Paul doesn't own Yesterday," it would surprise him. The trouble is having to ask permission to sing it in a movie. That gets you. The publisher is quite fair, actually. I think they only charged me a pound. I think they saw the irony, too.

Question: What groups do you like?

Paul: I like the ones who can *play*. There are few of them emerging. Groups like the Police, the Thompson Twins, a guy called Howard Jones. They make very good records and they're very competent musicians. So that's who I tend to sympathize with. I like Stevie Wonder, Michael Jackson I like a lot. It's very good music. If you analyze it, it's well done. Michael's stuff is all Quincy Jones anyway and he's a hell of a musician, Quincy. So I tend to appreciate the music. I like Culture Club because George sings well, I think. There's a group in England called Wham and they also make good records. I identify with them more easily than the punk era when it was just sensation.

Question: Do you feel the Beatles were pioneers of rock video?

Paul: To go on TV, you went on and did your song. They made a video, just a little live video. Then later on if we couldn't be at the thing, people started to suggest, "Maybe you'll make something and just send it to us?" And once that happened we started to get a bit imaginative. I remember one night meeting this Swedish director in a nightclub and he started saying, "We could be really far out, you know. Psychedelic. Up in a tree!" So we said, "Yeah, you got it, and have another drink. *Wooo!*" And that turned out to be "Strawberry Fields Forever," which was pretty far out for its time. And from there we just continued. We liked the idea of putting on strange clothes and riding white horses through ruins.

Question: Why did it take so long for you to make another film?

Paul: Scripts, I think. I talked with many people trying to make a movie and got involved. To me there's a certain amount of luxury in making a movie. There's such a big team and, I dunno, you get pampered, hair, make-up, all that. And I like that kind of stuff where everyone looks after you. So I wanted to be involved in that kind of scene again. And I had happy memories from *A Hard Day's Night* and *Help!*, which are the kind of two movies we made. *Let It Be* to me was more of a psych trip. We might as well have sat on a psychiatrist's couch for that one! That was kind of like deep insight, whew! That was the breakup of a group, that movie. I talked to a lot of people, but we could never quite pull it off. We could never quite come up with something we could all make as a film. There were people like David Puttnam actually writing me saying, "This will be a retrograde step." Thanks, Dave! So it tends to put you off when you get all that. I talked to Gene Roddenberry because I wanted to do the all-time space thing. That was before *Close Encounters* and it was to involve the old-time flying saucer. I wanted to do that, but that didn't quite work out because Gene was actually getting Star Trek ready. The idea was kind of nice. It was *Aliens Invading*. It doesn't sound so good when you just say it. Anyway, wait for it. *Aliens Invading and Taking Over Through Music*. It was a big group. Culture Club may well be aliens for all we know. There were some nice ideas in it. For me what was going to be nice was, "What kind of music would aliens make to take over the world?" Obviously it couldn't be anything you'd ever heard before. It was more than contemporary, it was other-worldly. But we just couldn't get the script nailed down. I'm used to being rejected. You'd assume someone would just snap me up, but it's not like that. But you hear about *Star Wars* and *Bonnie and Clyde* as movies they didn't want to make. So I kind of clung to that. I thought maybe they just don't know. And you know what? They really don't.

Question: What's the hardest part of writing?

Paul: Keeping my hand going. It kept stopping and wanting to think. I said, "Stop it. Just write!" There is no style necessary. The first thing was actually an account of my bust in Japan. I was in jail for nine days and being kind of artistic. So I got back from that and forced my hand to keep writing. And it didn't want to. I wanted to have time off. I wanted to think about this thing. But I couldn't do it. So I just forced myself to write, write, write. And I ended up with 20,000 words on this thing and when I read it I thought, "That's not too bad."

When I read it I just kind of convinced myself that this was the way to write. And what confirmed it was when I was over in L.A. with Quincy Jones. Quincy was telling me about something he'd found a few years ago which said, "There are two aspects of writing: the creative and the judicial." The problem with most people is they try to do both at once. And that had been my problem at school, I realized. I'd try, "The train pulled into the station." "The sleek, silver train pulled into the. . . ." I just couldn't get past the first paragraph which was later to be axed anyway. I just couldn't get going. John and I once tried to write a play when we were just starting out. I think before we wrote songs, we tried to write a play. We got two pages. We couldn't go any further. It just dried up. It would have been great actually, it was like a precursor to *Jesus Christ, Superstar.* It was about a guy called Pilchard who you never saw, who was always upstairs in his room praying. And the whole play was the family saying, "Oh, God, is he praying again? I don't know." It was quite a nice idea. We could never get him out of that room and downstairs talking, so it dried up. So I've always had that problem.

Question: Isn't there a scene in *Broadstreet* where you're busking on a street corner?

Paul: I talked to the director and I said, "Once, just for a little laugh, when we were recording an album, I went out into the street and I was busking." I really enjoyed it. I think it's just the basic thing you do if you're a performer. Like Marvin Hamlisch, always, at any party, at the drop of a hat, "Oh, why sure, I'll play my entire repertoire. Hey, wanna hear this one?" Okay, Marvin, we've *hearrrrd* it. So for me, the guitar, that's the little thing that I do. So to get out and busk in front of people just passing on the street was really exciting. The grotted me up as much as they could to make me look streety. The worse they made me look, the better I looked. There was filth everywhere and torn jackets. I was looking quite contemporary for a minute.

Question: Did you make any money?

Paul: Yeah. Now you gotta believe me on this. I said to the assistant director, I said, "Someone's probably going to throw some money in here. And I know what they're going to say, 'And guess what? He kept it!' You know, 'The skinflint, he kept it!'" So I said, "Whatever we do, this is going to the Seaman Commission. I don't want that money." So we did. We got quite a little bit. There was this fabulous old Scottish guy who was drunk out of his skull in Soho. He didn't know who I was. He didn't look at me or anything. He just unloaded all his change.

I enjoyed it. I did it for about three-quarters of an hour. I was getting going. I did a couple of others besides "Yesterday." I did "You Are My

Sunshine," too. There was a lady on the radio, Gloria Hunniford, the next day who said, "You know what? He kept the money!" I'm lucky. I make my money really cleanly. I don't have to exploit anyone, which is pretty rare, you know, to make a lot of money really cleanly.

Question: Don't you risk unearthing a lot of ghosts doing such a massive publicity blitz?

Paul: Sure, but that is the risk you run going out in the morning. It would be easier to stay in all day and just send out videos and reruns, but that's not what I'm here for. This is life, the main event and stuff. I'm only sort of living a legend. I'm just bringing up a bunch of kids and going from dawn till dusk. I'm here to have as good a life as possible.

PAUL McCARTNEY
Questionnaire
LONDON, 1990

Birthdate: June 18, 1942

Hometown: Liverpool.

First Kiss: Grace Pendleton, when I was eleven, at Belle Vale School. I went past her house in Speke, where I used to live, and I saw her navy blue knickers on the washing line. When I got to school I said, "I saw your knickers on the line," and she said, "Well, they're clean and they're paid for!" An immaculate response.

Claim to Fame at School: I could draw naked ladies. I could do them on folded paper, so that when it was closed up the lady had her clothes on, and then when you opened it up . . . wey-hey! The only trouble was, before she did the washing, my mum used to go through my pockets for school dinner tickets and, of course, one day she found one of my naked ladies. I came home and my dad said, "I want a word with you. Did you do this?" It was like death. Anguish. Tears.

PAUL McCARTNEY
Press Conference
CHICAGO, 1990

Question: Tell us about placing the Martin Luther King speech you mixed into the live version of "Fool on the Hill."

Paul McCartney: When I wrote "Fool on the Hill," the idea for me was someone who had the right answer, but people tended to ridicule. I was looking for a speech from someone like that. I think the greatest recording in that vein is the Martin Luther King speech, which is so moving. It fit perfectly in the solo on "Fool on the Hill." It was quite a stirring thing to include.

Question: What would you have done if you hadn't been in the Beatles?

Paul: We were lucky. When we first got into rock'n'roll the great thing was that the National Service stopped, so we were able to have the Beatles and our success. We wouldn't have got any of it, if not for that. If I hadn't gone into rock, I probably would have become a teacher, because that's where I was heading, but I don't think I would have been a very good one.

Question: Are you happy now?

Paul: I am, actually. I used to dread that question at the end of the Beatles. People used to ask me and I'd go, "Ugh," and break down. It wasn't much fun. It was difficult to know what you were going to do in life, and the Beatles are a very hard act to follow! But I've done pretty well since. Yes, I'm really happy. I've got a great family and a great band.

Question: What led to the breakup of Wings?

Paul: The thing that led to the breakup of Wings was a disastrous concert we did for Kampuchea. We thought our performance was dreadful. I've listened to the record since and realized it wasn't so bad, but at the time we hated it so much it put us off being in a band for a couple of years. That's what led to the breakup.

PAUL McCARTNEY
Press Conference

New York, 1991

Question: How did it feel to play all the old Beatles songs?

Paul McCartney: It felt great for two reasons. One, we never did these songs much with the Beatles. "Get Back" we only did in the *Let It Be* film, we played it on the roof and never really did it again.

So it's nice playing these songs, because they're fresh, for me at least, and I think the audience likes them. You actually see grown men crying. There's really a lot of emotion because it's a reminder of a better time, or perhaps, when couples were first courting each other.

Question: It was said during the last press conference that you were considering collaborating with George Harrison and he has been quoted as saying that will never happen—any comment?

Paul: I don't think he said that. The only time I've heard that is through you guys. I think the question he was responding to was, "Do you think the Beatles will re-form?" to which he responded, "Let sleeping dogs lie," which is fair enough because without John you can't re-form the Beatles.

Question: I think he *was* referring to any sort of collaboration with you.

Paul: Well, I haven't heard it from him, so I don't believe you guys. When I hear it from him, then I guess it won't ever happen.

Question: What memories does New York hold for you?

Paul: Good memories. I've always liked it here, and plus my wife was born here. I actually met Ed Sullivan once on the street and he didn't recognize me. I said, "Hey, don't you remember me, oohh, I was on your show, we got big figures!" He said, "Oh yeah, of course." Some things touch me different nights. For instance, when I had just finished writing "Hey Jude," I was playing it for John, looking for his comment, in case he hated anything in it. I got to the part where I sing, "The movement you need is on your shoulder" and I said, "Don't worry, I'm changing that." He said, "Change it! That's brilliant, it's the best line of the song!" "What's it mean?" I said. He said, "I know what it means." The other night I got to that part and found it very difficult to sing it.

Question: What influence has classical music had on you?

Paul: When I was younger we never listened to classical music. My father was a jazzer, so when classical music came on the radio, it was something we turned off. It was George Martin's suggestion to do a string quartet on "Yesterday." I said, "You're kidding, a string quartet in the Beatles?" He said, "Trust me, let's just try it." So we sat down at the piano and worked out an arrangement. I put in a couple oddball things just to stamp my identity on it. I was really pleased with the way it turned out. We went on to do "Eleanor Rigby," "She's Leaving Home," and John's "I Am the Walrus," so we messed around quite a bit with it.

Question: Do you get nasty letters from Pete Best?

Paul: No, I haven't actually got one, I might after this.

Question: What are your recollections of meeting Elvis?

Paul: I've heard people say that when we met him he was real weird and we were all drugged out, but we weren't. It was a very straight evening. We were big fans of Elvis, particularly his work before he joined the army. He was really brilliant. He was the first guy I had ever seen who had a remote control on his television, that's how long ago it was. He played "Mo' Hair Sam" on the juke box all night because he was totally into that. Priscilla was wheeled in about half past ten for about five minutes as if she was a doll, and she looked like one. We were totally in awe of him. He was a real regular, nice guy.

Question: With all the trouble you've had with the law, do you favor the legalization of marijuana?

Paul: I favor the decriminalization of it, because I think there are too many people that get into it innocently and become criminals. The minute you're caught and the minute you go into the slammer, you learn worse tricks. I think it's a very difficult issue because I don't want to defend it too much, because if my kids ever asked me I'd say, "Stay away from it, don't ever do any drugs." People will bring up the point that scotch is legal and pot isn't. I think at that point there is probably a good argument for decriminalization.

Question: What about the material in the archives?

Paul: I think the best thing from the archives is "Leave that Kitten Alone," which is an old EMI thing. Me, John, and George singing harmony on "Three Cool Cats" is quite nice, as well. The rest of it are just takes that we turned down. Now they're bringing them back as real interesting takes, but they're really just the takes we rejected. They probably could get another *Gone with the Wind* out of the outtakes.

PAUL McCARTNEY
Press Conference
LIVERPOOL, 1991

Question: For people who don't quite know what an oratorio is, could you please explain it, and what is yours about?

Paul: An oratorio is a choral work for choir, orchestra, and soloists. I wasn't quite sure myself when we started writing it, but I think that's about the nearest definition. It's basically a choral work, and what this one's about is it starts with someone being born in 1942 in Liverpool, which is when I was born. So the first movements are autobiographical, and then it just takes off into a story which is really not me. It's about someone going through life trying to deal with all the ups and downs, and you've got to come and see if he wins or not.

Question: Having been involved in this work for the last two or three years, do you think it's going to have any bearing on your future work, or will it be easy enough to revert to the kind of songs we associate with you?

Paul: While I was writing this with Carl Davis, I was on my world tour, so I was actually doing two things at the same time. Doing the rock-

'n'roll stuff keeps the classical stuff nice and flexible, and doing the classical work allowed me to be a bit freer when I was writing some of the pop stuff. The bearing it may have on my future work is that I might like to do more of it. I've always had my eye on going a bit in this direction. When I wrote "Eleanor Rigby" I remember thinking, "What am I going to do when I'm thirty? That's very old, thirty." And I did have this image of myself, maybe moving into this kind of thing. Yes, it's taken until now (more like fifty than thirty) to actually come to grips with it. I suppose it was because I was asked by the Philharmonic to do it that made the final decision. The way I've approached things with Carl is similar to how George Martin and I used to work. So I think that will have a little bit of bearing on my next pop album.

Question: Could you explain the difference between writing a five-minute song and composing a ninety-five-minute oratorio?

Paul: The main thing is when we started writing, Carl and I, I started to fall into all my normal tricks. If you're writing a three-minute piece, you'll do your first verse than immediately look for a chorus, then a middle and you repeat the chorus. There's a kind of formula most people stick to, with maybe an instrumental section in the middle of it. But Carl pointed out to me that there didn't have to be any formula. We could do anything we wanted. We could have a verse then we could go to a completely different tune in a completely different key. It's very flexible, so it was very interesting to write. I think the basic difference is, you don't have to stick to any structure. You're a lot freer, you've got more time to explore.

Question: Wasn't the first classical music you wrote for the film *The Family Way*, back in 1966?

Paul: I've always been interested in music besides just rock'n'roll. I use to like jazz, I like people like Cole Porter, and I would listen to people like Bach, The Nutcracker Suite, all the popular classical stuff. I've been interested in that sort of stuff for a while, so I did a couple of things with people like the Black Dike Mills Band. I did a record with them [for Apple]. That was a little away from what I'd done and then, as you say, I did the soundtrack for a film called *The Family Way*, with

George Martin. So we started to explore those other areas just for fun really. It's very interesting if you're interested in music to go outside of your own field. When we started out to do the Oratorio, we did our session, and I gave Carl an idea how I wanted it to be. Then he said, "Let me go off and arrange it and the next time I see you I'll have it all done." I said no, we can't do it like that because it's going to be too much input from you, which didn't seem to be a good way to do it. So I said, let me be with you through every single second. He said, it's going to be really boring. I said it wouldn't, because I'd done this before and I like it. I sat with George Martin arranging the string quartet for "Yesterday" and the arrangements for "Eleanor Rigby." I sat with him through everything, the arrangements, the text, the violin solo. I didn't actually let him have one minute on his own. I thought it would start to become more his work, and he was happy to do that, but Carl kept warning me it would be very boring. He said, "You're going to have to sit there while I write out thirty parts or whatever it is." It was very interesting for me. Very educational, actually, I learned a lot.

Question: Did you sometimes feel like a student of Carl Davis? And is it true that on July 14 you will play the Cavern?

Paul: Second bit first. I don't think so. Is it open? It keeps opening and closing. Dear me, am I a student of Carl's? Not really, because I've been in the business a long time now, and even if you don't know how to write it down, you can't help picking up things, and if you work with great musicians you see them working and you begin to understand what's going on, so I think Carl was probably a bit surprised to find out I had a bit of musical knowledge. I don't look like it, but obviously I've been around quite a while now. Carl would occasionally say, let me give you a little lesson. Depending on what mood I was in, I'd sometimes say, "No, Carl, we won't do that because it felt too much like being a student." Occasionally, however, when I was in a receptive mood I'd say, go on. For instance, he'd say the last movement, the eighth movement [which is called PEACE], is based on the rondo form. So I would say to him, "What's a rondo?" Carl would say, "Let me give you a little lesson," and he would. He'd explain to me what the rondo form was, and if I was interested, if I thought it would be a good idea for us to use, then we'd use it. So we used it in the eighth movement. It's roughly based on the rondo form. We did a little bit of it, but he tried to sit me down with Benjamin Britten's *A Young Person's Guide to the Orchestra* and I wouldn't do it. I refused, I said, "No, Carl, it's too late for all that, luv!"

Question: Were there any parts in particular you were having a rougher time with?

Paul: Probably the most challenging was the violin solo, because I think that if you're going to write a solo for an instrument it helps if you play it. Of course, I can't play violin, so it was very interesting. Carl could keep me straight if I was going to a very awkward position for a violinist or a note that would not read well, he'd be able to keep me in the right framework. It was great, great fun, but it was a challenge for me. I'd never done that kind of thing before. But I looked at it this way, I'd come to Carl and say, okay, I really think this is the time for a violin solo, so the way I do it, I've imagined the orchestra quiets down, the violinist stands up and now he plays and in my mind, I think, "What does he do?" And luckily an answer always comes. I never really got too stuck.

Question: As a pop musician you have freedom of expression, but you don't have the same freedom as a classical musician. What's your appreciation of the orchestra as an apparatus?

Paul: When I went to see this orchestra at the Albert Hall two years ago, a little phrase stuck in my mind, that it was the ultimate synthesizer. You look at the orchestra as you normally look at synthesizer, you say, "Give me some brass sound, give me the string sound," well, there it all was. The absolute, ultimate synthesizer. That's the way I approached it. I just thought, there's no need for anything other than the orchestra, it's complete. You can do anything you want with it. Once I understood what kind of ingredients I had and what the limitations were, I just had fun with it. If I want the violinist to play some very high notes (there's some very high notes in the violin solo), which the first violinist was telling me he's not been asked to play before in his career, so it's pretty challenging for him as a player. I did that just to give him a challenge, just to see if he could do it, and to see if I could go that far. I think it works.

Question: Do you see this as a natural progression for yourself, and have you been worried about alienating your huge fan base?

Paul: Obviously, it might be a worry. There might be people that say they liked him better when he rocked and rolled. As I said, I was out on tour while I was doing this, so I've actually kept the two things going. I don't really know if it will alienate people, but I don't think it will. I think most of the people who like what I do are interested, as I am, in lots of music. I don't think they're just rap fans, or reggae fans, I think it's more varied.

Question: Why do you call the main character in the Oratorio Shanty, and how close is he to Paul McCartney?

Paul: I'd hear people talk about other composers and they'd say things like, "Oh, she's singing Brynhilde" and immediately classical people know what that part is just from the word Brynhilde. There's not *two* Brynhildes. I didn't want to have a name like Harry in case there was another opera, "Wee, he's playing Harry." *Which* Harry? So I wanted a distinctive name. I was looking for a Liverpool name with a ring to it. And I thought of shanty as being like a sea shanty and also an old shanty town, as a tumbled-down shack. One of the choir boys was telling me that one of the lads is called Shanty. I wanted that name for those two reasons, to evoke Liverpool, but also for a tenor to say, "I'm singing Shanty" and you'd know what piece it is.

Question: I understand the Philharmonic is going to be touring the States next year. Are they going to be performing any of your movements?

Paul: Yeah, I think they're going to take the whole piece. At the moment, they have a couple of dates booked. I think they've got the Hollywood Bowl and they've got one in Cleveland. We're waiting to see how this is accepted. If people want it then they'll ask the orchestra to do it, but they're certainly doing it a couple of times in the States next year.

PAUL McCARTNEY
Oratorio Press Conference
CANADA, OCTOBER 22, 1992

Question: Why weren't you intimidated when approached by the Royal Liverpool Philharmonic?

Paul McCartney: I don't know. The first time I thought about that was about half way through the writing. I was in a pub, just killing some time before going to see Carl, who lived around the corner. I was having a drink with this Irish actor and he said, "Boy, you must be intimidated by this." And I remember, I thought, "No, not really."

Question: But didn't you worry what the critics would say? Any rock star stepping into the classical area is a big target, especially a former Beatle.

Paul: It's hard to explain, but I just didn't think about it, even the night of the first performance in Liverpool. In some sort of innocent/ignorant way, I'd forgotten I would be putting it out there for every Cambridge matriculation exam on the planet. I was foolish not to expect the critics to go after it, but I suppose it was just a safety valve in me, something that says, "Don't worry about it." If I had been worrying about the critics' reaction, it would have taken a lot of the excitement and fun out if it. In the end, you just do the best you can and let everyone else have their say. It was the same with the Beatles.

Question: Why haven't you gone to other productions of the "Oratorio"?

Paul: I didn't want it to have to *depend* on my presence. I wanted it to be able to stand on its own so I could go on with other things I want to do. I would like to check in once a year just to see how it is going, but my own schedule takes over, which is the case now. I'm just finishing the sequencing on the album today, and then there's the tour planning. But I understand some of the productions have been quite amazing. In Tokyo, for instance, I would loved to have seen the Japanese chorus singing, "I was born in Liverpool."

Question: Did you set out to make it autobiographical?

Paul: The first three movements were basically memories from my childhood. I don't really remember the war, but I have the image of Hitler's bombers going over Liverpool, the kind of pictures you see when you are a kid on the telly . . . millions of bombers and the black city beneath, then seeing little puffs as the fire bombs go off. We thought a lot of it in movie terms. Those first three movements are pretty personal, but after that, I just thought, "I don't want to tell my story. Let's move away from it, make it not quite so literal."

Question: What do you see as the dominant message?

Paul: Hope . . . hope for the future. . . . the same old thing about giving peace a chance.

Question: How emotional was it for you to go back to Liverpool for the premiere?

Paul: The thing about the Oratorio was that it was in the cathedral, which is the second biggest in Europe, and right next to my old school. So, I had memories of childhood . . . memories of my failing the chorus audition. My dad had sent me to try and get a scholarship because free books came with it. But I didn't manage to do it. It was kind of strange to see all these kids in the chorus the night of the premiere, because they had gotten the gig.

Question: How different was the feeling when you played Liverpool on the last world tour?

Paul: That show was equally as emotional, especially when we did the tribute to John . . . "Give Peace a Chance," "Strawberry Fields," and "Help." But it reminded me of another period in my life, the teen-age days and dreaming about being in a band and getting people to listen to our music.

Question: Why are you going on tour again so quickly? After all, it was thirteen years between tours before the last one.

Paul: We had a great time and we had a real good band, which is a central point.

Question: Do you feel it helped you regain your place in the Beatles legacy? Do you think your contribution was underappreciated for a while?

Paul: That's a touchy one. When someone like John dies, you can't help but lionize him. I missed him, too. But, yes, it is nice when people look at the overall picture and say, "Yes, John was great, but this other geezer is not so bad either."

PAUL McCARTNEY
Press Conference
LIVERPOOL, 1993

Question: On the European tour will you be going to Greece, and with the new film on the Beatles will there be a revival?

Paul McCartney: I'm not sure if we are going to Greece, we have no plans as yet. I'd like to, but it's really up to the promoter. The revival of the Beatles is not a tour or anything heavy like that. They're making a ten-part series on the Beatles, and I suggested that if they needed some music they should ask me, George, and Ringo to work on a fresh piece. It would be a nice chance to get together without the heavy pressure of all the press saying the Beatles are reforming. At the moment we only plan to do one piece of music.

Question: What are your best memories of recording?

Paul: I remember the mid-Beatles period where John and I would go in with a couple of guitars, play the song for the guys, and within about an hour we'd have a decent version. Then we'd use that live take to build on. That was very important, a strong foundation like a good take.

Question: How much of an albatross is the Beatles?

Paul: I don't really feel they were. I used to feel that way after the Beatles had just broken up, you know, "Is there life after the Fabs?" As time has gone by, though, I've rediscovered the songs and instead of the anger and pain we all felt, I just like the songs and they're a pleasure to do.

Question: You are known as a writer of great love songs. Is there a secret to writing them?

Paul: I think it's a compliment if I *am* thought of as a writer of great love songs. I've also written songs that are nothing like that, such as "Helter Skelter" and "I'm Down," which are pretty hard-edged. People seem to forget that because the ones they think of me writing are "Yesterday" and "The Long and Winding Road." I still haven't worked out how to do it, that's the attraction. It's like magic every time I sit down to do it. I think, "Oh, will it happen again?" If it does, I'm very grateful.

Question: In the *Daily Mirror* last week you made some rather strange comments about Mick Jagger. One: you used to steal his girlfriends. . . .

Paul: True.

Question: Two: he still has an eye for the young ladies. . . .

Paul: True, both true. I used to steal his girlfriends and he used to steal mine, and it appears he still seems to have an eye for young ladies, good on him.

Question: There's talk about you trying to buy back the Beatles' songs from Michael Jackson.

Paul: You know the story on that. When John and I were kids, under the age of twenty, we signed a deal, as we didn't know you could own songs, it was a surprise to us. We just thought they were in the air, we didn't see how you could own them. We saw how you could own a house, but we couldn't see how you could actually own a song. I think the publisher saw us coming. They said, "Good lads, come sit in my office if that's how you think!" And we got signed to an old-fashioned deal, pretty much a slave deal, which I'm still under to this day. My argument is that it should be varied a bit since we've been pretty successful. What happened was Michael bought the songs because they were on the open market and he had a lot of money after the record "Thriller." Actually, I was the one who advised him to get into music publishing. He said, "I'm gonna buy your songs," and I said, "Ha ha, good joke." So that's that!

PAUL McCARTNEY
Press Conference
ORLANDO, FLORIDA, 1993

Question: What is your most cherished possession?

Paul McCartney: Probably my Hofner bass. It was an instrument I got back in the sixties and it's still got the old gig list on the side of it from the last Beatles show. It's a cheap little instrument, but it's my favorite souvenir from those times and it sounds good, too.

PAUL McCARTNEY
Press Conference
MEXICO CITY, 1993

Question: Why do you think Beatle music has lasted so long?

Paul McCartney: I feel pretty grateful people are still interested in Beatle music because it's been thirty years, and that's a long time. If there's a reason it's because John and I wrote some good times back then. Also, some of the things we said in the songs are still important now. The sentiments of peace and love are still the message. I'm very grateful.

Question: Explain the new *Paul Is Live* album cover.

Paul: I was looking for something involving the word "live" in it. An L.A. director sent me a film script based on the rumor "Paul is dead." You know when I was walking across Abbey Road and didn't have my shoes on and several American DJs said I was dead? It was a crazy publicity thing. So I said, "Paul is dead," we'll call this *Paul Is Live*. So I went back to the crossway (this time with shoes on) and the god is my son's dog called "Arrow."

Question: Is there anything you'd like to do musically you haven't done yet?

Paul: I've been lucky enough to do everything I've wanted to musically. I've done ballads, love songs, and at the same time, write rock-'n'roll. What I enjoyed doing recently is a classical piece for the Liverpool Orchestra, *The Liverpool Oratorio*. That was real interesting because it's kind of pure music and not so much pop music. I'd like to do some more of that.

Question: Do you have any regrets professionally?

Paul: No, I haven't really got any regrets. I can look back and see the little things that happened that weren't so good at the time, but it's all worked out really well for me. Think about it, I'm just some kid from Liverpool and now I'm this big, famous person, it would be crazy to regret most of it. So I don't have any regrets. I've been very lucky. I love music, my father loved music, and I'm still in music.

PAUL McCARTNEY
Press Conference
New York, February 11, 1993

Question: One of my favorite songs off your new album [*Off the Ground*] is actually "Cosmically Conscious." I also heard that it was written quite a while ago, in India.

Paul: Yeah, it was. It's kind of on the end of the record, as one of those little snippets, almost an afterthought. But there is a full-length version and it was written maybe twenty-five years ago, when we were with the Beatles in Rishikesh with Maharishi and he used to always say, "Be cosmically conscious. It is a joy." That's pretty much the entire lyrics of that song, which is why it's a snippet on the end.

Question: I was wondering how you might try to top the 184,000 people you played to in Rio de Janeiro on the last tour this time around.

Paul: Probably we're not, that's the answer. But somebody did invite us back to Brazil. And they say there's a bigger place in São Paulo. But it's not on the itinerary this time, but maybe that could top it.

Question: We hear you're doing something as a patron of the arts in Liverpool, what is that?

Paul: A few years ago I went back to my old school and found it going to ruin. So I was hoping that something could be done for it, because it was built in 1825. Even though I hated it while I went there, like most kids, looking back on it now it was a great experience. It gave me a very good footing in the world. So what we're hoping to do in 1995 is re-open it as a performing arts center for local and overseas kids.

Question: We understand there was a documentary about Linda's work as a photographer broadcast in London around Christmastime. Will one have a chance to see that here?

Paul: I'm not sure, but the BBC did make a great documentary on Linda which featured her photography. Normally she gets a bit eclipsed by the fact that we got married. I always say I ruined her career. A lot of people think she was sort of freeloading and just hanging on my coattails, which is actually not true. She had a very great career and the sixties book, I think, has proved that. I'm not sure if it's going to be over here in the States, but I hope so.

Question: It appears that with your recent tour and some of the work you've done since, you've become very comfortable going into your past, particularly the Beatles' songs. Another era of your career that musically was very, very successful and meant a lot to me was Wings. I was wondering how you feel about that, because you really don't delve too much into those songs in your current repertoire.

Paul: It's difficult, you know, when you've got as much material to choose from as I have and you want to play some of your new album. But then again you want to do some Beatles stuff, which is probably what I'm most known for. There's always people in the audience who really want to hear that and it's true that the Wings stuff tends to get a little bit squeezed out. There's always people like you who say, "Why don't you do something off *Ram,* man?" It's just that there's only so much time. We do a few from that period, but it's true they get squeezed out because of the Beatles and the new stuff.

Question: We spoke to Carl Davis recently and he said you might be working on a guitar concerto. Is there any truth to that?

Paul: That was a thought we had, and something I wouldn't mind doing. But in actual fact it turned into some piano pieces. It may be something we'll do at some point, but what I've just finished with him is six piano pieces. After having done that very full-blown thing, the Oratorio, or as someone called it yesterday, the Horatio, I've gone back to just one person sitting at a piano and some very simple piano pieces. So that's the next thing. Then I think Carl and I might write something together, maybe later in the year.

Question: Can you tell us the message of your new song "Hope of Deliverance"? Is it true it was written in very little time?

Paul: Yeah, it was written quite quickly. If you're lucky some songs just tumble out, you just write them down and you've found you've written it. I just went up into my attic and wrote it quite quickly. I'd like people to make their own decision as to what the message is, but for me it's just that these days there's a lot of stuff out there that's dangerous if you're bringing up kids. There's a lot of fears, a lot of worries, a lot of people homeless, a lot of recessionary stuff going on, and disease. So really all I'm saying is, "Hope of deliverance from the darkness that surrounds us," whichever particular darkness your is. It might be a girl whose boyfriend's left or it might be something more serious, some sort of tragedy in the family or whatever. But it's really a kind of prayer, I suppose.

Question: I know that there's an elite like yourself who can sell out stadiums and arenas, but where do you perceive the live concert industry going and what kind of trends do you see happening with it?

Paul: Yeah, I don't really know about trends. People always used to ask us when we were the Beatles, "What's going to be the new thing next year?" And we'd say, "We don't know." I just know what's going on now or what's in the past, but I don't read the future, so I couldn't tell you about that. I think people will always like to hear somebody live, or see somebody live. It was really brought home to me before our last tour when I went to see Dustin Hoffman in London in a production of *Merchant of Venice*. When he walked on stage it was like, "Wow, I'm in the room with Dustin. You got this great feeling, you know, I'm really in the room!" Welcome to my parlor! It's a special thing, you're not just watching him on video, you're actually there with him and if you shout, "Hey, Dusty!" he'll hear you. I just think there is some attraction in that. People hopefully will keep going to concerts, I would think they would.

Question: What do you think about the fact that your album is hitting stores the same week as Mick Jagger's latest solo album and critics have reviewed them by comparison? Do you consider Mr. Jagger competition?

Paul: Well, yeah, I suppose so. You know, we always used to ring each other when we were in the Beatles and the Stones and say, "When's your album coming out?" And we used to delay our releases, but I didn't do that this time. No, he's good, Mick, he's a good friend. I like him a lot, I like his music. I think he's written some great stuff. You can't really control who's there as your competition. So I don't mind, really. I think it's inevitable. It's actually a cheap shot if (critics) don't do their homework. They kind of just review both of them quickly and go, "Well, he's hard and he's soft," which is not right. I haven't heard his album, but I hear it's good. And I think ours is good, so we'll see.

Question: Does it bother you when people say you haven't been able to get rid of that wonderful soft image?

Paul: Not really, no. There's a lot of people who would like a soft image. I don't think I've particularly got a soft image actually, it depends if you know my work or not. Things like "Helter Skelter" are certainly not soft, or "I'm Down," or some of that stuff. Maybe I'm better known for songs like "Yesterday." But listen, I'm not knocking it, it's great to be known for both, anyway.

Question: Why are you surprised that you're catching so much shit for "Big Boys Bickering"? I mean, it's just your expression about the environment and everything else. Are you surprised at the attitude?

Paul: Not really. The thing is, I've never used swear words in my songs—it just never occurred to me, really. I never felt I needed to. Actually, before we released this I talked to my sister-in-law about it. She's bringing up young kids and she was saying, "Oh, you're known as the guy who doesn't swear. And now finally you're swearing and it's kind of a letdown." I said, yeah, but I'm trying to make a point. This is a protest song about people, men mainly in smoke-filled rooms running our lives, telling us whether or not we can close this ozone hole, and I sense that a lot of people would like them to really get on the case and quick. So what I do is say that in the song, basically, that they're "mucking" it up for everyone, but I use the "f" word, which I'm not going to use now because there's kids watching. But it doesn't really fuss me. It's no big surprise to me. I hear it in everyday common language. I've heard it since I was a kid. You've only got to switch on a movie and there's like fifty times worse stuff than that. I think if it's essential to the plot (it's a bit like nudity in plays), than it's valid. In this case, for what the song was saying, which is that people ought to get on with it and stop messing around, I think it's valid.

Question: I've read recently about Linda having her own food line that's not only health oriented, but is not animal based. Are you going to be taking these ideas further than say, just that song, on to the tour and translating that mindset into the shows?

Paul: When you grow up, when you're a father of four as I am, these things become important, ecology and stuff like that. So on the last tour instead of saying nothing about it, we tried to be the people's voices. We meet a lot of people who are interested in this kind of thing. We figured that rather than just being flippant when you're on a TV camera, it's actually allowed to talk a bit of sense about something you really care about. So yeah, we'll continue to do this. I don't know about writing songs about it. You can never say whether you'll be able to write another song about that because they're not easy to write. But certainly we'll be plugging it. And in our tour booklet this time, we've given a couple of pages to Greenpeace, Friends of the Earth, and PETA, the animal rights organization which we're members of and we believe in what they have to say. I think going into the next century these ideas are really interesting. Their time has come. So yeah, we'll be plugging them.

Question: What's it like being a pop star and trying to raise normal kids? And can you tell us anything about this potential music project with George Harrison and Ringo Starr?

Paul: First bit first. When me and Linda got together we decided we'd try to raise the kids with their feet on the ground, even though now we're trying to get "off the ground." We made that a big priority because we realized that having the money that I had and the fame, the kids could become snobs real early. You see a lot of kids like this, you know, rich kids, and they're really snotty. So we just decided that we'd send them to ordinary schools like we went to, and try and give them some good values until they're roundabout twenty-one and then forget it as you've got no control over them anyway. But then at least they've got a grounding and, touch wood, I think that worked. They're really nice kids, but I'm biased. But they're good kids, they're sensible and not snobs. And what was the second part of this mammoth question?

Question: The work with George and Ringo.

Paul: Yeah, well, normally when I'm asked this question, "Will the Beatles ever get back together?" we've just sort of said, "Well, no. It's absolutely impossible and without John it wouldn't be the Beatles." That's kind of an easy answer and it's always been true. But at the moment, they're making a ten-part series on the Beatles in England and it's going very well. We've got involved in it. It gives us a chance to give our own point of view, rather than everybody speaking for us. "You know why he was walking across that crossing [on the *Abbey Road* LP] with no shoes on?" "Because it was hot, man!" It was a real hot day in London, I had sandals on and I kicked them off, big deal. But we're always answering stuff like that. In fact, I met a little kid who'd been to a Beatles summer camp and she was telling me all about how you turn the record backwards. And I was saying, "no, no, no, *I was there.*" And she said, "No, it's not true." She wouldn't listen to me. So we're taking this opportunity with the series to try and put over our own point of view. What happened was, we were talking to the director and I said if there's a piece of film you've got, I was thinking in terms of maybe a montage of John material, him just looking great, nice memories of John, I thought, well, you'll need a piece of music to go with that, so we volunteered to do that. I kicked it around with the others and asked would you mind doing that? Would we hate to do that, is that a definite no-no? George said, "Well, that'll be good," and Ringo said, "That'll be great." So we thought, that's a nice start, rather than trying to get the Beatles back together. We'll probably get together and maybe try and write or record something for this one piece of music and just see where that takes us. We're not looking for anything big, I don't think anyone really wants to re-form the Beatles. But just to get together as friends and make a piece of music would be nice.

Question: A lot of your contemporaries like Eric Clapton and Bob Dylan have released box sets of their outtakes, rarities, and B-sides. Have you given any thought to that as far as your solo work? You've also done a lot of videos—how about a video anthology?

Paul: Yeah, well, that's one of those things that I think will happen. What happens with me is I've got a new album out, so I'd rather put out new material than outtakes of old stuff. For years, we were going to try and put together an album called *Cold Cuts,* which was all the things that didn't get on *Ram* and *Red Rose Speedway,* all through the years, which I think would be interesting for collectors and real fans who've got all the other stuff. But as I say, when you're going on tour, it becomes nicer to write new stuff an do that. Plus, *Cold Cuts* is now a bootleg. Someone's put it together anyway.

Question: When you write your music now, are you writing for your fans who grew up listening to you, or for younger fans? If it's the latter, how do you stay in touch with the younger generation?

Paul: Well, if I do stay in touch with the younger generation it would be through my kids, because I've got kids of that age and that's where you get your clues. Just watch them and see what they're into. But in truth I don't actually write for anyone but myself. I've tried that. You think, now I'll write for the modern people or I'll write for the old fans or something. And it's not the way to do it. You shouldn't do anything like that. It's really best to just write for yourself, so that what you care about, what you love, comes onto the page or onto the demo, whatever you're doing. And then you take your chances with people. You just hope some young people will like it as well as some older people. So I write for myself, really.

Question: Are you writing anything now?

Paul: This second? Yeah, I've got a couple on the board. Sure, I've always got a couple. I'm always working on stuff. Are we being given the big windup? That's a wrap, folks. Thank you.

PAUL McCARTNEY
Press Conference on Linda
MAY 18, 1993

Paul McCartney: We're together an unholy amount of time.

Question: Doesn't that get boring?

Paul: Occasionally it does. We go to different rooms. She'll take photos and I'll paint. We're not in each other's hair. Unlike most couples, we seem to actually enjoy each other's company. We're very honest with each other. We try to deal with our problems really quickly. I remember after we'd first met I was cruising around London with my new bird and I said, "I'm really tired, I'm so sorry." She said, "It's allowed." That's who she is. That's maybe another reason we stuck together. She's comfortable to be with.

PAUL McCARTNEY
Earth Day Press Conference

Los Angeles, May 18, 1993

Question: How did you get involved with this concert?

Paul McCartney: Somebody phoned me up and asked me if I'd like to play an Earth Day concert at the Hollywood Bowl and I said, "Yeahhhh, man." And that was it.

Question: How do you feel?

Paul: Great. How do you feel? It's great to be back. I played here before. A long time ago. It's a great bill. It's about the best cause there is. And it's Earth Day. So happy Earth Day.

Question: What message do you want to send out?

Paul: Enjoy Earth Day. In this universe, this is the planet we live on. We must be aware and take care of it.

Question: Why did you decide to write songs about the environment instead of just doing love songs?

Paul: Well, you haven't heard my new album now, have you? Admit it. You gave me a real blank look. The album does address these kinds of issues on one or two of the tracks. I am writing a little bit more that way now.

Question: Why now?

Paul: Because I think it's more necessary now than ever.

Question: Love you, man!

Paul: I love you, too. I don't even know you, and I love you!

Question: What's the reaction to "Big Boys Bickering," [a song on the album *Off the Ground*]?

Paul: Pretty good. It's the first song I've written with a swear word in it. One or two people were slightly shocked by that.

Question: "Hi Hi Hi" [a Wings song from 1972]?

Paul: There's not a swear word in that. Unless sex is a swear word. "Big Boys Bickering" is just a message song that says, "Hey, guys, all these people who run our lives are in these smoke-filled rooms and make decisions generally contrary to our wishes." That songs gets mad at that.

Question: Paul, any messages for the Native Americans of Southern California?

Paul: Generally I'm not a guy with a lot of messages. I'm a supporter of theirs and an admirer of the whole thing. I feel a bit presumptuous talking because I don't know any of them personally. I say, "Hang in there and let's hope things get straightened out and we're going into a good phase." Fingers crossed. Guys, I can't be here all afternoon. I've got to do a show later. I'll see you later.

PAUL McCARTNEY
Selected Quotations
on the Maharishi Mahesh Yogi
London, 1993

"No, it is not a gigantic hoax. A lot of people are going to say I left because I was disillusioned, but that just isn't so. The Academy is a great place and I enjoyed it a lot. I still meditate every day for half an hour in the morning and half an hour every evening and I think I'm a better person for it. I'm far more relaxed than I have ever been. If you're working very hard and things are a bit chaotic, you get all tensed up and screwed up inside. You feel as if you have to break something or hit someone. But if you spend a short while in the morning and evening meditating, it completely relaxes you and it's easier to see your way through problems. If everyone in the world started meditating, then the world would be a much happier place." (1967)

"John and George were going to Rishikesh with the idea this might be some huge spiritual lift-off and they might never come back if the Ma-

harishi told them some really amazing things. Well, being a bit prag-
matic, I thought, 'I'll give it a month, then if I really like it, I'll come
back and organize everything to go out there for good,' but I won't
burn my bridges."

"Prudence Farrow got an attack of the horrors and wouldn't come out
of her chalet. We were all a bit worried about her so we went up and
knocked. 'Hi, Prudence, we all love you. You're wonderful!' But nobody could persuade her out. So John wrote, 'Dear Prudence, won't
you come out and play . . .' We walked up to her chalet, a little delega-
tion, and John sang it outside her door with his guitar. And she looked
out, she improved after that. I think it was quite sensitive of John to realize she needed showing that she was okay, for someone to tell her she
was all right. You know, if you're used to McDonald's and Howard
Johnson's, India is a bit different. Looking at it from a nineties per-
spective, there was probably therapy needed for a lot of people there.
We were all looking for something. Obviously you don't go to
Rishikesh if you're not looking for something. It's a long schlep otherwise. Prudence probably needed to talk about it rather than meditate."

"A week before the British elections of 1992, the one where the Maharishi's Natural Law Party took double-page ads in all the papers,
George asked me to stand as the Natural Law Party Member of Parliament for Liverpool, just one week before the last general election.
George rang me giggling from LA. He said, 'I've been up all night and
you may think this is a bit silly, but Maharishi would like you, me, and
Ringo to stand as Members of Parliament for Liverpool.' He said,
'We'll win.' I said, 'Yeeeessss!' He said, 'It'll be great.' I said, 'Why,
what'll we do?' He said, 'Well, we'll introduce meditation for everyone.' I said, 'Wait a minute, this is a quite far-out idea.' As George's
wife pointed out, he wouldn't want the work. If you send George a
bunch of papers, he says, 'I'm not looking at that!', but if you're an MP,
you've got to look at those papers, there's no getting round it. I said,
'George, let's get one thing straight. No way am I gonna do it. I don't
want to rain on your parade or anything. You do it if you want. I'll support you. I'll back you up. But there's no way in heaven I am going to

stand as a Member of Parliament a week before the election!' George was saying, 'You know places like Bradford, Blackburn, or Southall where they have a big Indian community? They're going to bring in Indian guys, holy men to be candidates.' He said, 'They'll definitely win in all those Indian communities.'"

"Looking back, the Maharishi experience was worthwhile. It was the sixties, I'd been doing a bunch of drugs and I wasn't in love with anyone . . . I think maybe I was looking for something to fill some sort of hole. I remember feeling a bit empty. I don't know whether it was spiritual, it was probably just staying up all night and doing too many drugs. I was probably just physically tired.

"The whole meditation experience was very good and I still use the mantra . . . It's always in the back of my mind if I ever want to. For instance, when I was in jail in Japan it came in very handy; I meditated a lot and it was very good. I wasn't allowed to write and I didn't want to just sit there and do nothing. My brain was racing, as you can imagine, so meditation was great . . . I imagine the more you get into it, the more interesting it would get."

PAUL McCARTNEY
Selected Quotations on God and John
December 4, 1997

"Tragedy makes you talk to God a little more often. The idea that there is someone to hand it over to is very good. Unless you're very religious, you live your life not thinking there's anyone you can hand it to, and that was quite a blessing for us to find.

"When we were kids we always used to say, 'Okay, whoever dies first get a message through.' . . . When John died I thought well maybe we'll get a message, because I know he knew the deal. But I haven't had a message from John."

PAUL McCARTNEY
Press Release on Linda's Death
LONDON, APRIL 21, 1998

"This is a total heartbreak for my family and I. Linda was, and still is, the love of my life, and the past two years we spent battling her disease have been a nightmare. She never complained and always hoped to be able to conquer it. It was not to be.

"Our beautiful children, Heather, Mary, Stella, and James, have been an incredible strength during this time and she lives on in all of them.

"The courage she showed to fight for her causes of vegetarianism and animal welfare was unbelievable. How many women can you think of who would singlehandedly take on opponents like the meat and livestock commission, risk being laughed at, and yet succeed?

"People who didn't know her well, because she was a very private person, only ever saw the tip of the iceberg. She was the kindest woman I have ever met;

"All animals to her were like Disney characters and worthy of love and respect. She was the toughest woman who didn't give a damn what other people thought. She found it hard to be impressed by the fact that she was Lady McCartney. When asked whether people called her Lady McCartney, she said, 'Somebody once did—I think.'

"I am privileged to have been her lover for 30 years, and in all that time, except for one enforced absence, we never spent a single night apart. When people asked why, we would say, 'What for?'

"As a photographer, there are few to rival her. Her photographs show an intense honesty, a rare eye for beauty.

"As a mother, she was the best. We always said that all we wanted for the kids was that they would grow up to have good hearts; and they have.

"Our family is so close that her passing has left a huge hole in our lives. We will never get over it, but I think we will come to accept it.

"The tribute she would have liked best would be for people to go vegetarian, which, with the vast variety of foods available these days, is much easier than many people think.

"She got into the food business for one reason only, to save animals from the cruel treatment our society and traditions force upon them.

"Anyone less likely to be a businesswoman I can't think of, yet she worked tirelessly for the rights of animals and became a food tycoon. When told a rival firm had copied one of her products, all she would say was, 'Great, now I can retire.' She wasn't in it for the money.

"In the end, she went quickly with very little discomfort, and surrounded by her loved ones.

"The kids and I were there when she crossed over. Finally, I said to her: 'You're up on your beautiful Appaloosa stallion. It's a fine spring day. We're riding through the woods. The bluebells are all out, and the sky is clear blue.'

"I had barely got to the end of the sentence, when she closed her eyes, and gently slipped away. She was unique and the world is a better place for having known her. Her message of love will live on in our hearts forever.

"I love you, Linda."

PAUL

PETA
Press Release on Linda McCartney's Death
APRIL 1998

Linda McCartney was an angel for the animals: She lived and breathed animal rights. An anti-vivisectionist, vegetarian, and long-time PETA supporter, Linda, together with her devoted husband, Sir Paul, took every opportunity to help spread the word about animal rights. Linda first called PETA in 1988 to offer her and Paul's help with PETA campaigns when she heard about PETA's Rock against Fur benefit in New York. Since then, the dynamic duo have helped stop General Motors' crash tests on animals, Gillette's product tests on animals, helped ban fur prizes on *Wheel of Fortune* and invited us to have information booths on their worldwide tours. She and Paul edited a graphic video to shock stadium-sized crowds into understanding the cruelty behind the fur trade, the meat trade, and animal testing laboratories.

Last winter, PETA asked Paul and Linda to help rescue 126 beagles from a U.K. animal breeder who planned to sell them to a laboratory where they would be poisoned. The McCartney's donated 15,000 pounds sterling to rescue fifty of the dogs—lucky animals who are now a living legacy reminding us all of Linda's good works.

Linda was also a tireless advocate of vegetarianism. She published several cookbooks and even marketed her own line of meatless meals. She sent crates of her veggie sheperd's pie to the PETA headquarters for staff to enjoy, and even shipped tons of her vegetarian food to feed starving children in Bosnia.

In Ingrid Newkirk's book, *Save the Animals! 101 Easy Things You Can Do,* Linda wrote: "A long time ago we realized that anyone who cares about the Earth, really cares, must stop eating animals. The more we read about deforestation, water pollution, and topsoil erosion, the stronger that realization becomes. Of course, anyone who cares about animals must stop eating animals. Just the thought of what happens in a slaughterhouse is enough. We stopped eating meat the day we happened to look out our window during Sunday lunch and saw our young lambs playing happily, as kittens do, in the fields. Eating bits of them suddenly made no sense. In fact, it was revolting. If you want to live a longer and healthier life, the conclusion is exactly the same, naturally."

Remembering Linda
Selected Quotations from Friends

LONDON, APRIL 1998

"Cherie and I are very saddened for Paul and his family. Linda showed extraordinary courage throughout her illness. She was someone who made a tremendous contribution across a whole range of British life."

BRITISH PRIME MINISTER TONY BLAIR

"Because Linda was a private person, many people did not know the many sides of her. Not only was she a great and natural photographer and a brave campaigner for animal rights who single-handedly made vegetarianism a mainstream diet, she was also an incredible mother and a very loving friend to all who were privileged to know this unique lady. Linda was not only very kind and loving, she was also a courageous and pioneering woman who made stand after stand for those not as strong as herself. For us, her friends, the brightest light has left our lives, but she has left us a shining inspiration."

McCartney Family

"I'm absolutely devastated. Gerry and I had known her for years. We used to see her all the time. It's unbelievable. We all thought she had got over it. She was such a lovely lady. Paul really adored her."

Pauline Marsden
wife of the singer Gerry Marsden from Gerry and The Pacemakers

"A remarkable woman who was half of a remarkable marriage who brought up some remarkable children. Everything she did with life was positive."

Sir David Putnam

"Linda had a passion and a desire to change people's attitudes. Her positive outlook and dedication to promoting a diet that would bring about the end of animal suffering was absolute."

"She was an icon for animal protectionists because of her outspokenness. Now that she's gone, I think she'll inspire legions more to realize that animals are our neighbors, not our slaves.

"In her spirit, we'll fight harder in her memory."

The Vegetarian Society of Great Britain

GEORGE HARRISON

PART FOUR

It's Been a Long, Long, Long Time

GEORGE HARRISON
Letter to Stuart Sutcliffe
LIVERPOOL, EARLY 1960s

25, UPTON GREEN,
SPEKE, LIVERPOOL. 24.
FRIDAY DEC 16TH

Dear Stu,

I hope you are going on okay there with Astrid. I arrived okay (24 hrs exactly), but spent a packet on porters, taxis, etc.

I went to see your mum & dad the day after I arrived and they were pleased to see me. Your dad doesn't seem to mind the idea of you being engaged, but your mum seemed a little disapointed [sic] in you, (that is as far as I could make out). Your new home is fab and your dad was busy adding the finishing touches to the paint work. I was shown your room to be, which is about the size of the room you and John occupied at Gambier, and your mum has moved in all your paintings, photos, record player, bed etc. . . . like the painting you did of 'you on the bins,' I believe it was one of your earlier creations!

I saw John last night for the first time since he has be [sic] home, although he's been back a week or so. He never let on to us!

I was at the 'Jac' last night as well to pick up the letter you sent, and found out we have bookings for Christmas Eve, Boxing day, New Years Eve, and some queer bloke was almost on his knees, asking me if we would play for him. Can't you, or won't you, come home sooner, as if we get a new bass player for the time being, it will be crumby, as he will have to learn everything. And its no good with Paul playing bass, we've decided, that is if he had some kind of bass & amp to play on! Anyhow, I would like to have the whole group appearing for our first few bookings at least, so as to go down well from the start. So how about coming home soon! This hasn't been talked about with the others in the group and is just my opinion. Wouldn't it be good, Astrid's first Christmas in England!

If you aren't coming home for a while, can you send some money to keep Frank Hessey laughing. I want to get an Echo for Christmas, £34, or £6 down, the rest when Frank catches me, so if all my other stuff is up to dak [sic] I will probably be able to get it with no guarantee. I believe 'Gerry' has one, only he ruins it by using it on every number.

I bought Eddie's *Singing to my Baby* L.P. "Man of Mystery," "Lucille," "Only the Lonely," "Like Strangers," (Everly's new one) "Perfidia," (Ventures new one) and may buy an instrumental called "Chariot." I am learning everything I can get my hands on now!

Anyway Stu, get home here smartish, and remember me to the wife, Jurgend & the blonde as well. Remember, the trip is quite good even alone, and you too can be in Uller RD in exactly 24 hrs.

Cheerio

George

GEORGE HARRISON
Selected Quotations
NORTH AMERICA, 1964

"I met a Spanish guitarist who taught me a Segovia piece. It was unbelievable, absolutely marvelous. I'd love to be able to play Spanish guitar—unamplified—you know, where it sounds like eight people playing at once. Ever since my introduction to that kind of music, I've been trying to find a really good Spanish guitar. I've bought about four so far. The best one cost me around 250 pounds. But I don't get enough time to practice, traveling about the way we do. It's all we can do sometimes to find time enough to eat. Once in a great while, when I do find an hour or two to myself, I try [to play] the Spanish guitar, but it's pretty difficult doing it on your own. To do it well, one really needs to study and work under a good teacher. Before I know it, I find myself playing the same old things. Fumbling about on the strange instrument makes me feel like an amateur. I guess I just go back to what I know to restore my ego."

"[I once saw President Kennedy.] It was sheer accident. I had just come out of my hotel and walked to the corner one evening and I was standing there waiting for the green light, when I heard a lot of sirens.

A policeman appeared out of nowhere and strode out to the middle of the street and halted all the traffic. Then came a squadron of motor-cycles with officers wearing crash helments and a few big black limou-sines following along. The whole motorcade had to slow down to turn the corner right in front of me and in one of them, smiling and waving at the people on the sidewalk was President Kennedy, just as big as life. I recognized him right away. He looked exactly like his pictures, only younger, even.

"What an exciting man! It was the biggest thrill of my entire holi-day."

"I didn't actually grind away at the books as a kid. Oh, I did some study-ing, of course, one had to. But I wasn't at all like some of the kids, you know the type, the ones who always boast about having spent five hours doing their homework. I never spent five hours on homework in my life. It just sort of came easily to me, I guess. Whatever tasks the masters gave the class, I'd take 'em home and zip through 'em. I have to give my parents credit for a lot of that. If they hadn't been strict about us kids doing our school work, I probably would have fobbed off com-pletely and done nothing. As a kid, I was built like a garden rake, but I was mad keen on soccer, cricket, swimming, and all sorts of athletics. The day before my birthday every year, I develped tonsillitis. The first couple of years I thought it was just coincidence, but as time went by and it kept happening year after year, I began to get a complex about it. I remember saying to my mother, when it happened again just be-fore my eleventh birthday, 'I'm doomed, Mum!' The day before my thirteenth birthday I woke up fit as a fiddle. No sniffles. No cough. No watery eyes. No sore throat. I felt so good I was worried and I decided I'd better go and see the family doctor. The minute he saw me he said, 'I've been expecting you. Had a good year? Open your mouth.'

"He stuck one of those wooden paddles on my tongue, peered down my throat and said, 'Ah hah!' Then he took one of those long shiny metal things with a light on the end of it and pushed it down my throat. When he pulled it out I said, 'I'm okay this year, right, Doc? My throat is fine.' 'Your throat is so fine that you'll have to go to hospital right away, my boy. I'll get in touch with your mother.' He didn't sound like he was kidding and he wasn't. I went to hospital and stayed there for seven weeks. They said I had nephritis."

GEORGE HARRISON
Interview
LONDON, SEPTEMBER 1969

Question: Are you happy with the way Apple is going now?

George Harrison: Quite happy, but if you say to the wrong person, 'such and such' and he says it to somebody else, by the time it comes back to you it has nothing to do with what you originally said. That's the main problem with Apple and I'm sure it's the same with any business. That's the difficult thing, if you say to somebody, "Okay, now here, do that," and it comes back just slightly different, it takes up a lot of time. Really, what Apple was trying to be is as Derek says, "It's just for our whims."

Question: Derek, how do you describe Apple?

Derek Taylor: It's an organization which has developed, without anyone really planning it this way, as a service which exists to implement the whims of the Beatles, which, fortunately, often turn out to be very commercial. However, if they didn't, we'd still have to do it, and that's okay. That's the gig. The gig is not Apple, the gig is working for the Beatles!

Question: Organizing the whole thing.

Derek: You come here and you work for the Beatles. Now the latest whim is to take the worst minority, religionist cult in England, the Radha Krishna Temple, and get them a top thirty record within ten days. It's nothing else and that's what it will ever be.

George: The thing is to service our whims as Derek said, which sometimes are not totally our whims. Because of circumstances you tend to get over involved, and that's the hard thing. For example, take Jackie Lomax. I became his record producer purely because I happen to walk into Apple one day and some people said to me, "Oh, Jackie should record," and, of course, I remembered him from years ago, and I knew he could do with recording, but I put it off because I was going to India. When I came back I just happened to walk into Apple again and there he was, so people were asking me to do something with him, so I said, "Yeah, okay," and we did it. Then it comes out in the press like I'm committed to be his record producer for life. He knows how I feel about that, we talked about it and in the end he should do his own thing and he will, you know.

Question: What about the Indian scene, are you still very much committed to it?

George: Do you mean musically or generally?

Question: Intellectually and anyway really.

George: Yeah, it's my karma. It's like saying Brian Epstein did die, we did go to America, and we did get Apple. Everywhere you go you've got a number of choices. There's a crossroad and you can go left, right, but if you just follow yourself—natural instincts—you don't have to really decide. You'll naturally go down one of them, and there's always choices and many different ways to go, but if you just keep following yourself and what you feel, you automatically go down the right road. It happened with me just through constantly experiencing action, reaction, action, reaction. I got into Indian music, which was very remarkable because the first time I ever heard it was on a Ravi Shankar album, which it had to be really, looking back. I played the music, and although it's sort of intellectual, it is technically and spiritually the most amazing music I have ever heard. I listened to the music, and even though I didn't really understand it, I felt within myself as though I knew it back to front. It seems so obvious and logical. Ravi Shankar is probably the person who has influenced my life the most. Maybe he's not that aware of it, but I really love Ravi and he's been like a father figure and a spiritual guide to me. Later, I realized Indian music was like a stepping stone to the spiritual path, because I also had a great desire to know about the yogic path. I always had a feeling for that, and the music lead me there. I got involved with Hinduism because Ravi

Shankar was a Hindu, and because it just happened that it came my way, and I went to India. I got to understand what Christ really was through Hinduism. Down through the ages there has always been the spiritual path, it's been passed on and it always will be, and if anybody ever wants it, in any age, it's always there. It just so happens that India was the place where the seed was planted. The Himalayas were very inaccessible to people, so they always have peace there. The Yogis are the only people who can make it out there. It may be something to do with my past lives, but I just felt a great connection with it. In this age the West and East are becoming closer and we can all benefit so much from each other. We can help them with our material attributes, and they can help us with their spiritual things. We need them both, you need the outer aspect of life as well as the inner, because the outer is empty if you don't have any spiritual side to life, and vice versa. The western people needed to go through this material life, well, they've been through it now, and we've got so many material things it's got to evolve into the other now, you know. We can give to each other, it's all a part of the evolution; taking the best from both sides. Not only do we have the yogis coming over here, but our business people are now going over there.

GEORGE HARRISON
Note to Brute Force
LONDON, 1969

Dear Brute,

You have got a great name, a lovely voice, and a beautiful record on Apple called *King of Fuh*. I felt I should make contact with you (until we meet someplace when we will really make contact), as I have been involved with it all so. Hello! I dig the "Nobody Knows" side, too. Thanks for being patient [sic] with us and for Being:

GEORGE

GEORGE HARRISON
Letter from
A. C. Bhaktivedanta Swami Prabhupada

LOS ANGELES, FEBRUARY 16, 1970

Sriman George Harrison
c/o Apple Record Co.
3 Savile Row
London
England

My Dear George,

Please accept my blessings. I am so much obliged to you for your val-
ued cooperation in spreading my movement of Krsna Consciousness
throughout the whole world. I beg to acknowledge receipt herewith of
your contribution of $19,000 (nineteen thousand dollars) for publica-
tion of my book, *Krsna,* now going to the press within the week.

I know that both you and John are very good souls. Both of you are
pledged to do something for the peace of the world. By the grace of
Krsna, you have already realized to some extent about the necessity
and importance of the Hare Krsna Movement in the world. Similarly, if
John also does so, it will be a great event.

John and his wife were very kind upon me when I was staying at Tittenhurst Park as their guest. I always prayed for them to Krsna for understanding this great movement. Please inform him this message on
my behalf. I have dreamt something very nice about John which I shall
disclose in proper time. In the meantime, please ask him to cooperate
with this movement as you are doing, and he will be very happy . . .
Hope this will meet you in good health and shall be very much pleased
to hear from you.

Your ever well-wisher,

A. C. Bhaktivedanta Swami

GEORGE HARRISON AND A. C. BHAKTIVEDANTA SWAMI PRABHUPADA
Conversation

LETCHMORE HEATH, NEAR LONDON, JULY 26, 1976

A. C. Bhaktivedanta Swami Prabhupada: We are inviting everyone, "Come here. Such a nice house [has been] donated by George. You live here comfortably, eat nicely, and chant Hare Krsna." We don't do any factory work here, but still, people do not come. They prefer to go the factory and work the whole day in hell!

George Harrison: I suppose some day the whole world will just be chanting somewhere out in the country.

Prabhupada: That is not possible, but if some leading men take it seriously, others will follow. Just like in our *Krsna* book, your signature is there, "Oh, George Harrison. Yes." They take it without any consideration.

George: Where will you be in India when you go back?

Prabhupada: Most probably Bombay.

George: I am going to Bombay for a wedding. Some friends are getting married. December the fifth, I think. I think you met Laksmi Shankar, the singer? Her daughter, who is also a singer, Viji Sri Shankar, she's marrying a South Indian violin player, L. Shankar.

Prabhupada: He's also called Shankar?

George: Well, he's called L. Shankar. You know in South India they have a funny way about them, they have a surname. He's just called L. Shankar. His brother is called L. Subramanyam.

(The two men are discussing the problem of pollution.)

George: I think the whole world's changing. Somebody said it's the pollution, there's so much in the ocean now with oil on the top, there's not so much evaporation anymore.

Prabhupada: It is actually the sinful activities of the populace. That is the real problem. They are all engaged in sinful activities. Especially this innocent-animal killing. This is simply the reaction. Here is some cauliflower. Please take a little.

George: I'm trying to finish one [dish] so I can start on the next! I was also sick lately. I had something and I went yellow. I had jaundice. I don't know why, just had food poisoning or something and it affected my liver.

Prabhupada: Who cooks for you?

George: Sometimes me. I think we had Chinese food that evening.

Prabhupada: Oh, you should not take.

George: Because I was working as well, so I was pretty tired.

Prabhupada: Better you cook simple food yourself and take it.

George: The only thing I could eat was papaya.

Prabhupada: Papaya is very good, yes. You like that preparation?

George: We used to have this with milk in Rishikesh. Every day they'd leave it outside the door.

Prabhupada: Are you reading my books sometimes? Which one?

George: Mainly *Krsna*. Mukunda gave me the new books, but there's just so much to read. I don't know how anybody could have written it, it's difficult even to read that amount.

Prabhupada: Sometimes they are surprised one man can write so many books, but it is by Krsna's grace. Otherwise it would not be possible for a human being, it is not possible. You are in the same house?

George: Hm? Henley. I work from my house. I have a recording studio in the house. So I don't have to go to London anymore.

Prabhupada: Oh, you have all arrangements there. That's very nice. How many acres?

George: It's about thirty-five. My compliments to the chef!

Prabhupada: I am very much pleased you take so much trouble to come here.

George: It's my pleasure. Are you ever going to stop traveling?

Prabhupada: That is Krsna's desire. I don't want to, personally, but if Krsna wants, that is everything. We now have a very nice house in Detroit. If you sometimes go there . . .

George: Ah, Detroit. They need one there. Crazy place. Did you have a temple in Hamburg? I was there once, but they just had a little tiny house and they were trying to get another.

Prabhupada: Hamburg temple, has, I think, closed? So what is the difficulty sprinkling water? It is costly?

Jayatirtha: We'll try to sprinkle more, but there's a lack of water pressure.

George: We had a little Honda pump, but you had to start it off. It's a gasoline engine, I think. We just pumped out of the lake and we had a sprinkler on the other side. Makes a noise, though, that's the only thing. You could use the water out of the lake, then nobody could really complain. That probably wouldn't be enough, it would take the water level down. How do you fill that up?

Mukunda: You don't have a well at your place?

George: No, just, that pond. Originally the lakes were all filled, just like this, as well as flooding the drains. When it rained the house and everything would go, but we have a big storage tank. Underneath that big bank of rhododendrons was a room which was actually a storage tank. But these days they have meters on the mains, so you have to pay for every gallon.

Mukunda: What about getting one of those water diviners to come and find water?

George: Well, you can find it anywhere if you just bore a hole. What we did was drill at the end of the lake. But you have to go down to the depth of the riverbed, and there there's not much water because it's all chalk and limestone. That's the problem with watering in the summer.

Prabhupada: Your house is near the river?

George: Yes. The Thames is there, but we're on the hill, so we bored a hole down to three hundred and fifty feet, to the level of the river, and then a pump, we can pump that. But when it rains or if you water the ground, it's so chalky it runs right through it. It's very hard to keep a lot of moisture in the water. At the same time all the rain water runs through, then it hits the rock level of the riverbed, there must be tons of water down there. We can pump out of there all day long for months on end and nothing seems to dry up.

Jayatirtha: Around here you have to get permission.

George: We did, too. You put your name on a list, put a public notice in the local papers, and if somebody wants to complain they have a chance to. And once it's been up there for a few days and if nobody's made any formal complaint you go ahead.

(Here Harrison and Bhaktivedanta Swami discuss the death of George's mother.)

George: When my mother died I had to send my sister and father out of the room, because they were getting emotional, and I just chanted Hare Krsna.

Prabhupada: Oh, very nice you chanted, so she could hear?

George: I don't know, she was in a coma or something. It was the only thing I could think of.

Prabhupada: When did it happen?

George: In 1970. It was the only thing I could think of that might be of value, you know.

Prabhupada: So are you reading the *Krsna* book repeatedly?

George: I read it every so often. I always take the *Gita* with me wherever I go. But you know, I sometimes read a little of something and a little bit of something else. I've never been a great reader.

Prabhupada: On account of your chanting "Krsna," so many people are chanting.

George: I don't think it's on my account.

Prabhupada: No, they say, "George chants Hare Krsna." You have got many thousands of followers.

George: It's nice, but I think we all . . .

Prabhupada: I take little rest during daytime. But actually I do not like to sleep.

George: No, it's a waste of time.

Prabhupada: When I go to sleep, I think, "Now I'm going to waste my time."

George: They call it a little death. Sleep is the little death. . . . I remember, we were in Vrndavana and we were singing in the morning, singing "Jaya Krsna," and this person said to me, "You should make it into a song in English." So I wrote several verses, each chorus went, "Jaya Krsna, Jaya Krsna, Krsna Krsna, Jaya Krsna, Jaya Sri Krsna; Jaya Radhe, Jaya Radhe, Radhe, Jaya Radhe, Jaya Sri Radhe." It was on *Extra Texture,** you know that album? I wrote the English words. "He whose eyes have seen what our lives have been, and who we really are, it is He, Jaya Sri Krsna." Then it has a chorus. "He whose sweetness flows to any one of those that cares to look His way, see His smile, Jaya Sri Radhe," then the chorus again.

Mukunda: This is on George's new record.

George: No, it was last year. "He who is complete, three worlds at His feet, calls up every star, it is He, Jaya Sri Krsna." It's a nice song. I took the tune we sang in Vrndavana and just made it slightly different with chords, chord patterns.

Prabhupada: So on your next record, you can present this.

---

*Actually, this song appeared on Harrison's *Dark Horse* album.

GEORGE HARRISON
Press Conference
AMSTERDAM, FEBRUARY 4, 1976

Question: I thought you could have had a *'Best Of'* album from your solo career.

George Harrison: I gave them a list of songs I would have used, but they just did their own record. There were too many old Beatles songs. I don't have any say about the old songs.

Question: Are you still a member of the Hare Krishna Movement?

George: I was just friends with them.

Question: But you produced their album?

George: That was just that record and I bought them a temple. But I never actually joined. I just tried to help them out . . . Krishna is simply another name for God. He has many names and each of us is a part of the whole creation and we all have a little quality of Krishna in us and so in the technique to awaken that awareness it is recommended we repeat this mantra: "Hare Krishna, Hare Krishna, Krishna Krishna, Hare Hare, Hare Rama Hare Rama, Rama Rama, Hare Hare." Devotees chant that over and over. It makes one feel very good and if you do it all the time then you have more knowledge.

Question: Why didn't your deal with A&M records work out?

George: I was ill and I was supposed to give them an album at the end of July, but they knew I was sick and they said it didn't matter. But then later they decided it *did* matter and so I decided I had to leave them.

Question: What are the plans for the future?

George: Just to try and be a better person, write more songs, and make more records.

Question: Can you tell me why you chose the name Dark Horse for your record company?

George: Because I needed a name to call the company and somebody suggested I use the name of a song, so I thought of "Dark Horse."

Question: What do you think of Allan Williams's book, *The Man Who Gave The Beatles Away*?

George: I think it's stupid. Ten percent is true and ninety percent is what Allan Williams dreamt.

Question: How do you feel about the Hamburg Tapes?

George: As John said to Capitol Records about the sleeve of the Beatles' new repackage: "You can't make a silk shirt out of a pig's ass!"

Question: Are you ever going to visit a Beatle convention?

George: There was a convention in California and we gave them several films and lent them a big Dark Horse and gave them some posters. But I couldn't be there.

Question: What do you think about a Beatles reunion?

George: I don't know. We are always in different parts of the world. Would you like to go back to high school? It's okay for people who just watched, but when you went through that experience, and it is difficult to imagine doing it again, and then shatter everybody's illusion. It's probably better not to.

Question: Was that fifty million dollar deal from Bill Sargent a serious offer?

George: He approached everybody's lawyers.

Question: But you couldn't do it because of the Allen Klein case?

George: It has nothing to do with Klein. We were all busy at the time. We are not thinking of Beatles all the time. It's only everybody else who does! We are just busy living our lives.

GEORGE HARRISON
Interview
HAMBILDEN, OXFORDSHIRE, 1983

Geoffrey: How do you remember your guru, Srila Prabhupada?

George Harrison: Prabhupada always used to say that he was "the servant of the servant of the servant of Krishna." He was very, very humble. The thing about Prabhupada, he was more like a dear friend than anything else. We used to sit in this room in my house and talk for hours.

Geoffrey: I understand that on his deathbed he called you "his archangel," took a ring from his finger, and instructed his disciples to make sure you got it. Did you?

George: Yes, I got it. I have it.

Geoffrey: Were you his disciple?

George: As far as being a full-fledged devotee, no. I was never really into it that far. I liked him and his philosophy, though. I never followed all the rules and regulations that strictly, however. Except for maybe a few months.

Geoffrey: Anything else to say about the Hare Krishna movement?

George: Well, I love the food. When I visited their place in India [Mayapur] last year, I got up with them at four in the morning and after mangal arti [prayers] they brought me a forty-course breakfast. All on silver and everything. I was the honored guest. Which, of course, is better than being the unhonored guest!

Geoffrey: What is your attitude towards spiritual life these days?

George: I was at the airport in Honolulu and I met a guy dressed in these old saffron corduroys. He approached me with a book and said, "My guru wants you to have this." I couldn't make out if he recognized me or not. I said, "What do you mean, your guru wants me to have this book? Does he know I'm here?" The book said, "Something Something Guru, the World's Spiritual Leader." Now, I read the book and this guy doesn't like anybody. He ran down Sai Baba, Yogananda, Guru Maharaji, and everybody. Although he did quote Prabhupada's books (and everyone else's for that matter). It seemed very dogmatic. I'm just not into that. It's the organization of religion that turns me off a bit. I try to go into myself. Like Donovan said, "You've got to go into your own temple once a day." It's a very personal thing, spiritual life.

Geoffrey: Tell me a bit about the new book [*The Love You Make*] on the Beatles by your former Apple attaché Peter Brown.

George: Peter came by with this guy [co-author Stephen Gaines] for about ten minutes to Friar Park, had a cup of coffee and they left.

Geoffrey: What did he ask you?

George: Nothing. There was no interview, nothing. They just had a coffee and split. Then he goes away and acts like the three of us sat him down and said, "Right, Peter, you're the one! You should be writing this. You tell the story." The guy made millions, you know.

Geoffrey: Millions, really?

George: Yeah. It's one of the best-selling books in the world. Well, a million anyway. But it's crazy.

Geoffrey: What do you mean?

George: We took this guy from Liverpool. Made him. Gave him a job. Helped him establish himself. After all those years, then he comes out with his rubbish.

Geoffrey: I've heard that Mal Evans's diaries were stolen and are soon to be published by an American magazine.

George: Well, Mal certainly kept diaries for years. He always wrote down everything that happened. The problem is the legal ownership of those diaries.

Geoffrey: I've heard that the woman he was living with at the time of his death had them.

George: Yeah, but the rights are so unclear. They'll probably never be published.

Geoffrey: How do you feel about the Beatles' myth today?

George: All this stuff about the Beatles being able to save the world was rubbish. I can't even save myself. It was just people trying to put the responsibility on our shoulders. The thing about the Beatles is that they saved the world from boredom. I mean, even when we got to America the first time, everybody was running around with Bermuda shorts on, brushcuts, and braces on their teeth. But we didn't really create any great change, we just . . .

Geoffrey: Heralded it?

George: Heralded that change of consciousness that happened in the sixties. We went along with it, that's all.

Geoffrey: Gave it a voice, maybe?

George: Yeah, I guess.

Geoffrey: I met Yoko recently. She seems fine, you know. She seems to be trying to carry on with life, her and Sean, who, by the way, is a very bright kid.

George: Yeah. I'd love to meet Sean. I bet he is. I don't know, the whole Beatles thing is like a horror story, a nightmare. I don't even like to talk about it. I just hate it.

Geoffrey: Sorry. What about gardening? I know you love that. Don't you have all kinds of exotic plants and trees from around the world up at Friar Park?

George: No, not really. I get all my stuff from a local nursery here in Henley. I've got a few gardeners working the place. Trying to spruce it up a bit. It was let go for years, but it's coming along, little by little. Getting better all the time, you might say.

GEORGE HARRISON
Press Conference
Toronto, 1988

Question: You've said you aren't especially taken with today's music, and that the spirit doesn't seem to be there as it was in earlier years. When you were getting ready to record *Cloud Nine*, what did you do to get away from that?

George Harrison: Well, I set out not to use drum computers and MIDI keyboards for a start, because most things these days are done like that. I wanted to make records like in the past, and basically make things a bit more human.

Question: George, how did you and Jeff Lynne meet and come to work together on this project?

George: I thought he'd make a good producer for me, and Dave Edmunds, who was a neighbor of mine, had worked with him before, so I asked if he ever saw Jeff to tell him I'd like to meet. That was back in 1985. So he came over, had dinner, and we just kept in touch and by the end of '86 I said, "Well, I'm going to make a record soon, do you want to do it?"

Question: Were you familiar with his work with the Electric Light Orchestra?

George: Oh, yeah, that's why I wanted to call him up and meet him. I thought he'd be perfect for me, which he was.

Question: I had a dream last night that you and everybody on your new record decided to go on tour. Is there any chance that dream is going to come true?

George: Possibly. But I don't fancy being the star of the show. I wouldn't mind being part of a show doing some of my tunes, but I wouldn't like the responsibility of being out there all on my own. If I'm going to do anything at all I had better do it pretty soon, otherwise I'll be on crutches or something.

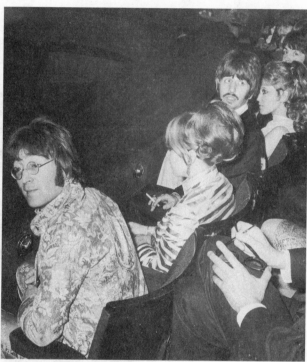

*Arriving in New York to announce
the formation of the Beatles'
Apple Corps, 1968.*

*Lennon recording "All You Need Is
Love." EMI, Abbey Road Studios,
Summer 1967.*

Lennon and his young son, Julian, board a plane to Athens for an extended holiday with the other Beatles. July 22, 1967.

Julia Baird in Ireland as a young mum. She shared a loving but distant relationship with her famous elder brother.

CLOCKWISE FROM TOP:

Making the scene in London are (left to right) Cynthia, John, George, and Pattie. 1967.

A rare shot of Pattie Boyd, the future Mrs. Harrison, as a young model.

The Beatles and company at the Isle of Wright festival in the late sixties.

John and Yoko at a London gallery opening, 1968.

*Ono in the very early sixties
while on a concert tour of Japan.*

*A rare copy of Yoko's
alien registration papers.*

COUNTER-CLOCKWISE FROM TOP LEFT:

Out on the town together in London, 1968.

London, 1968.

At the infamous Bed-In in Montreal, 1969.

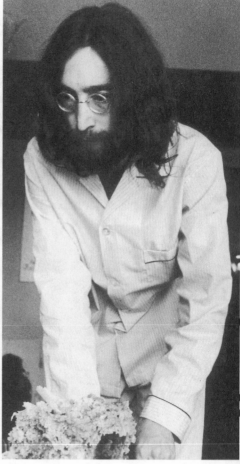

*John and Yoko meet with the family of convicted
murderer James Hanratty at their Apple offices in
London, 1969 — another of the couple's do-good deeds
that went awry, as Hanratty was later hanged.*

*Arriving at the Ontario Science Centre
in Toronto for a press lively conference, 1969.*

TOP TO BOTTOM:

*Relaxing in a Toronto hotel during
Lennon's peace politician years, 1969.*

*On Top of the Pops performing
"Instant Karma," 1970.*

Question: You've said you weren't crazy about doing a big video, but "Got My Mind Set on You," I think, is hilarious. I wondered how much of your own sense of humor was actually a part of that, and do you feel better now about the possibility of doing more videos?

George: Well, you know, my humor is such that I have to be able to have something funny happening around me so I can be deadpan, as I'm not really into acting. That works very well for me. The director was a guy called Gary Weiss, who incidentally directed *The Rutles*, so he's a very funny fellow himself. He thought of having a simple setting like that room and making it move so I could just play it straight and everything else would be the joke.

Question: What gave you the idea to do the video for "When We Was Fab"?

George: I just thought it would be nice to write a song with the sound of the '67 or '68 period. It was just a whim, really. Especially since at that time I was with Jeff in Australia and I know how much he likes the old stuff, so I started out to write it. I didn't have any lyrics at the time, so it was tentatively called "Aussie Fab" because it was reminiscent of the Fabs and written in Australia. So it was purely a trip down memory lane.

Question: I read where your song "Just for Today" came to being after you saw a pamphlet from Alcoholics Anonymous.

George: Well, really, if you're into the songwriting mood, then anything can trigger it. I had these three friends who were all in AA at my house one night back in 1983, and this guy showed me a brochure called "Just for Today." It seemed so nice, to try and live through this day only. I mean, it's not just for alcoholism. It's good for everybody to remember that we can only live today and the only thing that really exists is now. The past is gone, the future we don't know about. So it's an extension of the "be here now" idea. I thought it would make a nice song, so I wrote it. But it's good also for AA, I think. Maybe we could make it into a TV commercial.

Question: George, at one time you considered calling your latest album *Fab* and then you changed it to *Cloud Nine*. Why?

George: If you know about the connotations of the past, of the sixties and the Fab Four and all those things, then it's a good little joke. But if you don't know about all that, it sounds a bit pretentious. Also, when I looked at the photograph on the album sleeve with me and all these clouds, it looked more like *Cloud Nine.*

Question: Now that you're a solo performer, how different is it for you?

George: Well, it's totally different, really. In those days, it was the four of us. We just went into the studio and made some records, went out on tour, then went back in the studio to make more records, went out on tour, then went back in the studio to make some more records. That was it, really. Nowadays, it's a big business and it has to be coordinated. With the Beatles, after around 1964, we only had to put the records out and people rushed to buy them. It's not like that these days. You have to work with the record labels and coordinate releases and do a lot of promotion work. I'm on my own, whereas in the past I had three other smart-asses with me all cracking jokes.

Question: Do you miss that?

George: I miss that side of it, yes. We used to have good fun at press conferences. They used to be really great because there would always be somebody with a wisecrack. I do miss that side of the Fab Four, I admit.

Question: George, do people treat you as some sort of religious icon these days?

George: No, not really. I think people seem to give me some respect, however, which is quite nice.

Question: The last couple of years you seem to have had some reservations about getting too involved with the record business.

George: Yeah, I got a bit tired of it back around about 1980. I just felt there was no point. The way the music was going, I couldn't relate to it. I just thought, "Well, I've got a lot of other things to do, so I might as well have a rest." Nowadays, I never consider that I'm going to be out there with this record and people may not buy it. I didn't even think about that. I mean, if you have a flop, it's a flop. I think you just have to make something you enjoy yourself and see what happens. And I've had enough success in my life that if I fail, it's okay.

Question: What's more difficult, being a Beatle or an ex-Beatle?

George: I think being one was much more difficult. I mean, it was fun for a long time, but there was so much pressure on us. It became really tiresome and it was good, in a way, to dissipate that energy that there was with the four of us together. You know, let it go away so that we could have some semblance of a life. Otherwise, it would have just been madness continually.

Question: Has your attitude about today's music changed?

George: Yeah, I think the main reason for the problem, you know, was the recession. It went through all kinds of businesses, though radio, the music industry, and people didn't seem to know what was happening. They were confused about what was supposed to be good. I think they lost all direction, and I just didn't want to be a part of that. Maybe the only change was that I've changed, and I just felt it would be fun to do an album and see what happens.

Question: Do you hear anything today that you like, any artists that capture your imagination?

George: Bob Dylan! I do, but unfortunately not so much in pop music or the top forty. My favorite music at the moment is this Bulgarian choir. It's called the *Mysterious Voices of Bulgaria* and it's the most brilliant vocals, it's quite beautiful.

Question: How did you get involved with Monty Python?

George: Well, I've been friendly with them for a long time and when they were beginning *Life of Brian*, the original film company backed out as they were right into pre-production. A friend of mine asked if I could think of any way to help. I asked my business manager [Denis O'Brian] and he thought about it for a few days, then he came back and said, "Yeah, okay, we'll be the producers." So we borrowed the money from the bank and formed Handmade Films. I did it because I wanted to see the film. I couldn't stand the idea of it never being made.

Question: Could you tell me what a typical day in the life of George Harrison is like?

George: It's different all the time. Like last week I've been just getting up, going for a run round my garden, eating a bowl of Scotts porridge oats, and then right into the recording studio. Go out for dinner, finish off what I was doing, and go to bed. That kind of thing. Or get up, go to London to the office. There's no typical day, really. Get on the Concorde and fly to New York!

Question: Paul McCartney is currently working with Elvis Costello. I was very surprised and I thought, what a combination, to have the intelligence of a Costello with a great songwriter McCartney. Do you think that Paul was in a bit of a rut and was looking for someone to work with similar to John Lennon?

George: I wouldn't say that Elvis Costello is like John Lennon at all. Personally, I don't think he is. I don't think he even comes close, anywhere near John. I mean, Elvis is pretty good *but.* . . .

Question: I just meant that he was a very thoughtful writer.

George: Well, he wears glasses! And I think Paul was definitely in a rut. In a *Rutle.* And yeah, I think it's good. He should work with various people and hopefully he'll find somebody who will actually tell him something because most people who work with Paul are afraid to say anything to him. And I think that's no good. You need to have somebody you can work with who'll tell you you're no good when you're no good. Otherwise, it's no help at all. So I look forward to hearing what they come up with.

Question: That brings us to the inevitable question. I read something a couple of weeks ago where you said that there was a possibility that you, Paul, and Ringo might do some work together.

George: Yeah, well, Paul has asked, you know. Suggested maybe the chance of me and him writing something together and, I mean, it's pretty funny really because I've only been there about thirty years in Paul's life and now he wants to write with me. But I think it may be quite interesting sometime to do that.

Question: Would you tell him if he was no good?

George: Sure. For the last few years I've spoken my mind to him. Whenever I felt something, like [Paul's film] *Broadstreet,* which I thought was a big mistake. Not making the film, because I quite enjoyed it myself, but the idea of trying to write and do everything yourself. That's the mistake. I think the only barrier between us now is our astrological signs. Some of the time we get on pretty well and the rest of the time I find that I don't really have anything in common with him.

Question: Does that surprise you, after all these years together?

George: Well, I think if you have a relationship with somebody else, you have to be able to trust each other, and to do that you have to be able to talk to each other straight. The thing with Paul is one minute he says one thing and he's really charming, and the next minute, you know, he's all uptight. Now we all go through that good and bad stuff, but I think by now we've got to find somewhere in the center. Anyway, he's getting better. *Broadstreet,* I think, humbled him a bit.

Question: What about pop's so-called new social conscience?

George: I haven't heard it yet.

Question: Like Live Aid. . . .

George: I like anything like that. Sometimes I feel it's a shame that it's down to musicians to go around saving the world, however; I think some of the politicians should get their fingers out occasionally.

Question: Can you tell us about your son, Dhani? Is he a budding musician?

George: Yeah, he's nine and a half and he's got a pretty good ear. He enjoys all kinds of music. From Mozart to Ravi Shankar to Little

Richard and Chuck Berry. He's playing the piano a little bit and I think he's going to be okay. I'm not saying that's what he's going to be in his life, but he's hopefully got a good musical ability for his age.

Question: Does he understand his father was a Beatle?

George: Now he does. You can't turn on television without seeing something to do with the Beatles, can you? As I was just saying to somebody earlier, kids pick up on the Beatles through the old movie *Yellow Submarine*. I made a point of not saying anything about them to him. But by the time he was five he wanted to know how the piano part to "Hey Bulldog" went, which completely threw me because I didn't understand where he'd heard a song like that. I haven't heard that myself, really. Then I realized it was from *Yellow Submarine*.

Question: If you did go on tour, how much of a consideration would your feelings about being out in public bother you?

George: I'm not really worried about being in public. I'm not crazy about crowds, though. This is even just walking in an airport or being in a football match or something. It's nothing to do with people looking for me or threatening me. I just don't like crowds. I don't like traffic jams, either. I don't like that situation. I prefer peace and quiet. But I don't really worry about anything like that. The only time is if you get a mob of people who know you're going to be somewhere. I mean, there's always fanatics at rock concerts. But to do a tour wouldn't be any trouble because you have all the security and you know the way in and the way out and it's no bother, really. I don't fear for my life like some people try to suggest. They've said, since John Lennon got killed, I would go and hide and I've had a big fence built around my property. I had a fence around my property back in 1965, so there's no change, really.

Question: So you don't have any bodyguards?

George: No. Absolutely, on my honor. I don't even have a roadie!

Question: When you have jam sessions at your home studio, do you do Beatles tunes and do you remember all the words?

George: No, I don't know *any* of the words. Occasionally I can remember one or two, but we don't do Beatles tunes. More likely to do Everly Brothers or Chuck Berry tunes.

Question: You've proven yourself to be an astute businessman away from the music business. Do you feel you have rounded out your life more at this point in your career? Do you feel satisfied with what you've done?

George: Having done the film company and the various things we're talking about, I think they impress everybody else more, so their *concept of me* is now more rounded out. They all think, "He's smarter than we thought," but it doesn't impress me.

Question: I'd like to know about your religious philosophy. Are you still promoting it or do you keep it to yourself these days?

George: Well, I keep it to myself unless somebody asks me about it. But I still feel the same as I felt back in the sixties. I lost touch with the Krishnas when Prabhupada died, maybe ten years ago or something. I know one or two of them, but I don't really hang out with them anymore. I used to go and see the old master, you know, A. C. Bhaktivedanta, quite a lot. He was real good. I'm still involved, but it's something which is more a thing you do inside yourself. You don't actually do it in the road. It's a way of just trying to get in touch with yourself. I still write songs with it in there in little bits and pieces, but lots of songs that are unfinished say various things, but maybe I say it in different ways now. There's a song on this album which is straight out of Yogananda, "Fish on the Sand," it's called.

Question: Do you think you were underused during the Beatles years?

George: Yeah, possibly, but George Martin said recently how he always felt sorry because he concentrated more on them and he should have paid more attention to me. He said, "I hope you'll forgive me." But I'm quite happy with my role in the Beatles. You know, it split up because of all those problems, there were too many songs. Because we got too close to each other, but I'm quite happy with the way things went. I feel that whatever I am now, I always have been that, you know. Maybe things have taken longer to reach the surface or whatever, but I'm who I am and I am not really that much different to how I was then. Maybe

I'm more able to express it or perhaps people are more interested now in what I have to say. Because in the sixties and the early seventies they thought I was a loony. Because I just went to India and did all that bit.

Question: George, you seem like such a modest person despite the incredible events of your life.

George: I'm not a fanatical person. About astrology or anything, really. I don't want you to get me wrong, but I'm a Pisces, and Pisces is like that. One half going where the other half's just been. I tend to be more withdrawn. If you look at Pisces, they're the spiritual ones who often get pushed around, but these days it's really mostly clear sailing.

GEORGE HARRISON
Selected Quotations on *Cloud Nine*
1980s

"Everybody's looking for something good, aren't they? It's all about that; if there's any love around, you can have it, but if there's anything bad about it, well, I'll keep that bit to myself . . . and I'll see you on cloud nine!"

"I love playing on stage, but I'm not sure I'll be touring this time around. On the last tour [1974], I'd get up in front of all these people and after a while it was obvious half of them were there to see me and the other half because it was what was happening in town that night. I wasn't sure I even really liked all these people. I'd rather play for twenty friends who really care than a stadium full of yobbos."

"The guitar on the cover of *Cloud Nine* was the first really good American one I'd ever owned, back when the Beatles first started out and we were still in our leather gear. I bought it for seventy-five quid off a sailor in Liverpool. Eventually I gave it to Klaus Voorman who took it to L.A. when he moved. Using that particular guitar on the cover seemed like a good idea because we set out to do a record that was of today, but also echoed that late sixties feel."

"It's always nice to do a record, but who could I get to help me? There were not many people I could think of, but I thought of Jeff Lynne, he'd be perfect. But I'd never met him. Fortunately, Dave Edmunds had worked with Jeff, so I said, 'Tell him I'd like to meet him.' Dave called me back some time later to say, 'Jeff's coming to London,' so we arranged to have a meeting with him, just dinner . . . Then over a time I got to know him better. Eventually, I sort of tricked him into producing the thing. Jeff's input gave me a lift. He's put so much time into the record, in a very selfless way. It still sounds like my record; his contribution was tastefully done. Jeff has a way of getting the best out of me and it helped to have a friend to hang out with in the studio for all that time."

"I started 'When We Was Fab' while Jeff and I were messing around in Australia last November at the Australian Grand Prix. The idea was that it would evoke a Fabs song. It was always intended to be lots of fun. Every so often we took the tape of 'Fab' out and overdubbed more and it took shape to where we wrote words. We put wacky lyrics in the last line of each chorus."

"I asked Jeff to write me a tune for the record and he wrote 'This is Love.' When he brought it to me, he had a choice of several different versions of the same song, and there are still enough bits left to write another two tunes. I chose the bits I liked from his versions and then wrote some words with him for it."

"'Got My Mind Set on You' is something I've had in the back of my head for twenty-five years. It's a very obscure song I heard off an old album by James Ray. If you listen to the song now it's very different from how I've done it. I've updated it and changed the chords because I preferred it the way I heard it in my head. Jim Keltner got this drum pattern going one day that was a cross between swing and rock. Gary Wright turned round and said, 'Hey! Doesn't that remind you of that old song?' I was surprised anybody else had ever heard the tune!"

"'Just for Today' was written three years ago after I had some alcoholic friends over to the house. I can drink large quantities of wine because I'm not alcoholic, but they can't drink anything because they are. One of them gave me a brochure from AA from which I borrowed the title. It says 'Just for today . . .' and you open it up and it tries to give people a bit of solace. It was saying not to try and deal with everything all at once, which I think is good advice for everyone. You don't need to be an alcoholic to be reminded to stay cool just for today."

"I've got this big room, which is an oak hall, it's got an oak floor, oak walls, an oak ceiling, and it's about thirty-five-feet-high. There's this old piano I bought off Gary Wright and I happened to get it tuned in case we needed it. It's not a great sounding piano, but in the ambiance of the hall, I keep listening for it, saying, 'Now does it sound like it's in the hall, or does it just sound like we put it through some box?' So that's what that is."

"I don't know if people actually think along the lines of, 'Well, he's getting old,' but I've thought people must be thinking that. It's a funny song, very tongue in cheek. I was brought up in that period, people would say you look like the wreck of the Hesperus . . . Actually, it was a poem, an old Victorian poem.

"When I started writing it, I just opened my mouth and the first two lines came out. I continued along that theme until the middle eight and I suddenly go into a vicious attack on the press!"

"I passed a little church in England near where my boy Dhani goes to school. There was a poster on the side of the church saying, 'Gossip! The Devil's Radio! Don't Be A Broadcaster!' I've always kept away from that—though I've done my share—because with my past I've tended to be one of the people being gossiped about! I just thought it was a dead ringer for a rock tune. . . . 'Don't be a broadcaster' . . . I like to remind myself of this, because I'm just as bad as everyone else."

"Jeff dislikes the things I dislike about current music and certain sounds. We only used drum machines on two tracks on the album. Like the drumming on 'Got My Mind Set on You' is all machine. Jim

Keltner is the best I've ever heard on the drum machine . . . Jim can make it swing, so it's not rigid."

"Eric Clapton plays on four tracks. The end solo on 'That's What it Takes,' he also plays on 'Devil's Radio,' 'Wreck of the Hesperus,' and on the title track. Gary Wright plays keyboard, the piano, on a song called 'Just for Today.' He also plays on 'When We Was Fab.' Elton John plays electric piano on 'Cloud Nine' and he plays piano on 'Hesperus.'

"On drums we've got Ringo, Jim Keltner, and Ray Cooper plays on one track. Ringo plays on about four tracks.

"All the horn parts were played by Jim Horn. That's his real name. All the remaining stuff. . . bass is Jeff, keyboards, Oberheim is Jeff, and guitars are me and Jeff. All the little twiddly parts that just crop up, like autoharps, is just me and Jeff, and we also do all the backing voices."

GEORGE HARRISON
Interview
HENLEY-ON-THAMES, 1980S

Question: How would you describe Srila Prabhupada's* achievements?

George Harrison: I think Prabhupada's accomplishments are very significant; in fact they're *huge*. Even compared to someone like William Shakespeare, the amount of literature Prabhupada produced is truly amazing. It boggles the mind. He sometimes went for days with only a few hours sleep. I mean even a youthful, athletic, young person couldn't keep the pace he kept himself at seventy-nine-years of age. Srila Prabhupada has already had an amazing effect on the world. There's no way of measuring it. One day I just realized, "God, this man is amazing!" He would sit up all night translating Sanskrit into English, putting in glossaries to make sure everyone understands it and yet he

*His Divine Grace A. C. Bhaktivedanta Swami Prabhupada, the founder of ISKCON (The International Society For Krishna Consciousness), was born Abhay Charan De in Calcutta in September 1896, and left this material world on November 14, 1977.

never came off as someone above you. He always had that childlike simplicity and what's most amazing is the fact he did all this translating in such a relatively short time, only a few years. And without having anything more than his own Krishna Consciouness, he rounded up thousands of devotees, set the whole movement in motion, which became something so strong it went on even after he left. And it's still escalating even now at an incredible rate. It will go on from the knowledge he gave. It can only grow and grow. The more people that wake up spiritually, they'll begin to realize the depth of what Prabhupada was saying, how much he gave.

Question: Did you know that complete sets of Prabhupada's books are in all the major colleges and universities of the world?

George: They should be! One of the greatest things I noticed about Prabhupada was the way he would be talking to you in English and then all of a sudden he would say it to you in Sanskrit and then translate it back into English. It was clear he really knew his philosophy. His contribution has obviously been enormous from the literary point of view, because he's brought the Supreme Person, Bhagavan Sri Krishna, into focus. A lot of scholars and writers know the *Gita,* but only on an intellectual level. Even when they write "Krishna said . . . ," they don't do it with the bhakti, or the love required. That's the secret, Krishna is actually a *person* who is the Lord and who will also appear there in that book when there is that bhakti. You can't understand the first thing about God unless you love Him. These big so-called *Vedic* scholars, they don't necessarily love Krishna, so they can't understand Him or give Him to us. But Prabhupada was very different . . . He has definitely affected the world in an absolute way. What he was giving us was the very highest literature, the highest knowledge. I mean there just isn't *anything* higher!

Question: What about trying to solve the problems of life without employing the spiritual process?

George: Life is like a piece of string with a lot of knots tied in it. The knots are the karma you're born with from all your past, and present life, and the object is to try and undo all those knots. That's what chanting and meditation in God consciousness can do. Otherwise, you simply tie another ten knots each time you try to undo one. That's how karma works. I mean, what we are now is simply the result of our past actions and in the future we'll manifest the results of the actions we're performing now. A little understanding of "as you sow, so shall you reap" is very important, because then you can't blame the condition you're in on anyone else. It's by your own actions you're able to get more in a mess or out of one. It's your own actions that relieve or bind you.

Question: Is there any special way you like to think of Krishna?

George: I like seeing Krishna as a baby, the way He's often depicted in India. And also Govinda, the celestial cowherd boy. I like the idea that you can experience Krishna as a baby and feel protective to Him, or as your friend, or as the guru.

Question: I don't think it's possible to calculate just how many people were turned on to Krishna Consciousness by your song, "My Sweet Lord."

George: I wanted to show that Hallelujah and Hare Krishna are really the same thing. I sang "Hallelujah" and then the change to 'Hare Krishna' so that people would be chanting the maha mantra before they knew what was going on! I had been chanting Hare Krishna for a long time, and this song was a simple idea of how to do a Western pop equivalent of a mantra which repeats over and over again. I don't feel guilty or bad about it; in fact it saved many a heroin addict's life. "Hallelujah" is a joyous expression the Christians have, but "Hare Krishna" has a mystical side to it. It's more than just glorifying God; it's asking to become His servant. And because of the way the mantra is put together, with the mystic spiritual energy contained in those syllables, it's much closer to God than the way Christianity currently seems to be representing him. Although Christ, in my mind, is an absolute yogi, I think many Christian teachers today are misrepresenting Christ. They're supposed to be representing Jesus, but they're not doing it very well. They're letting him down very badly and that's a big turn off. My idea in "My Sweet Lord," because it sounded like a "pop song," was to sneak up on them a bit. The point was to have the people not offended by "Hallelujah," and by the time it gets to "Hare Krishna," they're already hooked, and their foot's tapping and they're already singing along "Hallelujah," to kind of lull them into a sense of false security. And then suddenly it turns into "Hare Krishna," and they will all be singing that before they know what's happened, and they will think, "Hey, I thought I wasn't supposed to like Hare Krishna!" People write to me even now asking what style that was. Ten years later they're still trying to figure out what the words mean! It was just a little trick really. And it didn't offend. For some reason I never got any offensive feedback from Christians who said, "We like it up to a point, but what's all this about Hare Krishna?" "Hallelujah" may have originally been some mantric thing that got watered down, but I'm not sure what it really means. The Greek word for Christ is Kristos, which, let's face it, Krishna and Kristos is the same name actually.

Question: What would you say is the difference between the Christian view of God and Krishna?

George: When I first came to this house, it was occupied by nuns. I brought in this poster of Visnu. You just see His head and shoulders and His four arms holding a conchshell, lotus, and various other symbols, and it has a big om written above it. He has a nice aura around Him. I left it by the fireplace and went out into the garden. When we came back in the house, they all pounced on me saying, "Who is that? What is it?" as if it were some pagan god. So I said, "Well, if God is un-limited, then He can appear in any form, whichever way He likes to appear. That's one way. He's called Visnu." It freaked them out a bit, but the point is, why should God be limited? Even if you get Him as Krishna, He is not limited to that picture of Krishna. He can be the baby form, He can be Govinda and manifest in so many other well-known forms. You can see Krishna as a little boy, which is how I like to see Krishna. It's a very joyful relationship. But there's this morbid side to the way many represent Christianity today, where you don't smile, because it's too serious and you can't expect to see God, that kind of stuff. If there is God, we must see Him, and I don't believe in the idea you find in most churches, where they say, "No, you're not going to see Him. He's way up above you. Just believe what we tell you and shut up." I mean, the knowledge that's given in Prabhupada's books—the *Vedic* literatures— that's the world's oldest scriptures. They say that man can become purified and with divine vision he can see God. You get pure by chanting, then you see Him. And Sanskrit, the language they're written in, is the world's first recorded language. Devanagari* actually means "language of the gods." It's a matter of being open. Anyone who's open can do it. You just have to be open and not prejudiced. You just have to try it. There's no loss, you know. But the intellectuals will always have problems, because they always need to "know." They're often the most spiritually bankrupt people, because they never let go; they don't understand the meaning of to transcend the intellect. But an ordinary person's more willing to say, "Okay, let me try it and see if it works." Chanting Hare Krishna can make one a better Christian too.

GEORGE HARRISON AND JEFF LYNNE
Press Conference
May 5, 1988

Jeff Lynne: [Our name was the] Trembling Wilburys at one point. Me and George were doing *Cloud Nine* and we had this fictitious group called the Trembling Wilburys. It's the kind of thing you do in the studio at about four in the morning.

George Harrison: Yeah . . . somebody was making these guitar picks and they asked what they should print on 'em. Everybody has some smart little thing written on their picks, so as we'd just been talking about these Trembling Wilburys, I had Traveling Wilburys misspelt on this guitar pick. At that point, it was just a drunken thought in the back of my head. The way the actual record came about was I had to do this song, which is now the single, "Handle with Care," because Warners needed a third tune for a twelve-inch single. I was in Los Angeles while Jeff was producing Roy Orbison and we were having dinner and I said, "I'm gonna have to write a song tomorrow and just do it." I was thinking of the way John recorded "Instant Karma." And I said, "Where can

*The Sanskrit alphabet.

I get a studio?" and Jeff said, "Well maybe, Bob, you know, because he's got this little studio in his garage." He just went back to his house, phoned up Bob and he said sure, come on over. Tom Petty had my guitar and when I went to pick it up, he said, "I was wondering what I was gonna do tomorrow." And Roy said, "Well, give us a call if you're going to do anything, I'd love to come along." We wrote this tune the next morning when we got to Dylan's house, just the tune and then I thought, "Well, let's stick a bit in here for Roy."

Jeff: We were just on the lawn in Bob Dylan's back garden, all strumming away, and we said let's write a bit for Roy. And then Roy tries it out and it's perfect for him. It all came together like that, because everybody was there who wrote the song.

George: I always think it's a bit daft having all these people standing round and only I end up singing, you know. When they actually were doing the vocals, at one point, I just said to Jeff, "Hey, Jeff, this is it! The Traveling Wilburys!" It was like magic, it just happened. If you'd have tried ringing everybody up, saying, "Hey, we've got this idea, will you do it?" you would never have gotten though all these record companies and managers, it would've been impossible. But it was so spontaneous, we were doing it even before we realized . . . The song was no use to me as a single for *Cloud Nine* because it wasn't on the album. And it was a bit of a throwaway simply to use as a B-side. The record company was afraid that in America they'd import the track and the radio might start playing it because of the novelty value. There didn't seem to be any point putting it out like that, so I just carried it 'round in my pocket for ages, thinking, "What can I do with this thing?" And ultimately the only thing to do was do another nine tunes and make an album. It was just a question of timing, because Bob had to go on the road at the end of May and this was early April, when we did "Handle with Care," so he said, "Well, I've got a bit of time in the beginning of May." We had like nine or ten days we knew we could get Bob for. Everybody else was relatively free, so we just said, "Let's do it, we'll just write a tune a day and do it that way," and that's what happened . . . There's a good little story about "Handle with Care," because we got the tune and we put it down, all the rhythm guitars, with just a click track and then we needed the words. I was walking round with a bit of pa-per and a pencil and I was looking 'round Dylan's garage looking at lists of his song titles, trying to think of a title . . . and I was saying, "Come on, where's the words?" thinking all these people are such great songwriters so give us some lyrics then! Anyway, I looked behind his garage door and there was this big cardboard box that said, "Handle with care." Once we got the title it just took off. I thought, "I've been beat up, battered round," and then the lyrics were flying. I mean, we could've had twenty-nine verses to that tune, it was brilliant . . . A lot of people take Bob seriously, but if you know Dylan, he's such a joker re-ally. And he just sat down and we said, "Okay, what are we gonna do?" And Bob says, "Let's do one like Prince!" And he just started banging away, "I love your sexy body!" And it just turned into that tune.

Question: It's going to annoy [Dylan's] record company, because he's come up with better songs on this Wilburys' album than he did on his own.

George: A lot of people say that and I'm inclined to agree. I'm a huge Dylan fan. I've got all his records, and I've always liked him, and I'll go on liking him regardless of how bad his records are! But I was really pleased because he was so into the mood. By being together, it loos-ened everybody up. It wasn't as heavy as when you have to do some-thing on your own. What I've heard is now, since the Wilburys record, he's really writing some fantastic tunes, and for his next album he's gonna get a producer and I've no doubt he'll make a great album. So even if that's all the Wilburys did, was help get Bob enthusiastic again, it was well worth it.

GEORGE AND OLIVIA HARRISON
Interview

London, June 22, 1990

Question: Why did you decide to speak out on the plight of the orphans of Romania?

George Harrison: Well, the wife asked me if I would do this song. She said, *"Or else . . ."* No, she asked if I could talk the Wilburys into doing a song. When you see the photographs and what's happening, the babies alone in their cribs, we all have to do something occasionally. And I thought it was a good thing to do.

Question: What was the single factor that started your Romanian Angel Appeal?

Olivia Harrison: It was sort of a gradual assault on my conscience. It was slowly wearing away at me and I decided that perhaps we should try to raise some money, so I began to write various charities and see what we could do. In the end, I found myself responsible for lots of money and felt I should go to Romania and see what would be the most effective thing to do. Especially since Elton, Linda, Barbara and Ringo, Paul, and Yoko had donated along with us. Anyway, I went to Romania and was just overwhelmed, devastated, and shocked by the situation.

Question: How many children do you think are involved? The kind of figures we're getting are around 15,000. Do you think it's more than that?

Olivia: I think there's far more than that. I've heard 40,000, I've heard 50,000, I've even heard 400,000. Virtually every few miles there's an orphanage. We had a list of 400 and we didn't see any of them on the list. We started to go to one and they'd just point us to another, and another, and another.

Question: What are the conditions?

Olivia: Shocking! It's very bad, far worse than you can imagine, especially now. I mean, at this point in time, everybody is enjoying such luxury in their lives, and then you see one hundred fifty children with no sanitation. On a practical level, that's what we're trying to do, make their lives more tolerable. Basically, they need to be taken out of the orphanages. Every child needs a family, some love, and nurturing.

Question: Why should there be so many children in Romanian orphanages?

Olivia: Well, Ceausescu felt that if Romania had thirty million people it would give him more power and the country would become a more formidable force in Europe. Women were forced to have five chidren. Both abortion and birth control were illegal. So the lucky ones in the orphanages grew up to be in his army, the Securitate, but those were the lucky ones.

Question: They were known as *his* children, I believe.

Olivia: They were turned over to the State. I saw a trolley of babies you know, like loaves of bread. The sad thing is, life goes on, politics change, but nothing really changes in their lives. Day after day, year after year, their entire lives are spent in these horrible institutions.

Question: Are you saying you'd like them to be adopted, and if so, isn't there a certain amount of resentment against the adoption of Romanian children over here?

Olivia: I've been steering clear of that question because it is a difficult one. I know a woman who just brought a baby back and was given the runaround, but she finally succeeded. If you feel that in your heart, then that's a personal decision.

Question: How much money have you raised so far?

Olivia: Through the *Daily Mail* we've raised £835,000, to the credit of the British public . . . I always remember Bob Geldof saying during Live Aid, "pity the man who did nothing because he could do so little." And really, the public haven't been shy in donating a pound or five. That's what's done it.

Question: George, how did you first become aware of what was happening?

George: Well, I was in Los Angeles so I didn't really know about it until Olivia told me by telephone. Then, to my amazement, she suddenly said, "I'm going to Bucharest tomorrow." When she returned she brought back a lot of photographs and said, "It'd be a nice idea if you would do a song and help raise a bit of money. Maybe you could put a single out." I thought, well that's easy enough, because I was in a room with tape machines and stuff, so we did something.

Question: All the proceeds will go to this Romanian Angel Appeal?

George: Yeah. We also had an instrumental from Dave Stewart to put on the B-side, and then somebody suggested we make it into an album. There's a fellow who manages a couple of people in the States and does Dylan's tours, [it] was his suggestion, so within a couple of hours we had Ric Ocasek from the Cars. He volunteered a track, so I got on the phone and now we have Eric Clapton and Elton John, plus Stevie Wonder, Mike and the Mechanics, as well as Guns N' Roses. So it's quite a fun album.

Question: Olivia, you've been back to Bucharest, have you seen any of the effects of the money you've brought in?

Olivia: This last trip I took, during the earthquake, I visited two orphanages. I'm very emotional about the whole thing, but to walk in there and see the children with no showers, hot water, heaters, or bathtubs, so little for us, things we wouldn't even think about.

Question: Do you hope to go there, George, to see what's happening?

George: Not particularly. I'm not saying I won't, but it's not really my idea to go . . . I can do more this way, to help get the money to the people who actually know what they're doing.

It's going to be better than it was, and it's just a matter of time to get 'round to all these places and get them all wash basins and toilets.

Olivia: George was going to be an electrician . . .

George: Or a plumber . . .

Question: What did you eventually become?

George: I don't know, really. Just some object for the newspapers to make fun of probably.

GEORGE HARRISON
Interview
LOS ANGELES, DECEMBER 14, 1992

Question: Have you had occasion to read any portion of Geoffrey Giuliano's book, *Dark Horse: The Private Life of George Harrison*?

George Harrison: Yeah, I did see it once. I opened it randomly and read about two or three paragraphs and that was it. I put it away. I don't recall where I saw it. It might have been in my office, I think . . .

Question: Have you ever met him?

George: Yeah, I met him briefly. I have no way of recalling what year it was, but I met him at the home of 'Legs' Larry Smith for possibly thirty minutes. I visited with Mr. Smith and he was in his flat.

Question: At some point did you become aware Mr. Giuliano was making it his business to do research, write books and articles about you and the other Beatles?

George: The first I heard about it was when my office told me they had been [contacted] by Giuliano for some kind of information, or some kind of acknowledgment . . . I don't recall exactly what it was, but I know my business manager spoke to him personally.

Question: At what point did you become aware Giuliano was actually writing books about you, Paul McCartney, and the Beatles as a group?

George: It was when his book on the Beatles was issued.*

Question: Have you read any of the other things he has written about the Beatles?

The Beatles: A Celebration, St. Martin's Press, New York, 1986.

George: No. The same goes for the book on the Beatles. I didn't read the thing. I thumbed through it and tried to get the gist of the layout and the photographs . . . I receive books all the time. People mail them to me occasionally, I come across [them] somewhere, you know, there [are] many books being written about the various members of the Beatles . . . I don't make it a practice to read them.

Question: Have you ever had any discussions with any of the other Beatles, Ringo Starr, or Paul McCartney, or John Lennon, before he was tragically murdered, concerning anything Mr. Giuliano wrote about any of you?

George: No, not really. I spoke to Paul McCartney last week when he was in Los Angeles . . . And I said [something] to him about [all] these books that are written on us, and I said, "I hear this fellow Giuliano has written a book about you, too." I said, "Do you know anything to speak of, about him?" There is a certain trick to the way Giuliano goes about his work. He acts as if he is kind of authorized, and [all] these people, not just him, but all these type of people, have a skill of wheedling their way into places that are going to be some benefit to them in getting their books written.

Question: What did Paul McCartney say to you when you told him to be careful?

George: He said, "Yeah, I have," he said, you know, "But I don't read any of that stuff," just what I would expect . . .

Question: The cover of *Dark Horse* which is, I take it, an unauthorized biography, has a quote attributed to you. It says: "Geoffrey Giuliano, that guy knows more about my life than I do . . ."

George: I made a statement when somebody asked me about Giuliano and his book . . .

Question: Has anyone [ever] told you they have read the book; that is, any friends, relatives, or business associates?

George: No. Anybody who is associated with me wouldn't bring up the subject because they know my feeling about these kinds of books. . . . I would like to add about Denny Laine that in connection [with] Mc-Cartney, Paul said Giuliano has been hanging out and romancing Denny Laine, who gave Giuliano a lot of negative stuff to be put into the book on Paul he was writing.*

Question: Have you mentioned Mr. Giuliano to anyone other than Paul?

George: I think there is one other person I had a conversation with, not a very long one, who works for the Beatles company, Apple. Neil Aspinall the name is, and I have a feeling I heard some story about Giuliano in connection with him trying to [make some] money out of Yoko Ono . . . I recall that Yoko tapped his phone line . . .

Question: In any event, you do recall that you made that quote [which] is on the cover [of *Dark Horse*]?

George: That may not be exact word for word, but something to that effect . . .

Question: Did you ever have a press officer or someone who worked for you in that capacity?

George: Derek Taylor was the Beatles' press officer in the sixties and early seventies.

Question: Does he remain a friend of yours to this day?

George: Yeah, but I don't see him very often. I don't think I have seen him for a couple of years.

Question: What jobs did he do for you, or the Beatles . . . ?

George: He worked in the Apple Records press office in the late sixties and early seventies. Then he worked with me on a book, and I worked with him on another book (as I edited a book he wrote and he helped to construct [a] book I did) . . .

Question: What other projects did you work on with Mr. Taylor?

*Blackbird: The Life and Times of Paul McCartney, Dutton, New York.

George: Derek held a job at a film company [of which] I am a partial owner, Hand Made Films . . .

Question: [I've read that] since 1966, you have been very involved with [several] Indian gurus . . .

George: My involvement in the Beatles with India and meditation is widely known.

Question: And that you spent some time in India?

George: Yeah, spent plenty of time. Yeah, I have met a few . . .

Question: Is it accurate that you hated or resented Beatlemania?

George: No. This is Geoffrey Giuliano's representation of me. It is not me.

Question: What were your feelings about Beatlemania?

George: It got [to be] too much, you know. It is not a secret . . . We got so famous to the point where we couldn't move and in that context it wasn't always comfortable. It was very uncomfortable at times . . .

Question: How many people work at your home [Friar Park]?

George: There are a couple of cleaning ladies. There is another person who used to be a nanny, but cooks now. I have two brothers who work on the premises and four gardeners. At times I have had up to maybe eight gardeners, but there are four at the moment . . .

Question: Did you or did any of the Beatles, during that period when you were actually in Germany, before all the enormous fame fell upon you, were there any joking references to any Nazi symbols at that time?

George: Nothing specific I could think of, no . . . Generally, we had fun. There was a lot of beer drunk in those days, we played a lot of rock'n'roll, and generally acted like drunken rock'n'rollers. Basically, we had a great relationship with the German audience and the club owners. They loved us and wanted us to play there all the time because we were good for business . . . A lot takes place when you are in a night-club for six months, or whatever . . . But we had friends, and still have friends who are Germans, and as I say, we had a good relationship with the audience . . . When somebody was drunk, it may have happened, but I certainly didn't do anything and I can't say I saw anything.

Question: [I've heard] there are photographs of Hitler in the proposed *Sgt. Pepper* layout . . . Was there was any discussion among the Beatles as to whether one of those personages whose pictures appear might be Adolf Hitler?

George: Absolutely not. Having said that, the artist, this guy Peter Blake, might have secretly wanted to put Hitler on, and didn't tell us.

Question: Who was in charge of determining who would be on the album?

George: No one person particularly. We all suggested names of people, or provided, in a couple of instances, pictures of people we thought would be good to put on there. Together with everybody involved, us four and anybody else—like our road managers, all the artists, photographers, and everybody who was involved in the conception of this photograph—they all put in people. You know, there are a lot of people on there I personally wouldn't have had on. But it makes no difference. It was just a huge cross section of people.

Question: Did that album cover go through a number of versions until a final cover was settled upon?

George: No. The only difference [was] when they were setting it up and moving things around, and as I say, there were people like Mahatma Gandhi and the Bowery Boys that come to mind. Some people felt offended to be called lonely hearts and so they were taken off. [Those are] the only changes I can recall.

Question: So you got some expressions of unwillingness to be included by the estates of certain people?

George: Yeah. Certainly, we had to write to everybody who was on the sleeve and see that they didn't object; make it all a legal cover . . .

Question: Are the two areas of your business you are principally focused on, recording and filmmaking?

George: Yes, but alongside recording, obviously, I am a songwriter. I write my own songs and those are published. So that is another part of the business of recording.

Question: Do you perform all of the songs you write yourself?

George: I do on my solo albums, but I have made albums in the past with some friends. You asked me earlier about the Traveling Wilburys. That has entailed four and five of us making a record, which we have written the songs and sung them together . . . Of all the time I put into business I would say probably about seventy percent [is] on the musical side and thirty percent on the film side, because my partner, who is my business manager, Dennis O'Brien,* is the one who actually goes and does [all] the deals and the business of Hand Made Films. I am not a negotiator. I don't involve myself with any of that. I just get involved with the artistic side.

GEORGE HARRISON
Selected Quotations on Indian Culture
LONDON, 1970S

"While the words to the 'Hare Krishna Mantra' don't alter, the tune it's sung to doesn't matter. You could sing to 'Coming Round the Mountain' if you wanted. All I've done on this is shorten it. The actual meaning of the words is not important, although there are various forms of addressing the spiritual Lord, God, if you like. It is a sort of magical vibration to bring about a spiritual awareness.

"God has many names, and, while I've always believed in the existence of a God, I never knew what to call him. This is just another way of finding spiritual communion."

---

*Dennis O'Brien was subsequently sued by George Harrison, who claimed financial impropriety on behalf of his former manager and longtime friend. Geoffrey Giuliano, however, assisted Mr. Harrison in a lawsuit against *Globe* magazine acting as an expert witness for the former Beatle as well as providing several key pieces of physical evidence. The case was eventually settled out of court with Harrison being awarded a large sum.

"The Maharishi and I are still great friends, I'm not forsaking him at all. Chanting Hare Krishna is just another way of reaching God. I don't think it matters that it's not the same way. Each person must decide for himself the way that best suits him."

"I met Ravi in 1965 at the house of Mr. Angbadi, who ran the Asian Music Circle in Finchley. We had dinner there and it was through that meeting he later came to my house to give me some basic sitar instruction.

"Later, because he was a Bengali, he came to me because he wanted to do something about the situation in Bangladesh. He wanted to put on a concert where he could raise around twenty thousand dollars, which was more than he'd normally make from a performance. He originally asked Peter Sellers and myself if we could introduce the concert or think of something to do. So I became involved and helped put the concert for Bangladesh together, and it has raised eleven million dollars to date.

GEORGE HARRISON
Selected Quotations on Ravi Shankar
NEW YORK, JUNE 1997

"To me, George is a son, a friend, someone very dear, and I love him very much. He has given me so much love and respect that my heart is *full* of it.

"We are such good friends, it's a beautiful, mixed feeling. I had heard of the Beatles, but I didn't know how popular they were. I met all four, but with George I clicked immediately. He said he wanted to learn [sitar] properly. I said it's not just learning the chords, like the guitar. Sitar takes at least one year to [learn to] sit properly because the instrument is so difficult to hold. Then you cut your fingers . . . George said he would try. He seemed so sweet and sincere . . ."

PUNDIT RAVI SHANKAR

"I was born in the wrong place to be a sitar player. It's a torturous thing. Even to sit and hold it is difficult. But I enjoyed it, even the punishing side, because I never really had any discipline before. The sitar playing on 'Norwegian Wood' was horrible. I didn't know how to tune it or play it . . . I like music that is not ego music. Real music doesn't make you think of cash registers. It should transport you somewhere nice."

"You just have to be open to the rhythms and the sounds of [Indian music]. You don't have to know exactly how they do it. Which, in some sense, is what led to the bastardization of Indian music, which, I suppose, I started with 'Norwegian Wood.' But, you know, all I was doing really was trying to get the sound. You can't resist the sound of Indian classical music if you're ready to surrender to it and not judge it. Just accept it and listen to it. Which is why I got into it. It was just overpowering in a transcendental way."

"Ravi figured everything out, how [*Chants of India*] was going to run and which order it should go in. The total concept was Ravi's, really. Basically, more or less everything we recorded is on the album, in the order he conceived it while we were doing it. So as a producer, that was one thing I didn't have to bother with . . . If this is successful, it would be a great bit of handiwork, to be able to get it through to the people. What it is, in disguise, is a great blessing, because the *Vedas* are pure spiritual energy in the form of sound."

"When I first got a record of Ravi's, a World Pacific recording, I put it on, played it, and inside of me I had an instinctive feeling I was going to meet him, which I did. And all the other things have been a by-product of that relationship. I went to India to learn some music with Ravi, but my main quest was that I wanted to know about the yogis. But Ravi was my input into it. Through him I was able to hear the best music, buy the best incense, read the best swamis, meet the best people. I was very, very fortunate to become friends with him. And consequently all the goodness which has come to me in my life is a direct effect of being plugged into that Indian tradition, or whatever, I gained through Ravi."

"If you don't know who you are and where you've come from and where you're going, what is life? You can have all the money in the world and all the glory. But if you don't know what the point is, then your life is empty. So, in that respect, Ravi, not just Ravi, but he was the main ingredient, patched me into the Vedic tradition. And from that I've learned all these things about yoga, meditation, about what it is, about the goal. I've come to understand incredible stuff, just through pursuing that. Without it, I'd just be a boring old fart."

"At my first [sitar] lesson with Ravi, the phone rang and I jumped up to answer it, quickly putting the sitar down. He slapped my leg and said, 'You must always respect the instrument.' He wasn't at all intimidated by who I was, and he was right. From the very beginning, he was the opposite of what I think of as a classical musician. He was always full of fun, went to all the plays, the movies, read all the books, and he explained to me that in India, when the audience hears a good lick, they will applaud and shout spontaneously, rather than waiting for the end as we do in classical concerts here. I know his relationship with us caused him intense embarrassment on several occasions. He was very against the drug culture. He felt the music should be enough to get you high. Our relationship is very complex. He's still my teacher, and he's like a father to me, and an inspiration because he's a deeply spiritual person, which is exactly what I needed at that time in my career. But he's also like a little boy in many ways, very innocent. I need to take care of him because he finds it hard to deal with the business side of things. I know he loves a lot of Western classical music, but I don't. There are bits of Debussy I enjoy and a few others, but too much of it I find pompous. I always remember Ravi telling me that when Yehudi Menuhin first heard him play Indian music he started to cry and said, 'I've wasted my whole life up to now.'"

GEORGE HARRISON AND RAVI SHANKAR
Selected Quotations on Indian Music

New York, 1997

George Harrison: During the Beatlemania days I first got involved with Ravi's music. I bought some of his records and although my intellect didn't really know what was happening, or didn't understand much about the music, the pure sound appealed to me so much. It hit a spot very deep in me and I just recognized it somehow. I just had a feeling I was going to meet him. At the same time, when I played the sitar, very badly, on a Beatles record, Ravi came to London. A lot of press were trying to set it up for us to meet, but I avoided it. I didn't want to be on the front page of a newspaper as a gimmick, because it meant more to me than that. So I thought, "I'll wait and meet him in my own time." There was a society called the Asian Music Circle and the fellow who ran that, who I'd got to know, said, "Ravi's gonna come for lunch," so we met that way. Then he came to my house and showed me how to hold the sitar and put me through the basics of sitar.

Ravi Shankar: I hadn't heard any Beatles music before I met George, but I saw the effect on the young people. I couldn't believe it, even in India. It was not only the West. They loved them so much.

George: In those days, we were growing very quickly and there were a lot of influences, I mean that was the best thing about our band. We were very open to everything and we were listening to all kinds of music. I'd bought a very cheap sitar in a shop called India Craft in London, and even though it sounded bad, it still fit on the song "Norwegian Wood," and it gave it that little extra zing, so they were quite happy about it. I went to India to be with Ravi to learn some music and just experience India, but I also wanted to know about the Himalayas. That is the thing that's always fascinated me, you know, what are we doing on this planet? Throughout the Beatle experience we had grown so many years within a very short span of time. I'd experienced so many things and met so many people, but I realized there was nothing really giving me a buzz anymore. I wanted something *better,* I remember thinking, I'd *have* to meet somebody who will really impress me, and that's when I met Ravi. Which is funny, because he's this little fella with this obscure instrument, from our point of view, and yet it led me into such depths. I think that's the most important thing and still is. I get confused when I look around at the world and see everybody's running around and, you know, as Bob Dylan said, "He not busy being born, is busy dying," and yet nobody's trying to figure out the *cause of death* and what happens when you die. To me, that is the only thing. In the Bible it says, "Knock and the door will be opened," and it's true. If you want to know anything in this life, you just have to knock. Whether that is physically on somebody's door to ask them a question, or, which I was lucky to find, is meditation, it's all within. And that's really why for me this new record, *Chants of India,* is important, because it's another little key to open up to within. For each individual to be able to sit and turn off your mind, relax, and float downstream, and listen to something that has it's root in the transcendental, because even the words of these songs carry a very subtle spiritual vibration. It goes way beyond intellect really. So if you let yourself be free to let that have an affect on you, it can be very positive.

Ravi: I'm ashamed to say I knew almost nothing about the Beatles when I first met them, except they were very popular. I was so impressed by George, who was so inquisitive, asking about so many different things—mostly about music, sitar and, of course, along with certain spiritual subjects. His enthusiasm was so real, and I wanted to give as much as I could though my sitar because that is the only thing I know. The rest I cannot express. George talks so beautifully. He writes poems and songs. I express myself through musical notes, so it's a different way. But when I met him I taught him how to to sit properly, how to hold the sitar, and how to handle the finger positions, all the basic things. He was so interested and so quick in learning and then we arranged for him to come to India and he did. We fixed it for six weeks, but unfortunately, it didn't happen because people recognized him after a week or so, and there was such a commotion in Bombay we had to run away to Kashmir and live in a houseboat. But unfortunately he had to leave.

George: I believe it was because of *Sgt. Pepper* or something.

Ravi: I thought, "My God, I couldn't believe any four people could create such a storm all over the world!"

George: The Spice Boys!

Ravi: It was not that I was unknown or anything. I was playing concerts in Carnegie Hall and different places, but as a classical Indian musician. But the moment it was known that George has become my disciple, it was like wildfire. I became so popular with the young people that all of a sudden I was rediscovered, and then I assumed the role of a superstar for a number of years because of him. You know the whole thing was not really to my liking because of the association with drugs and things like that. So I really had a very difficult time for the next few years putting my music in the right place, but because I did, that is why I am here today. Otherwise, I wouldn't have been here. People have really come to understand the depth and seriousness of our music along with the entertainment part. That is there, but the true root is also projected in this particular record.

GEORGE HARRISON
Press Release Interview
New York, July 7, 1997

Question: How did you come up with the idea of recording *Chants of India* with Ravi Shankar?

George Harrison: Steve Murphy, president of Angel Records, had heard some songs that were similar to this material on *In Celebration,* a Ravi Shankar retrospective I helped assemble last year. He suggested we go in the studio to record more. This music, which is based on ancient *Vedic* chanting, I very much enjoy. And, of course, it would give me an opportunity to work with Ravi, so it made perfect sense.

Question: What drew you to Ravi Shankar?

George: His music was the reason I wanted to meet him. I liked it immediately, it intrigued me. I don't know why I was so into it. I heard it, liked it and had a gut feeling I would meet him. Eventually, a man from the Asian Music Circle in London arranged a meeting between Ravi and myself. That meeting has made all the difference in my life.

Question: What did your role as producer of *Chants of India* entail?

George: I organized the recording of the album, and during the sessions I sang and played on a couple of songs—bass guitar, acoustic guitar, and a few other things, vibraphone, glockenspiel, and autoharp. The main thing was finding the right musicians, busing everybody out to my [home] studio, and making certain everyone was properly fed. Finding the right engineer, John Etchells, was also key.

Question: Why is now the right time to release *Chants of India*?

George: In a way it represents the accumulation of our ideas and experiences throughout our thirty-year relationship. To put it into a slightly more commercial aspect, the label asked us to do this, which would never have happened fifteen years ago. Indian music has become more accepted and more people are interested in what this music offers, [therefore] this project has become more commercially viable. This music is very close to me. This is something I very much wanted to do. I actively read Vedic scriptures and I'm happy to spread the word about what this project is all about. People also need an alternative to all the clatter in their lives, and this music provides that. Whether it's Benedictine Monks chanting or ancient Vedic chants, people are searching for something to cut through all the clatter and stress.

Question: How do you view yourself as a sitar player?

George: I'm not a very good one, I'm afraid. The sitar is an instrument I've loved for a long time. For three or four years I practiced every day. But it's a very difficult instrument and one that takes a toll on you physically. It disciplined me so much, which was something I hadn't really experienced to a great extent before.

Question: Looking back, how do you view the sitar on "Norwegian Wood (This Bird has Flown)"?

George: Very rudimentary. I didn't know how to tune it properly and it was a very cheap sitar to begin with. So "Norwegian Wood" was very much an early experiment. By the time we recorded "Love You To," I had made some strides.

Question: Were the other Beatles open to your explorations with the sitar?

George: That was the environment in the band, everybody was very open to bringing in new ideas. We were listening to all sorts of things, Stockhausen, avant garde, whatever, and most of it made its way onto our records.

GEORGE HARRISON
Selected Quotations
DATES UNKNOWN

"I don't go around thinking, 'I am George Harrison from the Beatles!' I try to balance my life with peace and quiet, because the other side is real rowdy. I'm a Pisces. I am an extreme person. One half is always going where the other half has just been. I was always extremely up or down, extremely spiritual or extremely drugged. Now [I have] a bit of maturity. I've brought the two closer to the middle. I don't get too far up or too far down anymore and that feels good."

"There was a magic that happened between us and somehow it got into the grooves on those records. Not every song we ever did was brilliant, but a lot of them are timeless, great songs that happen to have something in the grooves which appeals to each generation as it comes up."

"It was sad when we broke up because we had been so close for so long. Mick Jagger said at the Rock'n'Roll Hall of Fame dinner that the Beatles were a four-headed monster. We never went anywhere without each other. We shared all the miseries and the isolation of limos, hotels, planes, and concert halls, which is all we ever saw for years."

"You can take the Beatles separately and analyze all their energy, but when you put them together astrologically and chemically, something stronger takes place that even the Beatles understood. As Bob Dylan said, 'To understand you know too soon there is no sense in trying.' Dylan is so brilliant. To me, he makes William Shakespeare look like Billy Joel."

GEORGE HARRISON
North American Tour Itinerary

1974

November 2	Vancouver, BC, Canada, Pacific Coliseum
November 4	Seattle, WA, Seattle Center Coliseum
November 6	San Francisco, CA, Cow Palace
November 7	San Francisco, CA, Cow Palace
November 8	Oakland, CA, Oakland Coliseum
November 10	Long Beach, CA, Long Beach Arena
November 11	Los Angeles, CA, Los Angeles Forum
November 12	Los Angeles, CA, Los Angeles Forum
November 14	Tucson, AZ, Tucson Community Center
November 16	Salt Lake City, UT, Salt Palace
November 18	Denver, CO, Denver Coliseum
November 20	St. Louis, MO, Assembly Center
November 21	Tulsa, OK, Assembly Center
November 22	Fort Worth, TX, Tarrant County Assembly Center
November 24	Houston, TX, Hofheinz Pavilion
November 26	Baton Rouge, LA, Louisiana State University Assembly Center
November 27	Memphis, TN, Mid-South Coliseum
November 28	Atlanta, GA, Omni
November 30	Chicago, IL, Chicago Stadium
December 2	Cleveland, OH, Richmond Coliseum
December 4	Detroit, MI, Olympia Stadium
December 6	Toronto, Ont., Canada, Maple Leaf Gardens
December 8	Montreal, Que., Canada, Montreal Forum

December 10	Boston, MA, Boston Garden
December 11	Providence, RI, Providence Civic Center
December 13	Washington, DC, Capital Centre
December 15	Uniondale, NY, Nassau Coliseum
December 16	Philadelphia, PA, Philadelphia Spectrum
December 17	Philadelphia, PA, Philadelphia Spectrum
December 19	New York, NY, Madison Square Garden
December 20	New York, NY, Madison Square Garden

GEORGE HARRISON
Japanese Tour Itinerary
1991

December 1	Yokohama, Yokohama Arena
December 2 & 3	Osaka, Castle Hall
December 5	Nagoya, International Exhibition Hall
December 6	Hiroshima, Sun Plaza
December 9	Fukuoka, International Center
December 10, 11, & 12	Osaka, Castle Hall
December 14, 15, & 16	Tokyo, Tokyo Dome

RINGO STARR AND PETE BEST

RINGO STARR
Press Conference
AMSTERDAM, 1976

Question: Why did you title this album *Rotogravure?*

Ringo Starr: Well, it's in every newspaper. I first heard Judy Garland sing it in *Easter Parade,* she said, "You'll find my picture in the rotogravure," and I said, "What's she singing? Russian? What sort of language is this?" Anyway, I found out it was French and it was also the first color supplement, like in the big papers, *The Times,* or *The Observer* in England.

Question: Why are you in Europe?

Ringo: To promote *Rotogravure!* We started in France, Germany, Italy, Denmark, here, and then we'll go to Japan. I did all the promotion in America before I left, so I'm just going around to see the people in the company. That personal contact is very good. If you say hello to the girls in the office, I think they work harder for you. It's nice if they think you're thinking of them. It's the first time I've ever done it with a record, I usually don't bother.

Question: There is a photo of the front door of Apple on the back of the cover, where did you get it?

Ringo: Neil Aspinall took it and sent us one each and I thought, "I'm gonna put it on the back of the album." It's a front door, but it's a back door, too. It's a got all these names scrawled on it from Finland. That's why you're getting a magnifying glass with the album, so you can read it all. And I thought it'd be a nice bit of fun, especially for those who actually wrote on it. It used to be so smart, with a doorman and a pretty letterbox, and now it's just, yeah!

Question: What happened to Ring'O Records?

Ringo: Ring'O Records is closed for now and opens up again at the end of the year, or next year, starting properly, because I was trying to run it, but I'm not really a businessman. There was just this one man working in England, but now there'll be more people running it, so it'll be different.

Question: You were on stage with Paul, in Los Angeles?

Ringo: Yeah, well I just went to one of the shows and decided to give Denny Laine some flowers. It would be too obvious to give them to Paul or Linda, so I gave them to Denny. It was just a fun thing. And then we all went and had a drink.

Question: Did you already know Denny?

Ringo: Denny I've known for years. Denny and I once did a jam at a club, him on bass and me on drums. There wasn't much melody going on with just bass and drums. Also no guitars or nothing, but we were drunk at the time. That's probably one of the worst bands I've ever been in.

Question: I read you did something with fireplaces?

Ringo: Yeah, I designed furniture, but I've stopped that now. I did that for five years and now I don't do it, I just make music.

Question: I'd like to talk now about some people on the album; Lon Van Eaton, did you know him from Apple?

Ringo: Yeah, I was looking for a guitarist in L.A. and someone mentioned Lon and I said, "Okay, lets see what he's like," and he worked very well.

Question: You and Jim Keltner are both credited as drummers.

Ringo: We work well together. It started in England in 1970, we were on a Jim Price album, we did a track together, I didn't even know if it ended up on the album. And then we did Bangladesh and in America I'm not allowed to work there, so I don't put an American out of work if I have another drummer on the session.

Question: When you were with Apple you sometimes used another name when you played with other people.

Ringo: Yeah, but now it's *Ringo*. It used to be Richie, or Richie Snare, there was a few odd names, now it's Ringo Starr. They still have to give me permission, but everybody does it for everybody. I mean, if all the people who played on mine dared say I couldn't be on theirs, that would be terrible. They wouldn't stop me anyway, I'd just do it.

PETE AND MONA BEST
Press Conference
WEST DERBY, AUGUST 28, 1985

Question: Mrs. Best, what inspired you to open a club on the outskirts of town?

Mona Best: I used to have them coming in and out of my house as if it were a railway station, so I thought to myself, we've got a nice cellar, maybe the gang would all like to go down there? The boys said, "What are we going to do down there? There's nothing going on, let's make it into a little club." That *little* club ended up with nearly three thousand members. Every night it used to be jam-packed solid. We use to light the fire even if it was a hot night so they'd buy more Coke. They'd say, "It's hot, another Coke please, Rory!" The people would be enjoying themselves chotter-block. I've never seen a club with such atmosphere. It was all volunteers that helped get the club together. They put in a lot of hours. Including John Lennon.

Question: This was really before the Cavern Club, wasn't it?

Mona: Yes. Later, when I spoke to [Cavern owner] Ray McFall, he was doing jazz in his club. He said, "You've opened up a little rock'n'roll club. Why don't you come down to the Cavern?" I said, "I can't, I'm too busy with my own place. But there's a very good rock group over here called the Beatles. Why don't you put them on?" He said, "I'm thinking of changing over to rock. Maybe I'll do it." And that's how the boys eventually went on to play the Cavern.

Question: Could you give us some idea what it was like at the club?

Mona: Everybody use to call each other by their Christian names. My mother, who was very ill at the time, was Gran to everybody though she seldom came out of her room. It was an unusual place with a fantastic atmosphere, very friendly. We had a jukebox, in fact, one of the guys used to spin records for us. So from a little acorn a very big oak tree grew. I remember the day the Quarrymen first showed their faces, the four of them: John, George, Paul, and Ken Brown. We didn't allow any ale in the club, or any other drinks for that matter. Sometimes though the kids use to smuggle them in and we had to pitch them out when they got drunk.

Question: How much was a membership?

Mona: Half a crown. And threepence for a bottle of Coke. In fact, a lot of club owners in town would say, "Hey, you're spoiling it for us, at least raise the price to nine!"

Question: Pete, how did you become involved with the Beatles?

Pete Best: My first recollection of meeting them was just before the club opened. We needed a group to open on the Saturday. I knew George because there was another club down the road called the Lowlands and he use to play there with Ken Brown and their skiffle group. When you talk about skiffle, you're talking very small amplifiers. Anyway, Ken said the group had broken up, but George said, "I know a couple of guys who say they've played in a band before. If they're interested in coming down, would you let them open?" Mum said, "Yes, let me see them." Well, it turned out to be John and Paul. But there was no drummer. It was John, George, Paul, Ken Brown and they decided to play under the name of the Quarrymen. On that fateful night the Casbah opened, the Quarrymen took the stage as a foursome (without a drummer) and history began.

Question: So the night the Casbah opened, the first group to play there was the Quarrymen.

Pete: Yes, and I believe they subsequently didn't do too badly.

Question: What was your first impression of the group?

Mona: The Quarrymen were never a very smart lot. Whenever you saw them they looked scruffy, just as scruffy and untidy as when they went on stage. Out of them all, Ken was the cleanest. The rest had ruffled heads, dirty clothes, and filthy jeans. But they were a happy lot.

Pete: At the time John was still at art college so he was a typical Bohemian. He'd come in with his black jacket and chukka boots. He never use to wear his glasses. I remember he was helping out at the club and painted several murals on the ceiling. He painted his usual pot bellies and caricatures, but the Casbah had to be dark so one day he said, "I'll just paint the ceiling black," and they all went. Paul was a little more sedate, he'd wear jeans, an off-white shirt and a cashmere jacket. That's the way they knocked around. They were very relaxed in what they did. They were always laughing and joking. There was nothing serious about them. Somebody would crack a joke and they wouldn't work for two hours. They were scruffy, but don't get the impression they were tramps or anything.

Question: Did you think these guys really had something special?

Pete: Remember, they were a group without a drummer and very different in as much as their material was not the run-of-the-mill stuff. They weren't interested in the Top Twenty, they were playing Chuck Berry, Carl Perkins, and Gene Vincent. They were all harmonies and doing what they liked, it's as simple as that. They also had great charisma on stage. There was something about them. The way they stood, the things they did, made them stand out from the rest of the groups. Stu Sutcliffe used to come down and watch the Quarrymen. He was very much a Beatles man.

Question: How did you personally become involved with the Beatles?

Pete: They played the Casbah for nearly twelve months and one particular night Ken Brown wasn't too well and they played as a trio. At the end of the evening the princely sum of fifteen shillings was kept back by mum. There was a bit of disagreement as they wanted that split up amongst them. Which, by the way, would have only bought them another beer or something.

Mona: They were always like that where money was concerned.

Pete: After that, they disappeared and Stu joined them. By that time they had changed their name to the Silver Beatles. At the end of their first tour of Scotland, a guy called Tommy Moore was drumming for them and he told me, "The tour was a complete flop, it didn't go anywhere." When the Quarrymen changed to the Silver Beatles there was another group in the wings, which was my own funky outfit. I formed a band with Ken Brown called the Blackjacks and took on another couple of guys, Chas Nugan and Bill Low. We played skiffle at school as I knew some guitar stuff, but later I switched to drums and got a kit. I started off with a thirty-six inch bass, a ten inch snare, one cymbal, a pair of brushes, and eventually got a drum kit which happened to be blue. After Tommy Moore disappeared the boys never managed to find another drummer. I got a call from Paul one night, saying they were booked to go to Germany. Allan Williams closed the deal and he wondered if I would be interested in joining. I told him my group really wasn't professional, we were just doing it for kicks. Anyway, the offer was there so I just said okay.

Mona: He gave up school to go, he was going in for languages. He said, "Can I finish with school to go off to Germany?" I said, "If that's what you want." He said, "I want to go into show business, that's where my heart is." "Do what you want," I told him, and off he went.

Pete: So I auditioned and as the story goes: Two days later we were on our way to Hamburg.

Question: Is the Allan Williams book [*The Man Who Gave the Beatles Away*] accurate from what you recall?

Pete: I think he must have had a lot of fun writing it. You can see what he was trying to do, making out that Hamburg was this wicked city with all the crazy birds, over the top booze, and the rest of it. Read into it what you like.

Question: After becoming a Beatle did you think you were on your way to super-stardom?

Pete: Joining a band which was fully professional was one thing, and joining a bunch of guys with no real experience quite another, but we were still friends. No, I didn't think we were going anywhere, but it was a chance to break into show business. I mean the German audiences were going wild, and that's when the charisma really started to grow. I don't think that they, in their wisdom, thought they'd ever become mega-stars either. I think we knew we were going to get in the charts, and that was the first stepping stone, in fact, that was the ultimate at the time.

Question: I once saw a movie which portrayed the early Beatles and it had John saying, "Lads, where we going? Straight to the top!" Is that true?

Pete: Yes. When we were on stage and things were going well he'd shout, "Where we going guys?" And the reply was, "To the toppermost of the poppermost!" Which meant we were going to get there. He'd call that out even if we were in the middle of a number.

Question: Tell me about the song "Peppermint Twist"?

Pete: That was one of the first numbers Paul ever wrote. He use to sing "Peppermint Twist" and I would sometimes get up and take over on lead.

Question: Has it ever occurred to you that you might be the lucky one in as much as you've got your life to yourself?

Pete: Frequently. Though there's two sides to the coin. It would have been nice to be there with them for the work I put into it, over two years. Eight hours a night, jumping up and down, going over to Germany, playing the clubs and all that. But my lifestyle has changed now. I've still got a very close circle of friends. I still socialize and I've got a terrific family.

Question: Who actually made the decision to retire you from the band?

Pete: I don't really know because of the manner I received it.

Question: It seems they got Eppy to do their dirty work.

Mona: The Beatles never really had the courage to speak their minds, unless it was something to their advantage. If there was any dirty work to be done Brian had to do it.

Pete: As far as I'm concerned, there was no build up to it even though the conspiracy was obviously going on. It would have been nice if I'd been in the position to defend myself or ask the reasons why. In fact, while Brian was dismissing me, there was a call from Paul asking whether the deed had been done. It would have been very nice to have had them there and actually ask the reasons why.

Question: How accurate was the film *Birth of the Beatles* regarding the boys' reaction to Stuart's death?

Pete: They've taken artistic liberties. What actually happened was we were met by Astrid at the airport and we were expecting to see Stu. This is when we went over to open the Star Club. When Stu wasn't there we asked where he was, and we were told he had died. It had only been a day or two before.

Question: Why didn't anyone notify you?

Pete: Because Astrid requested we stay away from him. We had our commitments as well, we were due to open the Star Club and rehearse, so we thought it would be better to stay away.

Question: What was John's reaction?

Pete: For the first time I actually saw him physically break down and shed tears. The rest of us, too, had tears in our eyes. John respected Stu as an artist. I think it hurt him a lot more than us.

Question: Had Stuart lived, do you think he would have been one of our great artists?

Pete: Definitely, without a doubt.

Question: Professionally speaking, if you had one thing to change what would it be?

Pete: Well, since I was once a Beatle, I'd like to have found out what it was really like to be on top with the group.

Question: What were your feelings when you learned of John's death?

Pete: My wife, Cathy, actually heard it first. She called me upstairs while I was getting ready for work saying, "Pete, John's dead, he's been murdered." Due to the fact that I hadn't seen any of the Beatles for many years or even spoken to them, the name John didn't mean anything, but when Cathy said, "It's John *Lennon*," it was a sick feeling. I had known the guy personally, he'd come to the house, I'd befriended him, he spent time in the Casbah raiding the Cokes.

Question: How often did he stop by?

Pete: Very often. After the venues, John would be the guy running through the Casbah, raiding the stores, putting his head down for the night, and listening to records.

Question: Were the Beatles very different from the rest of the bands in Britain after you came back from Germany?

Pete: Oh yeah, without a doubt. The bands which were playing in Liverpool were mostly *Top of the Pops* type groups. You know, smart stage suits, doing cute little walks and dance routines, very prim and proper. We came back playing the music we liked the way we wanted to play it. When Brian took us over though the image really started to change. It may have been good management from his point of view, but at the time every group in Liverpool was copying our performance, mannerisms, and the material we were playing. Everyone was trying to outdo one another, and all of a sudden Eppy comes along and says, "Okay, you've got to tidy the act up. I'm going to put you in suits and you're going to have to play the same repertoire every night."

Question: Do you think Lennon actually sold out to make it?

Pete: I don't think "sell out" is really the right word. I think they realized that to keep on the bandwagon they'd have to emphasize material the public wanted. They may have been reluctant, but I think it was a matter of necessity.

Question: Do you think it affected the music?

Pete: Sure. They started to play their own material as opposed to before. If you look at the material John wrote, there's quite a lot of freedom lyric-wise. He couldn't actually portray the original sound we created as the Beatles, so he went more into the lyrics. If you listen to John's lyrics, that's where his true feelings were.

Question: I can't imagine allowing my son to go to Hamburg in a band. Didn't you ever have any regrets?

Mona: Wondering what Pete was doing? Was he safe? Was it wise to let him go? Thinking that maybe he'd come back with a trailer of kids! As my mother said to me, "If he's going to go into show business, isn't it better for him to go with your approval, rather than starting trouble at home, and he storms off and you don't know what he's doing?" Everybody in the club knew what was going on with him because if I didn't mention it, all his girlfriends would be asking, "What's Peter doing? Has he got a German girlfriend?" I've never had to worry about Peter. He's a very natural boy.

Question: What are your personal mementos from that era?

Pete: Memories, they're probably the fondest thing I have at the moment. In terms of memorabilia I have a leather jacket, a suede coat, and a pink hat we wore on stage.

Question: Did you all wear pink hats?

Pete: Yeah. We loved Gene Vincent. That was where the leather came from. You could get it very cheaply in Germany. Gene Vincent had a fantastic band called the Bluecaps. In the film *The Girl Can't Help It* Gene and the Bluecaps wore these flat pink hats. And so for the first time we went on stage in leather jackets, flat pink hats, and cowboy boots.

Question: What was Bob Wooler's involvement with the Beatles?

Pete: Bob was a Liverpool deejay and he spotted us from a very early stage. He did a lot for us. He wrote several great articles on us in *Mersey Beat*. He always said, "There is a group which is going to be much bigger than anyone else in Liverpool." He had that much faith in us. He would always give us a very big buildup on stage. We used to be introduced with a trumpet fanfare, which he did, and it started to become a Beatle trademark. So as far as creating the atmosphere and publicity, he had an awful lot of influence and never really got the credit for it.

Question: Was it Bob's idea for you to move your drums to the front of the stage?

Pete: I actually did on a couple of occasions. The first time the drum kit nearly disappeared off stage with the fans grabbing hold of it. Most of the time though I would stay at the back, often on a pedestal. Bob would inevitably say, "Oh no, Pete, you belong up front with the others."

Question: How much did your first drum kit cost?

Pete: The blue Premier was around £120.

Question: Who paid for your first trip to Hamburg?

Pete: Allan paid for the passport and everything, but we didn't have any money.

Question: Have you spoken to Ken Brown?

Pete: Since the group split I've had a couple of phone calls.

Question: With four hit singles in the United States, Julian Lennon is now extremely popular. Do you think Great Britain is ready to accept Julian without the shadow of his father?

Pete: I think we've already accepted Julian Lennon. His sound, family resemblance, and the way he carries himself on stage is uncanny. When I heard his first record I thought it was an early, unreleased tune of John's. Whether he'll reach stardom, even if he has his father's talent, I don't know.

Question: You've said you were the closest to John. What was he like as a person?

Pete: There was two sides to John. He would spend an awful lot of time by himself writing very lengthy letters and he'd talk about Cynthia and his family. But Aunt Mimi, he wouldn't open up about at all. As far as Cynthia was concerned, however, it was totally different. Some might say he was callous or crazy. But I think that was just his way of handling people, to make sure they didn't get too close. Once he was by himself or in the company of friends, then he was a very different John Lennon.

Question: The other four Beatles, John, Paul, George, and Ringo have had a street named after them. Would you like a street named after you?

Pete: I would be flattered after all the hard work I put into the group. It would be something if it happened.

Question: How was it writing your book [*Beatle*]?

Pete: The reason it's taken so long is that many years ago, after I was released from the Beatles, I had many offers to write a book, make a lot of money, and sit back and twiddle my thumbs. But I didn't want to be accused of being catty, or jumping on the Beatles' gravy train. It was only later, when I read different books and this particular era of Beatle history hadn't been explained properly, that I decided to do a book, as it didn't look like anyone else was going to do it.

Question: Mrs. Best, have you ever thought of writing a book?

Mona: If I put my true feelings in a book I think someone would shoot me! There would be an awful lot of bitterness, because I do feel bitter, and sometimes find it very, very difficult to answer certain questions. Especially when people ask, "How do you feel towards the Beatles?" My feelings towards the Beatles are nil. I can't possibly feel *anything* for them, although I do admire their music, don't get me wrong. They're good musicians, but as people, for what they did to Peter, I could never forgive them. I'm sure I will be bitter to the day I die, because you can't see somebody hurt as badly as Peter and not take a certain attitude against them.

Question: Someone once said that you probably played more hours with the Beatles than Ringo when you add it all up. Do you think that's an accurate statement?

Pete: Most definitely, because for an awful long time we were playing eight hours a night, and that mounts up compared with the tours they later played, with only forty-five minutes on stage.

FAMILY

PART SIX

When You're Listening Late at Night

MIMI SMITH
Selected Quotations on John Lennon
POOLE, DORSET, 1979

"It's so typical of John, he gives me some telephone number in the middle of the Japanese mountains, I don't know where, and expects me to call him. I don't know what time it will be there, whether he'll be in, or anything. If he wants to talk to me, he can jolly well call me!"

"Sometimes John rings up and announces, 'Hi, it's Father Christmas here!' He's the same old jokey John. He really seems much more set-tled and happy now than he used to be. He'll be doing something, just you wait and see, something that will surprise everyone. I only hope he doesn't go pouncing on stage anymore. He's nearly forty now, and if he went back on stage he'd be doing exactly what he was doing at nine-teen. You must go on. When he phones now he wants to talk about Sean, about when he was a little boy himself. When he phoned the other night, he was talking about the time I wrapped him in a blanket because it was cold and I brought him downstairs. He can't have been more than five then. He just amazes me with the things he remembers."

JULIAN LENNON*
Press Conference
1985

Question: Was it a foregone conclusion you were going to enter the music business?

Julian Lennon: There was so much music around my family, there were so many pianos and guitars, I couldn't avoid it. It was kind of a natural flow and I was happy to do it, because I like music so much.

Question: With a successful single and album, you're going to be very busy—do you mind the hectic pace surrounding the music?

*John Charles Julian Lennon is John's son from his first wife, Cynthia.

Julian: I will be busy, but hopefully, if I can work it out, I'll just make an appearance once in a while and concentrate on the music side. After all this big rush of publicity I'll be staying home writing. I don't want to be in the spotlight all the time. I'm not one for the commercial Duran Duran stuff. I'd rather just write and let people hear it. I'm not out to promote my face around town, although the record company is, but that's just for the moment.

Question: How do you react to the press you're getting?

Julian: It's okay if the press tells the truth when they write a story, but when they start lying it gets to be a real pain! I just ignore it. It's not worth retaliating.

Question: In May Pang's book she describes how Yoko reacted very strangely towards you and your mother when you went over there for a visit. What impression did that make on you?

Julian: Yeah, she was strange. Maybe she felt we were a threat, you know, now that she had got dad securely wrapped up in chains. I was easy to have a relationship with. It was just her: one minute she'd treat you like you were her brother and the next she'd put up a brick wall. I don't care to think too much about it, it's a waste of time.

Question: Do you ever feel a grudge against her?

Julian: Not really. I have my own life to live.

Question: There has been a lot written about you and money. What is fact and what is fiction?

Julian: Fiction is that I have a lot of money. Fact is that I have been earning my own money. All the money is tied up with Yoko. I don't have a say in what I get, so when she thinks I'm old enough I might get something. It's totally up to her. But I'm not in a hurry. I'd rather earn my own living. I'm content with what we are doing and I'm happy where I'm living.

Question: You live in London, do you have your own apartment?

Julian: A little flat. I am cozy there. I don't want a big flat, maybe when

I retire in ten years' time. I'd like to get something in the country with a little studio, so I don't have to go to another studio.

Question: Where did you record the album?

Julian: All over America, in five different studios. But I also worked in France in this fabulous castle called Valotte, hence the title.

Question: The production on the album is very similar to that of your father's—it's not a very modern sound.

Julian: It's very similar to the demo tapes I did at home. It's the sound I was looking for, which Phil Ramone came up with. I like what he did with Billy Joel on *Nylon Curtain*.

Question: When did you realize your voice sounded like your dad's?

Julian: When I was at school, I suppose, and I played in a rock band. Me and the bassist, Justin Clayton, who plays with me now, were in this band. I noticed I sounded like my father. I can't change it; I don't want to change it. Why should I? The only way I could change it is by putting a funny accent on! I'm proud of it.

PAULINE LENNON*
Selected Quotation
BRISTOL, 1990

On Saturday, 22 June 1946, Freddie Lennon was in the process of finalizing arrangements for John to travel to New Zealand with his friends, the Halls, in Brighton, when the last person in the world he had expected to see appeared at the door. It was his wife, Julia, accompanied by her boyfriend, Bobby Dykins, who hovered nervously at the gate whilst she announced herself to Mrs. Hall.

*The above was excerpted and condensed with permission from *Daddy, Come Home: The True Story of John Lennon and His Father* with the kind permission of author Pauline Lennon Stone, who was married to John's father until his death from cancer in Bristol in 1976. In addition to her writing, Ms. Stone is also a noted astrologer.

"How the hell did you find out where I was living?" demanded Freddie, coming to the door.

"We enquired at the Pool Office," she replied coolly, hardly looking at him, the meekness of her manner so unfamiliar that it caused Freddie to look at her more closely. She had always been very meticulous with regard to her clothes, but the ill-shaped costume she was wearing, which made her look positively matronly, was definitely out of character with the little girl Freddie knew or the wicked person Mimi pictured for him.

"What for?" asked Freddie.

"I want to take John back," she replied.

Evidently it was to be a long conversation, so he called to Mrs. Hall to take John into the kitchen and then asked Julia to come in.

"I'm not letting you take him back to Mimi," resumed Freddie as she sat down.

"Oh, no," said Julia, and then launched into a lengthy explanation that she had obtained a new home—a comfy flat in Gateacre—where she was settling down with Bobby and wanted John back with her.

"You know that you wouldn't be able to give him a proper home while you're away at sea," she went on.

Freddie was apprehensive that Julia would oppose his idea of taking John to New Zealand, but to his surprise she had no objections when he told her of his plan.

"You must love him, then," was all she said, moving towards the door with her eyes cast down. Then, on impulse, she asked, "Can I see him before I go?" Freddie called to Mrs. Hall to bring John into the lounge.

"Hello, Mummy," he said, a little shyly. It was nearly two months since he had last seen her, and life with Daddy had been so different she almost seemed like a stranger. Having gazed at his mother for a few seconds, he climbed on to Freddie's knee and put his arms around his neck as if to reassure Julia he was happy and well cared for.

Apparently satisfied with what she saw, Julia stood up and moved towards the door.

"It looks as if he's decided to stay," she said, but as Freddie opened the door for her John leaped after his mother.

"Don't go, Mummy, please," he sobbed, burying his head in her skirt and making as if to stop her from leaving.

"Look, Julia, for John's sake let's have another go," pleaded Freddie, still hopeful that they might become a family again.

"It's no use, I don't want to," was Julia's reply.

"Then John will have to decide for himself," said Freddie, and turning to John he addressed him slowly and clearly. "Mummy's going away and she won't be coming back again. Do you want to go with her or stay with me and go to New Zealand?"

Unfalteringly John took his father's hand. "I'm staying with Daddy," he said.

Julia didn't speak, but silently opened the front door and began to walk away down the street. Yet before she had gone fifty yards John, not understanding what was happening, wrenched his hand from Freddie's and ran after her, calling, "Come on, Daddy."

It was manifestly clear that John had made his decision and that Freddie had no choice but to abide by it. Turning sadly to Mrs. Hall, he asked her to quickly pack John's things; her son Billy then delivered them to Bobby Dykins, who was waiting uneasily at the end of the avenue. Julia had already disappeared round the corner, with John still clinging tightly to her arm.

Freddie spent the rest of the afternoon walking through the sand dunes where he and John had loved to play, trying to come to terms with the situation. For the first time in his life, except perhaps when he was sent to the orphanage, his irrepressible spirit was extinguished by a gaping emptiness. Despite the short periods he had spent with his wife and child, they had represented an important anchor in his life, and he had loved them dearly in his own way. Now he felt beset by an unfamiliar sense of loneliness which he found very hard to handle.

Later that evening Mrs. Hall entreated him to stop moping and join the rest of the family on an outing to the Cherry Tree, a large pub on the outskirts of Blackpool which they had often visited during Freddie's stay. The Cherry Tree boasted a stage area with a microphone where local talent was invited to perform and the showbiz atmosphere was enhanced by the frequent appearance of artists starring in the shows on the Pier or at the Tower. Freddie himself had soon proved popular amongst the regulars as a singer and had even been approached by a stage manager friend of Billy's who offered him a job as his assistant as a "stepping stone to the real thing," as he put it.

"I'm afraid I won't be very good company tonight," he apologized to his companions as they entered the convivial hubbub of the bar, and despite the efforts of his friends to cheer him up his heart remained heavy.

But once the entertainment began, the music did begin to loosen him up a little and when the call for Freddie went out, although he initially refused, Billy Hall was insistent that he should do his usual turn. "Get up there," he urged him. "It'll do you good."

Instinctlively, he asked for Al Jolson's number, "Little Pal," which he would often perform at the ships' concerts complete with black grease-paint, and without thought he found himself substituting "John" for "pal." Neither was he ashamed of his tears, joined by Mrs. Hall, as he returned to their table amidst sympathetic clapping and shoulder patting.

For Freddie, the music provided a release for the emotions he found hard to express. And in the weeks and months that followed, he found his thoughts constantly returning to the words of the song. Somehow the lyrics so aptly summed up his feelings; his hopes that "John might be the man his Daddy might have been" and that they might one day "meet again, heaven knows where or when."

JULIA BAIRD*
Back Door Beatles
1956–1960

As Told to Geoffrey Giuliano

"When I was about twelve I used to think
I must be a genius, but nobody's noticed.

*Julia Baird is John's maternal half sister. She works as a French teacher in Chester, England.

If there is such a thing as a genius, I
am one. And if there isn't, I don't really care."

JOHN LENNON

"My Mummy's dead
I can't get it through my head
Though it's been so many years
My Mummy's dead."

JOHN LENNON / from "My Mummy's Dead"

While our mother Julia's musical encouragement and Uncle George's death may well have helped propel young John into taking up the guitar, it was his first chance meeting with Paul McCartney which ultimately led him to seriously consider a career in music. There was magic between them all right. But just exactly why these two particular little neighborhood rockers were able to forge such a tight-knit, lasting relationship isn't for anybody's sister to try and guess. Suffice to say, that get it together they did, the dramatic results of which we're all still keenly aware of, well over three decades since they first became acquainted at the Woolton Village Fête on June 15, 1956.

McCartney remembers, "As it turned out, John and I were both mates with a fellow from Woolton, called Ivan Vaughn. One summer day, he invited me to come along with him to a fête at the parish church in Woolton. I think at the time John was sixteen, so I might have been maybe fourteen or fifteen. I remember coming up on the fête from across the field and hearing all this great music, which turned out to be coming from the Quarrymen's little Tanoy system. I just thought, 'Oh great, I'll go listen to the band,' because I was very much into the music. So Ivy says, 'I know a couple of lads in the group, after their set, I'll introduce you.' I remember John singing a lovely tune by the Del Vikings he'd heard on the radio called, 'Come Go With Me.' Anyway, he didn't really know all the words, so he just made up his own. Good bluesy stuff like, 'Come go with me down to the penitentiary.' As I recall, he was playing banjo chords on his guitar, (which only had about four strings at the time). Actually, he looked very good. He had his glasses off, so he was really quite suave. You see, until Buddy Holly came along, fellows who wore glasses always took them off to play. After that, anyone who really needed to wear them, could then conceivably come out of the closet. After it was all over I met the lads in the church hall. They were having a beer, I think. It wasn't crazy drinking or anything, but rather, just a bit of good fun. In those days, the line up of the bad was Len Garry, Pete Shotton, Colin Hanton on drums, Griff on guitar and maybe Nigel Whalley, who acted as their 'official' manager. In actual fact, we all used to really think John was pretty cool. I mean, he was a bit colder and would therefore do a little more greased-back hair and things than *we* were ever allowed. He had nice big sideboards and, of course, with the drake and all, he did look a bit of a Ted. As for me, that particular day, I just happened to pick up an old guitar that was laying around and started to play, 'Twenty Flight Rock.' I knew a lot of the words which was really very good currency in those days!

"Later, we all went down to the pub, and of course, I had to try and kid the barman I was really eighteen. As I recall, there was a bit of a panic on, because suddenly the word went round that all the lads might be needed, as there was a vicious mob forming up the street considering whether or not to invade the pub! Why, I have no idea. As a matter of fact, all I knew, was that I'd come for a nice day out and suddenly I'm with all these men who were about to begin hailing machetes at each other! Thankfully, all that blew over, however, and in the end, we had a very nice evening. A couple of weeks later, Peter Shotton came up to Allerton on his bike and invited me to join the group. The rest, as they say, you all know by now. Frankly, one of the most interesting things to me about John was that (by my standards anyway) his people seemed to have quite a lot of money. I mean my family was from the trading estate, you know, like the rest of the Beatles, but John's relations were really like another world from what I was used to. I remember being very impressed in Mendips with seeing the entire works of Winston Churchill, and knowing that John had actually read them! You see, my Mum was a nurse and my dad a cotton salesman, so we always lived in the mid-wives house on the estate. So to actually *see* this sort of middle class thing was just fascinating to me. Christ, I can even recall John getting one hundred quid for his twenty-first birthday off of one of his aunties. I mean, I say I'd still like that to happen now.

"I remember John talking to me about people his family knew who worked for the BBC. Personal friends who were dentists, and aunties and uncles up in Scotland, so it was all very exotic to me. As a child, the only places I had ever been were Pelheli, Scagness, and Lemington Spa. That had been the whole of my travels, but not that lot. Why, John apparently had been up to Edinburgh on his own several times by the age of twelve. What adventure!"

Contrary to popular myth, however, Paul McCartney actually first laid eyes on John Lennon sometime before the Woolton fête at, of all places, the local chippy! Beyond that, he has told me he thinks he may have actually seen him once or twice as a young Teddy Boy climbing aboard the bus in Liverpool bound for Menlove Avenue.

Having been invited to join the Quarrymen solely on the merit of his mastery over "Twenty Flight Rock" (as well as his famous Little Richard imitation), Paul McCartney's obvious talents were a welcome addition to the ragtag group of school boy musicians. "John was really the only outstanding member," says Paul. "All the rest sort of slipped away, you know? I suppose the drummer was pretty good actually, for what we knew then. Frankly, one of the reasons they all liked Colin was because he happened to have the record, 'Searchin,' and again, that was mighty big currency back then. I mean, sometimes you made a whole career with someone solely on the basis of them owning a particular record!"

John's eventual formation of the Quarrymen was but his first wobbly step into the previously unknown world outside the protective web of the family. I can still clearly recall Mummy being thrilled by the fact that he was actually able to organize such an ambitious undertaking totally on his own. As a matter of fact, young McCartney wasn't the only newfound Lennon fan in the audience that balmy summer's day in Woolton; our mum was there, too. Enthusiastically cheering on her hard-rocking son along with Jacqui, myself, cousin Michael, and our aunties, Harrie and Nanny. From then on, whenever and wherever they happened to play, Mother made it her business to try and be there if she could. Mimi, on the other hand, wasn't quite so enthusiastic about her favorite nephew's headlong foray into the all-too-uncertain world of show business. "The guitar's all right, John; but you'll certainly never earn your living by it!" She was known to ironically utter her now world famous quote, "If you don't settle down soon son, Lord knows what's ever going to become of you!" Asked about his early memories of the often very opinionated Mimi, Paul had this to say: "I remember Mimi as being a very forthright, middle-class woman. Most of the women I'd known previously were off the estate and, quite honestly, were rather common. But certainly not Mimi. I can just hear her saying, "John, your little friend is here to see you." You know, with that kind of tone that made it obvious she was really rather belittling you. Just when I was beginning to feel quite badly about the whole thing, though, I would look up and see just the slightest twinkle in her eyes, which let me know that actually, she quite liked me. Even though she had a habit of keeping people at arms length, I always felt she saw me as one of John's nicer friends. Inside the house, he'd often be busy writing at the typewriter in his famous *In His Own Write* style. Honestly, I never knew anyone who personally owned a typewriter before. As far as our music went, I recall playing our guitars out in the front inside porch. I think we might have even learned the chords to 'Blue Moon' in there as well. From what John has told me, Mimi banished him out there from about the first day he brought home his guitar on account of all the noise. But it ultimately worked out okay, I guess, as he also used to say he liked the echo in there with the guitars all bouncing of the tiles."

No one in the family is quite sure just exactly when John first became so enamored of the guitar, but once he finally latched on to the idea of playing in a group, there was no stopping him. From that moment on, whenever we saw our brother, it was almost always in the company of his battered old ten-pound, acoustic guitar.

The first time we ever actually saw him perform, however (that is, aside from his many impromptu "private" concerts for us in Mummy's kitchen), was in 1956, at the Empire Day celebrations on Rosebury Street. As I recall, Jacqui and I had been at a Sunday School outing to Helsby hill for the afternoon, but when we returned to the church hall, to our amazement, Mummy was there waiting to take us off yet again. "Two special surprises in one day Mummy?" Jacqui sang out as mother hurried us along to a nearby bus stop. "Yes, luv. We're going to see your brother's combo play. But we're scads late already and I've no idea at all where the street is. So do both be good girls and keep your eyes peeled for Princes Avenue. That'll be our stop." Needless to say, none of us had any luck at all in finding the place. And it was only after walking nearly the entire length and breadth of the road we finally arrived. As we struggled our way through the rowdy crowd, John suddenly caught sight of us and summarily hauled us girls up onto the makeshift stage (an old lorry parked sideways along the middle of the street) so we could watch the fun reasonably unscathed by the wound-up, rocking teenagers. My big brother, too, remembers the event. "Eventually my mates and I formed ourselves into a group from school. Our very first appearance was at a do they were having on Rosebury Street. We didn't actually get paid or anything, but we did have some good fun. That day I think we called ourselves, 'Johnny and the Rainbows.' I can't really be certain though, as we constantly seemed to be changing it to some daft thing or another. I remember one night it even got changed three times before our last number! Mostly we just played blokes' parties and things, or maybe occasionally a wedding, if we were lucky. That was always a good gig as it usually meant all the free beer we could guzzle, and generally a damn good meal to boot."

John's lightening rise to neighborhood stardom, however, also brought with it some rather unexpected complications for the popular young rocker—*girls!* Probably my brother's very first, full-fledged fan was a lovely strawberry blonde-headed beauty by the name of Barbara Baker. Unfortunately for Ms. Baker, however, John was by no means as smitten by her as she obviously was with him. Both Jacqui and I vividly recall her hanging around outside the house almost every afternoon, hoping to catch sight of our guitar-toting brother. There she stood, alone and friendless, hour after boring hour, rain or shine, intently watching the street for any visible clue to our Mr. Lennon's disposition towards her at any given moment. We could, in no way, even begin to understand the attraction, and mercilessly goaded and teased her virtually every hour of her silent, solitary vigil.

One day while she was standing next to a lamp post where we had installed a rope "Tarzan" swing, she called us over and asked me to go inside to try and convince John to come out. Racing through the front door, I was greeted by a deep groan from my brother who then begged Mummy to please go out and send her away. More than a little annoyed by all this nonsense, mother immediately waltzed out the door and politely, but firmly, asked the embarrassed teenager just what it was she wanted. "May we help you, dear?" Julia called out from the gate. But it was too late; by that time the poor girl had turned on her heels and was off and running up the road. Jacqui and I, of course, were in absolute stitches over the whole ridiculous affair. And, for some unknown reason, lit off after her, finally catching up to her in a nearby park. To our complete and utter surprise, however, instead of being put off by our never-ending torment, she seemed very pleased to see us, and incredibly, once again, requested I run home and attempt to convince John to meet her. This time, however, John's mood miraculously seemed to have swung completely to the other end of the extreme, as he very casually ambled out the front door and up the road for a first face-to-face encounter with his secret admirer. Once again, my sister and I followed behind, hoping to witness John giving the persistent young lady a good piece of his mind, but were shocked to see them suddenly both embrace and silently sink down into the long, willowy grass alongside an old stone fence. Both of us giggling like crazy, John sheepishly poked his head up over the wall and begged us to go get lost. Every mortal pleasure, however, has a definite price. So in the end, John bribed us with half a crown each not to mention anything to anyone about this little rendezvous. Later that evening over tea, Mummy went on and on about how sorry she felt for John having to put up with that dreadful little girl, as it was perfectly obvious to anyone that he was not the least bit interested. John, meanwhile, was in absolute agony trying to keep us girls from blurting out the truth by smartly giving us both a good, sharp kick under the table.

"Before Elvis," John was once quoted as saying, "there was nothing." And as far as our happy household was concerned, nothing could be more true. John attempts to explain his fascination for Presley. "It was Elvis who really got me buying records. I always thought that early stuff of his was great. The whole Bill Haley era kind of passed me by in a way though. When his records came on the wireless, my mother used to like them okay, but they didn't really do anything for me. I went to see *Rock Around the Clock* once and was most surprised. Nobody was screaming or dancing. I mean, I'd been reading that everyone generally danced in the aisles at that film. It must have all been done before I went. Anyway, I was all set to tear up the seats too, but nobody joined in. No, as I say, it was definitely Elvis that got me hooked on beat music." His *music* perhaps, but I'm not so certain he felt quite the same way about Presley's many motion pictures. As a matter of fact, I recall one occasion when he couldn't wait to beat it out of a Saturday matinee dedicated entirely to the King's first two cinematic endeavors, *Love Me Tender* and *Loving You*. In all honesty, as a teen, John didn't really make much of an effort to take us girls out with him very often. Which, of course, is really quite natural, and certainly fine with me, now. But in those days, wherever John went, Jacqui and I were generally more than willing to tag along. Anyway, this particular afternoon, after sitting through the first showing, John all of a sudden leapt up and ran out of the cinema hurriedly barking out orders for us not to say a word to anyone, or even dare move until he got back. So there we sat, obediently suffering through the Pathe News, local adverts, the non support film, and, of course, Elvis, yet one more rollicking time. Several hours later, John suddenly reappeared and hustled us both off to a nearby park for a lightning-quick spin on the round about, and one or two half-hearted shoves on the swings before unceremoniously returning us home to Mummy. "Well," said Julia, "Wasn't that nice of your brother to take time out to show you young ladies such a lovely afternoon?" "Yes, Mummy," we both replied, smiling weakly. "It was lovely." Rushing outside to stretch our legs after sitting still all afternoon, we never let on just how lovely. No, amazingly enough, even then, Jacqui and I somehow sensed that although John certainly loved us all, he was rapidly growing up and therefore away from the tight-knit family life we knew. And like many other independent teenagers of the day, music, his mates, and the ladies were rapidly becoming the focal point of his young life. "I used to have to borrow a guitar at first," remembers John. "I couldn't play, but a mate of mine had one and it fascinated me. Eventually, my mother bought me one from a mail order firm. I remember it had a label on the inside which said, 'Guaranteed Not To Split.' It was a bit crummy, I suppose, when you think about it. But I played it for a long time and got in a lot of good practice. Why did I get it? Oh, the usual kid's desire to get up on stage, I guess. Mummy did teach me quite a bit . . . most of our stuff in the early days were just twelve bar boogies and things like that, though. Of course, Paul came along later, and taught me a few other things as well. So all in all, I guess I was lucky to have had the little musical training I did. Still, I never actually thought of it that way at the time. All I knew was I was having one hell of a lot of fun!"

McCartney, meanwhile, says that if indeed Julia was John's earliest and most important musical influence, then his would have to be his late father, James. "My dad was a pianist, you know," says Paul. "He played by ear . . . his left one! Apparently he fell off a railing or something when he was a kid and busted an ear drum. But yeah, if anyone was my big musical inspiration, then it was him." As far as our mother was concerned, Paul fondly remembers her as a clever, carefree, intelligent person, steadfastly devoted to helping her son realize his musical ambitions. "You know, I always thought of Julia as being an exceptionally beautiful woman. She was very, very nice to us all, and, of course, John just adored her. First of all, obviously on the level that she was his mum, but also because she was such a highly spirited lady. I mean she taught him to play the banjo, and I mean, that's really very 'gay', isn't it? Of course, my family was musical as well, but there certainly weren't any women around who could play the banjo! That was left to the men, wasn't it? Julia, I think, was very ahead of her time. Actually, you used to get quite a lot of that going on in her era. She was extremely lively, and heaps of fun as well, not too many blokes had mothers as progressive as Julia. My own mother, for instance, was very into stuff like hygiene, but still wasn't really what you'd call prudish. Of course, that was in those days directly following the war, so she was a little strict on cleanliness and things like that. Later, however, I rebelled a bit by making a definite attempt to hang around in dirty jeans as much as I could! My mum loved to see us doing well, however, and wouldn't have really much cared how we did it. That was always one of my deepest regrets, you know. Because, obviously, she died when I was about fourteen—

well before this particular phase of my life. Looking back, you know, I can remember two tunes in particular, Julia taught us. Oddly enough, one of them was, 'Wedding Bells Are Breaking Up that Old Gang of Mine,' while another was definitely, 'Ramona.' Much later, during the Beatle years, John and I often attempted to write a few songs with that kind of similar feeling, with 'Here There and Everywhere' coming immediately to mind."

Now that John and Paul had "found" each other, there was only the inclusion of guitarist George Harrison into the group to complete the nucleus of what we would ultimately come to know as The Beatles. The band's youngest member, George, came to know McCartney through sharing the long bus ride to and from town to attend school at the Liverpool Institute. Paul, however, was two years ahead of him, and already a reasonably accomplished performer by the time he was first introduced to my brother as a potential member of the Quarrymen. McCartney takes up the tale from here. "Master Harrison was always my little mate. Nonetheless, he could really play guitar, particularly this piece called, 'Raunchy,' which we all used to love. You see, if anyone could do something like that, it was generally enough to get them in the group. Of course, I knew George long before any of the others. As they were all from Woolton and we hailed from the Allerton set. I can tell you we both learned guitar from the same book, and that despite his tender years, we were chums."

Lennon, however, was apparently quite skeptical about admitting such a veritable "baby" into the group. How would it look for someone as talented and popular as John to be caught consorting with someone so young and undistinguished as George? What would his mates think, let alone the ladies? He definitely had a problem. After all, the whole point of being in a band in the first place was to look like a big man, and that was admittedly a little difficult to do playing with a twelve-year old guitarist. In the end, however, Harrison's exceptional musical skill, coupled with McCartney's enthusiastic insistence he be brought on board, overruled John's initial reservations. Strangely, George's "formal" audition took place atop a Liverpool-bound bus one sunny summer's day in 1957. McCartney recounts the occasion. "George slipped quietly into one of the seats aboard this largely deserted bus we were riding, took out his guitar, and went right into 'Raunchy.' A few days later, I said to John, 'Well, what do you think?' And he finally says, 'Yeah man, he'd be great!' And that was simply that, George was in and we were on our way."

"Practice," as they say, "makes perfect," and that is exactly the path my brother and his comrades had diligently chosen to pursue. "Where are we going lads?" John was known to suddenly cry out during their impromptu practices. "To the top, Johnny!" would be their enthusiastic response. "What top is that then?" "Why, to the toppermost of the poppermost," the final exchange in this, the baby Beatle's rhythmic war cry. Often times, with no other family home willing to let the boys rehearse, John and his tea-drinking buddies would traipse along to our place for a little aid and comfort from Mummy. "Julia was fantastic," admits John's long-time crony, Pete Shotton. "She was a kindred spirit who told us all the things we desperately wanted to hear. She made us feel welcome and always encouraged John to try and go as far as he could with his music. We loved her because she did everything for laughs. To her nothing was really serious, except maybe having a good time. I can remember her walking up the road with us one day wearing an old pair of spectacles with no lenses in them. Whenever she happened to run into someone from the neighborhood, she would casually slip her finger through the glasses and rub her eyes. Meanwhile, we would all be falling about in the bushes, pissing ourselves with laughter. Julia was definitely one of a kind!"

As he grew older, John began to spend more and more time at our house. There were many hilarious bathroom jam sessions with my mother at home in Blomfield Road. In the first place, our toilet was probably one of *the* tiniest in all of Great Britain, and to see John, Paul, George, Pete Shotton, Ivan Vaughn, and Mummy all scrambling around inside trying to find a place to sit, was truly a wondrous sight indeed! Perched precariously atop the commode, tucked like sardines into the bathtub, or tentatively saddling up to the sink, they somehow managed not only to fit, but to actually *play!* The door shut securely behind them, they enthusiastically tucked into a bevy of now-classic tunes like, 'Maggie May,' 'Besame Mucho,' 'Alleycat,' or the sneaky theme from the 'Third Man.' Mr. McCartney remembers, "It was the best room in the house, hands down! Quite crowded too, as I recall, don't forget it wasn't only us in there, but also our instruments, as well as a tiny pig nose amp we used to carry around. Many a fine tune has been written in that little room, let me tell you. In fact, at home, I used to not only stand around with one leg on the toilet, but, if perchance, I had to actually go, I would lug my guitar in with me instead of a book. I remember my dad used to say, 'Paul, what are you doing playing the guitar in the toilet?' And I'd say, 'Well . . . what's wrong with that then?'" In our humble john, however, there were absolutely no objections, and the raucous, musical, free-for-alls, sometimes meandered on late into the evening.

Their reason, of course, for choosing to tighten up their chops in the bathroom was, like Auntie Mimi's front porch, the room gave off a kind of natural echo which somehow seemed to enhance their offbeat sound. Occasionally, Jacqui and I were actually unlucky enough to be taking a bath when John's Beatle buddies suddenly felt the overpowering urge to let loose with a little home made rhythm and blues. In that case, we were both unceremoniously hauled out of the tub to make way for the bathroom Beethoven. Of course, we certainly didn't mind, as it generally meant we were allowed to once again go outside and play for an extra hour or so. (Bedtime being quite reasonably postponed as it would have been virtually impossible for anyone within a one-mile radius to get any sleep!)

The lineup for these unusual sessions was generally John, Paul, and George on acoustic guitar, Pete Shotton on string bass, and our uninhibited mother on either washboard, or playing percussionist with the aid of her favorite kitchen utensils.

Looking back, I suppose we had become a kind of refuge for John in his ever-increasing struggle to live amicably with Mimi. I certainly do not wish to give the impression, however, that she was in anyway callous or uncaring towards any of her family. Actually, the opposite was true. In many ways, Mimi was the family. The unopposed, unspoken leader, and advisor to us all. An extremely well-read, cultured, and insightful woman, she was, nevertheless, very much the "elder" sister and therefore, naturally, took a loving interest in everyone's welfare. My brother was generally quite happy living with her, and it was really only the normal sort of everyday, teenage "uneasiness" about things that cropped up later in John's life that ever caused them any great difficulty. If anything, our family will always be deeply indebted to Mimi for looking after John so well when circumstances had so cruelly robbed our mum of that privilege. Frankly, as Jacqui and I grew older, Mimi's home, ironically, became a kind of refuge for us, as well, during our own troubled teenage years. A little story Leila likes to tell, I think, sums up the unusual nature of John's early years best. One day, John happened to be outside Mendips with both Julia and Mimi, when suddenly he quite unexpectedly turned to mother and said, "I do love you, Mummy." Then pausing pensively, he softly spun around and whispered, "But I do love you," to Mimi. Despite the apparent eccentricities within my mother's family, all five sisters genuinely seemed to have found a level of peace and contentment in their lives which I greatly admired even as a youngster. All that was to change dramatically, however, when, in the sultry summer of 1958, a very grim reality came thundering down upon us all.

It was sometime in the early evening, perhaps around six or seven o'-clock, when Mummy quietly stepped outside with our Grandma Dykins to tell me she was off for a visit to Mendips. "I'm just going to see Mimi," she said, bending down to give me a little peck. "Bye, bye," I replied. Jacqui, as I recall, was out in the back garden playing with some friends when she left. Daddy was inside with John, helping tidy up the kitchen after our tea. I had been out riding my bicycle with some girls and for some strange reason, just sat there on the seat watching them both ambling casually up the road. They were chatting, I remember, and laughing too. It was just another day, nothing special. I'd seen both my parents hiking up that same road dozens of times. My father, on his way to work, would often turn around and lovingly wave or blow us each a kiss just before turning the corner. But tonight it was very different. Something was terribly wrong, I just felt it. Without thinking I threw down my bike and ran like bloody fury to top of the road to try and catch her before she boarded the bus. By the time I got there, however, she had gone. I can still see them slowly disappearing into the twilight. Why I didn't ride my bike instead of legging it, I'll never understand, but I do know I desperately needed to see her again.

And what would I have done if I'd had caught up with her? Pull her off the bus? Plead with her to turn around and come home? No. Because, you see, I wasn't sure myself just what I was so afraid of. It was dread, that's all. Nameless, faceless dread. Arriving at Mimi's, as usual, the two sister's from opposite ends of the earth, sat down together in Mendip's cozy living room, for the traditional tea and chat session they had both so much come to enjoy. Julia adored Mimi for her bookish intelligence and insightful worldliness, while Mimi sat in envy of her younger sister's uncluttered wit and easy charm. Most nights, after an hour or two of conversation, Mimi would accompany Mummy across Menlove Avenue to the bus stop, but this particular night she said, "I won't walk you, Julia, I'll see you tomorrow." Mummy gave her a hug and replied simply, "Don't worry." Nigel Whalley, one of John's long time neighborhood friends, just happened to be walking down the street as Julia was crossing the road and paused for a moment to say hello. Stepping through the hedge in the middle of the dual carriageway, Julia was suddenly hurled high up into the air by a passing automobile. She died instantly.* "An hour or so after it happened, a copper came to the door to let us know about the accident," says John. "It was awful, like some dreadful film where they ask you if you're the victim's son and all that. Well, I was, and I can tell you it was absolutely the worst night of my entire life. I lost me mother twice, you know. Once as a child of five, and then again at sixteen. It made me very, very bitter. I was just really trying to re-establish a relationship with her when she was killed. We'd caught up on so much, Julia and I, in just a few short years. We could communicate. We got on. Deep down inside, I thought, "Sod it, I've no real responsibilities to anyone now. Anyway, Twitchy and I got a cab over to Sefton General where she was lying dead. Of course, there was no way I could ever bear to look at her. I remember rabbeting on hysterically to the driver all the way there. Twitchy went in to see her for a few minutes, but it turned out to be too much for the poor sod, and he finally broke down in my arms out in the lobby. I couldn't seem to cry, however; not then anyway. I suppose I was just frozen inside."

Later that evening, after Jacqui and I had been put to bed by our father,

*The accident occurred in July of 1958 at approximately 10:20 pm. Julia was just forty-four years old.

I awake to find Grandma silently climbing into my big, double bed. She cuddled up beside me, and sometime later, Jacqui was also brought in, so I knew John must be staying over in her room. A few minutes afterwards, the three of us were suddenly shaken by the horrific sound of daddy crying and moaning uncontrollably in the next room. Ironically, my sister and I hadn't been told anything, so we had no idea whatsoever why he was so upset. But we were terribly frightened, and as such, didn't dare go anywhere near him. The next morning when we awoke, he was gone. "Where is Mummy?" I asked Grandma on the way to school that day. "Oh, she stayed with Mimi last night, that's all. Nothing to worry, luv." Stayed with Mimi? Never in my entire life had I known her to do that. She was absolutely always there in the mornings. Something very, very peculiar was going on. Jacqui and I both felt it, but we had no idea what. When we arrived at school, I was called straight into the headmaster's office and spent almost the entire morning sitting on his knee with him gently stroking my hair and kissing my forehead over and over. Later, another teacher took me into the girl's loo and helped me wash my face and hands. Apparently, Jacqui's teacher was showering her with lots of extra attention as well, so between the two of us, we were now both completely bewildered. Finally, in absolute frustration, I screamed out at the headmaster, "What is going on? What's the matter with everyone?" "I'm afraid your mother's been in an accident, dear," he said. "She's in hospital." The next thing I know, I was running down the corridor to Jacqui's room as someone from the school had offered to take us home. When we got there, however, we were completely and utterly shocked to find our Aunt Mater and Uncle Bert in my bedroom packing up all our clothes into two large suitcases. "You girls will be coming up to Scotland with us for a holiday. Isn't that lovely?" Mater offhandedly told us as she bent down to tie Jacqui's shoelaces. "Your mother's very ill, children, so of course, you won't be allowed to visit with her just yet. In the meantime, you're coming home with us to Edinburgh." I remember standing there being so bloody polite to them all, when deep inside I just wanted to cry out, "No! I'm not going anywhere until I know just exactly what is going on!" A little later, Daddy suddenly reappeared to tell us both goodbye. It was obvious he was an absolute wreck, and only stayed just long enough to have a little something to eat, talk with Mater a few minutes, and then immediately go back out again, as we were told, to visit Mummy "at the hospital."

We did indeed end up in Scotland. We stayed at Mater's in Edinburgh for a couple of weeks, and then traveled on to their remote farm, far up north for another month or so. Still nothing further was said to us about either the accident, or even very much about Mummy for that matter. Certainly not a single word about the fact that she was dead. Still, as my brother John once said, "A conspiracy of silence speaks louder than words," and, I'm very sorry to say, that in this case anyway, he was quite right. I remember lying in bed at night, wide awake, just knowing she was dead. Jacqui, however, was probably a little more innocent than I, and relied on me quite heavily to reassure and protect her emotionally. Eventually, we did come back home to Liverpool, but the unforgivable charade continued. Unbeknownst to us, there was a funeral held at the cemetery in Allerton. While the rest of the family enjoyed the luxury of their grief, and were allowed to share with one another the full emotional impact of Julia's tragic death, Jacqui and I were still kept very much in the dark. Why this particular strategy was deemed to be the most satisfactory I'll never understand, but I do know it hurt us both deeply. One especially painful hurt in our lives that never really went away.

Leila summons up some impressions from that very unhappy time. "I was on holiday from university working a summer job as a chalet maid at Butland's that particular year. One night after work, I received a telegram which read, 'Judy . . . car accident, died Friday, funeral Tuesday.' Well anyway, I just dropped everything and got myself home as quickly as I could. All I could think of was poor John. I can remember us going to the funeral in a complete daze. There seemed to be lots of people there, but I didn't really recognize too many of them. I couldn't stand it. I hated the funeral and everybody there. I found it impossible to really believe it was Julia in that box. It was the first death, other than George's, any of us children had ever really known. It literally made me sick to see all these strangers walking up and throwing flowers and things into the grave. I could only think of Judy at home, happy and carefree as always, looking after her family. Afterwards, we all went back to the Cottage and John and I just sat there on

the couch with his head in my lap. I don't know why, but I cannot recall even telling him I was sorry. I never said a single word. There was
nothing you could say, really. We were both just numb with anguish."

Meanwhile, Paul McCartney, having lost his loving mother Mary to
breast cancer as a teen, remembers he and John, each struggling to
cope with their mutual loss. "When I look back on Julia's death, all I really see is just the word T-R-A-G-E-D-Y written in big, black, letters. The
only way I could really help was to empathize, as I'd had the same
thing happen to me. I mean, there wasn't actually anything I could say
that would just sort of magically patch him up. That kind of hurt goes
far too deep for that. There was, however, one rather funny (or, more
accurately, cruel) incident that happened about a year or so after Julia
had gone. John was just beginning to get his act back together again,
you know. (That is, he could bluff it out a bit better than before.) Anyway, this one time, I remember being with him and meeting up with
someone who happened to ask me how my mother was getting on.
'Well, actually, she died a few years ago,' I said. 'Oh, I'm awfully sorry
son. Oh my God.' Turning to John, they asked him the same question,
only to be told precisely the same thing. And as teenage boys often are,
we both, somehow, found their deep embarrassment rather amusing.
Actually, it was a wonderful way of masking our true feelings, and it
gave us both a bit more of a bond."

To make matters worse, the fellow that hit our mother just happened to be an off-duty policeman who was suspected of drunken driving. An official inquest was held, but the gentleman, whose name I
have never been told, was ultimately exonerated of any negligence or
wrongdoing. As far as the courts were concerned, Mummy died as a direct result of "misadventure." A verdict just as good as any other really,
considering that as Julia was now gone, nothing *anyone* had to say
could ever alter that tragic reality.

All these details, however, were still completely unknown to my sister
and I, who, by this time, had taken up residence with Harrie and her
husband Norman at the Cottage. Early one Saturday morning, though,
all that changed dramatically when Uncle Norman suddenly sum-
moned us both downstairs for what looked to be a very serious chat.
"You won't be seeing your mother again, girls, she's in Heaven," was his

straightforward, simplistic way of breaking the news. Even though we naturally both suspected the worst, actually hearing it in plain English drove us both into immediate, uncontrollable hysterics. Harrie, meanwhile, upstairs making our beds, heard the commotion and immediately rushed into the sitting room screaming, "You shouldn't have told them like that! What right have you to interfere with my family?" "Only the right of simple, common decency," fired back Norman. "You apparently didn't have the guts to tell them, and as it's been almost two months now, I did!" As well-intentioned as he was, however, Norman was Harrie's second husband, and quite frankly, we didn't really appreciate hearing it from him.

As far as we were concerned, it should have come from our father. Daddy, however, had his own personal demons to try and contain. "I'm really not coping very well children," he told us one day after suddenly showing up unexpectedly at Harrie's. "I love you both dearly, but . . . it's actually very hard for me at the moment." We both felt sorry for him, but at the same time knew this almost certainly meant we would be staying at the Cottage for quite some time. Daddy literally fell apart when mother died. Although he somehow managed to go through the motions at work, whenever we saw him, he generally seemed very depressed and withdrawn. For at least five years after Mummy's death, the mere mention of even Julia's name inevitably reduced him to tears. Eventually moving quite nearby, we did, fortunately, see him once or twice a week. Why, even John occasionally dropped by for a cup of tea and a little conversation.

"Once in a while, John and I would pop in and visit Bobby at his new place in Woolton," says Paul. "We used to borrow his record player to listen to the latest Carl Perkin's discs we'd dug up in town. In fact, I seem to recall catching hell from him once for accidentally damaging one of his records. He was basically a good bloke, though, and always seemed to enjoy seeing John. Frankly, I do know John had this sort of 'stepfather' thing about him though. I mean he liked him all right, but he couldn't quite associate with him as his dad. Actually, it was a problem I had later, when my father remarried. I think when you actually look back on it, it was quite strange for him really."

Life for my sister and I, meanwhile, was rather tenuously forging ahead. Initially, of course, the adjustment had been difficult, but gently guided by Harrie's loving hand, we were slowly beginning to settle in. One of the greatest things about living there had to be the fact that we had now somehow "gained" a little brother.* David was just eleven months younger than I, and therefore proved to be a lot of fun for both us "big" girls to spend time with. At last we had actually found someone in the family further on down the pecking order than us! David was an especially sweet child, who, not surprisingly, grew up to be an even nicer man. We are all still very close. Although we now certainly lived in a different house, every evening that same big, home-cooked meal was still there waiting for us, and the wounds, quite naturally, began to heal. All of this, I'm sure, tended to put our father in a very awkward position, but what else could he do? If we had stayed at home with him it would have meant giving up his job, which, of course, was virtually unheard of in those days. The final solution was, I suppose, in many ways the best for us, as we now had a stable mother figure in Harrie, as well as the comfort and security of a real home. Financially, we were still maintained by our father, which was a real blessing to all concerned, for at least it offered him a continuing sense of participation in our day-to-day affairs. In the summer of 1960, however, we did briefly move back in with him and his mother, but after about four months or so went back home to the Cottage.

It was around this time, too, that we started seeing less and less of John. By now, the Beatles were raging on quite successfully (for a scruffy local band, that is), and if he wasn't actually playing somewhere, then he was at least rehearsing or attending art college in Liverpool. Once in a while though, he would pop by for a quick meal, a little much-welcomed roughhousing with us girls, or maybe even a long chat with a girlfriend on Harrie's phone. This little trick, however, sometimes required more than a bit of treachery on John's part. Harrie, you see, was sometimes rather unreasonably skittish about people tying up the phone for what she liked to call "nonessential" purposes. So, as a result, if John wanted to absolutely assure his privacy, he would have to crawl through the front window, and then stretch the curly cord back

*David's sister, Leila, was in Edinburgh pursuing her study of medicine at the university.

outside into the bushes, so as not to be spotted by Harrie's eagle eye.

Later, he started bringing around a lovely young girl with him by the name of Cynthia Powell. They had met at the art college in lettering class, and soon became fast friends. She was very pleasant to everyone, and exceptionally kind to both Jacqui and I. Shortly after John started going out with her, though, he insisted she bleach her hair out of reverence for his own personal sex symbol, the fabulous Bridget Bardot. "Unfortunately for Cyn," says Paul, "she just happened to come along at the time everyone was trying to turn their girlfriend into a 'bargain basement' Bardot. You see, we all happened to be at an age when a ravishing sex goddess taking off her clothes was *the* fantasy for us boys. We were all smitten. So the girls had to be blonde, look rather like Bridget, and preferably pout a lot. John and I used to have these secret talks where we intimated that we would be quite happy for our girlfriends to become Liverpool's answer to Bardot. My girl was called Dot, and, of course, John was going steady with Cynthia. So, eventually, we both got them to go blonde and wear miniskirts. It's terrible really, but that's the way it is."

Quite frankly, both Jacqui and I grew up with Cynthia around. She and John courted at the Cottage, and always seemed very much at home there. Often visiting Saturday afternoons, they would sit quietly holding hands on the settee, while we all gathered round to watch the telly. Sometimes, we'd be sent out of the room by Harrie so that the two of them could be alone. This, of course, always engendered a lot of good-natured "oos and ahs" from us, as we sauntered into the kitchen to impatiently wait until they wanted tea. Then, at least, we were allowed in to serve them. Which also carried the added bonus of giving us both an opportunity to personally see what they were "up" to. There is no doubt in my mind, but that Cynthia was always very good for my brother. She loved him desperately and only wanted the best for him. Anyone could see how terribly in love they were. I've always felt it a great pity they eventually parted so unhappily. Seeing them there together at Harrie's, no one could ever have guessed how terribly cruel their ultimate fate would be. For back then, they were both the absolute picture of teenage love.

JULIA BAIRD
Interview
CHESTER, SEPTEMBER 14, 1986

Geoffrey: How were the Quarrymen as a group?

Julia Baird: To be honest, the music didn't really mean much to us then. It was just so exciting to know our brother was up there playing and singing. We all went to see them play, the whole family. They would play various garden fêtes around Liverpool, so we all tagged along to see him play, all the aunts, cousins, everyone.

Geoffrey: What about John's early relationship with Paul? Mike McCartney told me recently they use to argue a lot even back then.

Julia: They would have done, because they were two strong personalities, both trying to assert themselves. Still they made a very good team.

Geoffrey: I assume this is the first Beatle convention you've attended—what do you think of it all?

Julia: Well, a convention really wouldn't be something I would normally be interested in, but a lot of the fans seem like nice people. I'm sure John would have said, "Go out and get them! If this is what you're into, just do your best." He would never make a judgment on anything like that.

Geoffrey: As your older brother, did John look after you as a kid?

Julia: Well, my sister Jacqui and I were obviously his two younger sisters, so it was more like, "Take the girls with you to the park, and if you're going to play football, then take them along."

Geoffrey: You were obviously so close, and yet for so many years no one really knew you or your sister existed. Did John later go out of his way to insulate you from the madness of Beatlemania?

Julia: I think he tried very hard to keep his entire family private. Only Mimi has really chosen to be interviewed thus far.

Geoffrey: What prompted you to write your book?*

---

*John Lennon: My Brother. Published internationally, it featured a brief foreword and interview by Paul McCartney.

Julia: I wanted to set the record straight because of all the misconceptions about my mother. I've simply told the truth as I know it, as I was there.

Geoffrey: People often comment on your mother's alleged promiscuity in the period between leaving Fred Lennon and meeting your father, John Dykin. Recently we've also learned a female child was born to Julia around that time who was given up for adoption to a couple in Norway shortly after her birth.* How do you think John might want you to reflect on those years?

Julia: Well, it's really got nothing to do with what John would want me to say, as she was my mother, too. I do know she was deserted by John's father and was therefore forced to bring up her little boy by herself. Eventually, though, she moved into my Grandfather George's (whom we always called Pop). But as for making any comment on her life between Fred Lennon and my father, it's really something about which I know absolutely nothing.

Geoffrey: Yet people have much such a big point of it all, haven't they?

Julia: They have. I, myself, didn't even know there was another child until late last year. It was a very big shock to me as well, you know. As for Julia's single life, what might be called promiscuous in those days certainly wouldn't be now.

*Victoria Elizabeth, born on June, 19, 1945.

MIKE AND ROWENA McCARTNEY*
Interview
LIVERPOOL, JULY 1984

Geoffrey: What was your name again, McGear or McCartney?

Mike McCartney: *McGertney.*

Geoffrey: I went by your old home today, actually.

Mike: You know, they once offered me twenty thousand pounds to do an exclusive Beatle tour of Liverpool for all the executive Japanese, Americans, and Torontonians. For the Garden Festival. Can you imagine a £20,000 reward?

Geoffrey: So what's your name these days?

Mike: Mike McCartney. That's my name now. I've changed it from Mc-Fab to McCartney.

Geoffrey: Your brother's not Paul McGear, now is he?

Mike: Who's he? Oh, you mean Linda McGear's wife?

Geoffrey: How intimidating was it to get into show business with your group, the Scaffold, with Paul McCartney being your brother?

Mike: Paul McCartney! Darling, darling! He's going to say "Be Ba Bea, *Beat. . . .*"

Geoffrey: I'm going to say "Beatles" next, that's right. (*Laughter*)

Mike: Actually, it was no problem at all. The only way to survive was to choose a theatrical comedy concept. If I had chosen pop music I'd be dead by now.

Geoffrey: Would you have liked to go into pop music but thought you couldn't because of Paul?

Mike: Look, Brian Epstein once said to me at the height of the Beatles'

---

*Mike McCartney is Paul's younger brother. He and his wife Rowena reside today in the Wirtal district of suburban Liverpool. Mike is the father of six children.

success, "Michael, would you like to be a pop singer? Please, come and join our organization." This was when they were just getting Gerry and Cilla organized. I said, "Brian, you must be jokin'. We've got one up there already who is doin' rather well, thank you." To try and emulate that, to put myself up there and draw on Paul as a comparison would be a pretty dumb thing to do. I'm as good as he is. He's a natural singer and a natural player of instruments, but I'm a natural singer too, though I've never been relaxed enough to really let anybody hear it.

Geoffrey: I spoke to George Martin recently about the song "Her Majesty." I said, "Yeah, what about when you and the Beatles clipped off that last note on 'Her Majesty'?" And he said, "Oh, did we?" I said, "What do you mean, 'did we?' There's a million guys in America right now who were high on LSD during the sixties reading the meaning of life into your leaving that note off and you didn't even know you did it?"

Mike: That's exactly what the whole Beatle thing was, doing it in complete *innocence*. You are just a being, you do what you do because it's your job and you can't go into it any more than that. Sometimes they used to tease the listeners a bit. Particularly John, I think, would love to fool around with people's heads.

Geoffrey: Did the Scaffold ever play on the same bill as the Beatles?

Mike: No. We played the Cavern, but we didn't go down too well because they were used to pop groups, and we'd come on spoutin' poetry and bloody comedy.

Geoffrey: The Beatles were always edging towards comedy.

Mike: John was a great comedian all right, a natural.

Geoffrey: Paul was no slouch, either.

Mike: No, but John was the heavy one and Paul was a very good feed. Two good comedians. But then Ringo's a very funny guy as well.

Geoffrey: George came out with a few zingers, too.

Mike: Well, you've been to Liverpool now, and all the people reading your book will understand that when they come to Liverpool, they might actually see why the Beatles are so big. Liverpool life is the best apprenticeship in the world, because our families are virtually gold mines of upbringing. Without that grounding I doubt very much whether the Beatles would have stayed at the top for so long or kept their sanity when all about them so many died. Of course an enormous contribution to that longevity was their sense of humor. They always say in Liverpool: you've got to have a sense of humor to survive.

Geoffrey: I went around to their boyhood homes today and I can see where you'd have to have a sense of humor, because it all seemed so harsh.

Mike: Hold on. There's two ways of looking at it. Ringo's neighborhood was heavy. Now I don't particularly know what George's was really like, as he was in Speke and I only vaguely remember going up to his house. Paul would have known George in Speke when we lived in Harwood Grove. George lived about three streets parallel to us. I remember walking up the back alleyway with some fireworks under my arm going to George's one night. I can't remember George as a kid particularly. He lived very close to us, and from there we moved to Forthlen Row.

Geoffrey: Which is very near John's.

Mike: Just down the road. So the point you were making was about all this poverty we were brought up in? The reality was quite different! We were actually lower working middle class. My dad was a cotton salesman, which was a good job, very well respected. He was on good money. And my mother was a midwife, again, a highly respected position. Look at John's place on Menlove Avenue. It's bloody posh!

Geoffrey: I've met Paul and Linda and they're the nicest people. How can you take a guy, give him everything that most people just get a taste of, and have him end up so cool?

Rowena McCartney: The Beatles weren't particularly star-struck, you know what I mean? A lot of groups today seem to be.

Mike: The Beatles were immediate stars, too.

Rowena: Yes, but it didn't go to their heads. The Beatles still got around, I mean, they went on every chat show. They did most everything they were asked to do instead of saying, "No, we're far too big for that." They realized that being amiable was much better. I can imagine your father taking the piss out of Paul if he ever got too big for his boots.

Mike: Yes, that's right. But again that can only come from your upbringing. That's why you don't get thrown when you're at the top, when the pressure's really on. Paul was always in contact with his relatives. Families tend to cut one down to size, so suddenly it isn't that big a deal being rich and famous as in Paul's case. I know family life is more important to him. And when you get too big for the family, then that's very uncool.

Geoffrey: Was it the same for the rest of the Beatles? Did they have strong family roots as well?

Mike: Yes. You just said to me in the car what a magical, amazing place Liverpool is.

Geoffrey: So what you're telling me is that one of the most significant factors in the Beatles' success was simply being from Liverpool?

Mike: Yeah.

Geoffrey: Okay, next subject, what about the Maharishi?

Mike: I did his meditation for two years. But I suddenly realized it was costing me a fortune and taking two hours of my life every day! So I stopped, because that's the trick. That is what the Maharishi is telling you: "Okay, gang, what are you coming here for? Go get the answers for yourself! *Self*-realization is the whole thing and I am just a tool of my Guru Dev." You know, these TM people, God love them, are very nice, but they think of him as a god. There's also an idea Jesus was a god as well. But as soon as you think of any human being as a god, then you've lost the answer.

Geoffrey: When I met Paul I certainly felt a bit of a flutter in my throat. Same thing with George.

Mike: It's called "the reason John got killed," and it's a worrying feeling. It's in everybody who is enamored with anybody else. As soon as you are overly impressed, you're finished. What you don't realize is that the people you're talking about go through the very same thing. I know a few occasions in my life when I've been in the presence of people I admired, and I've done exactly the same. I lost me bottle, and suddenly you're not yourself. In a star situation, when you're with somebody famous, you naturally change, like a chameleon, according to your environment, fear, embarrassment, degree of adulation.

Geoffrey: When I met Paul, I could feel him trying to compensate for other people's nervousness.

Mike: He was trying to help them understand themselves. Listen, the Beatles themselves have been flipping out for years listening to Elvis, Chuck Berry, Ben E. King, and Ray Charles. In the old days Paul and I used to like the Everly Brothers, listening to every word, every nuance, every bit of feeling to get it exactly right. Paul imitated Little Richard and was one of the few white people Richard has acknowledged as being a good interpreter of him! Therefore we were influenced by our peers as well. Now the most important thing to remember when an idol comes around is that he's just a guy who picks his nose and performs all the other bodily functions every other little god on this earth does. Don't forget the person is still a human being.

Geoffrey: Mike, did you say you had a tape of the Beatles no one has ever heard?

Mike: I have.

Geoffrey: And no one ever will?

Mike: Someday. But I have to think of it in another light now. I've got four children, and it's their heritage, right?

Geoffrey: Did you collect a lot of things over the years?

Mike: I'm one of those terrible people that can't throw anything away. Ringo, I think, is one as well, but unfortunately his house in Los Angeles burned down.

Geoffrey: Do you ever see many people from the old days?

Mike: I saw John's mate, Pete Shotton, in Liverpool when Queenie Epstein opened Beatle City. I didn't meet him, though, but I did meet Pete Best. I thought he was very much like he always was, quiet, dignified, and shy.

Geoffrey: They say he got canned from the Beatles because he was too good-looking and Paul didn't dig it, so he said, "Let's find the ugliest drummer we can who's got a cool drum kit."

Mike: Nonsense. It was just fate that decreed he should go. It's like they said, "Something's got to happen. Somebody's got to go, and it's not us." It could have been any one of them fate chose. George could have been the one, you know. None of them was that fucking strong. But when they all got together, that's when the magic happened. The other three were very quick, but Pete was moody, magnificent, and good-looking. The girls screamed for him, and that was an *asset*. They wouldn't have sacked the sod for that! That would have been much bigger, a good-looking drummer with Paul, John, and George fronting him. It was basically down to his drumming ability in the end. There were quite a few drummers around Liverpool, and I used to go home and tell Paul about Ringo. I often saw him play with Rory Storm. We didn't think about how ugly he might have been or even about the little white streak in his hair. It was just that this guy with Rory was a very inventive drummer. He goes around the drums like crazy. He doesn't just hit them, he invents sounds.

Geoffrey: There's a nice story about you reopening Apple Studios in the mid-seventies. You guys went down and recorded something, and Paul couldn't believe he was actually back there.

Mike: It was his decision to join me.

Geoffrey: What did you record?

Mike: It was very good for him. It's called "Knocking Down Walls of Ignorance."

Geoffrey: Was that the name of the track?

Mike: It is now! We were in London but I couldn't find a drummer, so I was ringing around to different people. Linda was saying, "Get hold of John Bonham." So Paul came in on the conversation. "I'll drum for you down at Apple." The track he drummed on I presented to EMI, and the young A&R man then in charge listened to the track and said, "Very good, but the drummer certainly leaves a lot to be desired." (*Laughter*) I didn't tell him it was the drummer who played on their best-selling *Band on the Run* album. I just didn't have the heart. So I walked out, got on the train and went back home to Liverpool.

Geoffrey: You know, I walked around Matthew Street today and I could hear Beatle music rafting out of the shops and I saw all this wonderful plastic Beatle stuff everywhere for sale.

Mike: It's amazing that they actually knocked the Cavern down. What an extraordinary happening.

Geoffrey: Look, Mike, I spent eight years under the influence of various and sundry preparations with headphones on listening to *The White Album* and *Sgt. Pepper.* When I would do that I would go to "other places," I mean, it was wonderful. I could do it with other music, too—Hendrix's *Electric Lady Land* is probably my favorite. What these big artists have done is they've touched something that really isn't normal consciousness.

Mike: That's right. Absolutely, absolutely.

Geoffrey: That is heavy shit. This is high art! It's magic. But it came *through* them.

Mike: But where is the magic from? Human beings or a god? *It's only magic.* It's only pretend. It's an illusion and what they're presenting is a beautiful, intellectual, magical experience.

Geoffrey: Do you think they're just as flipped out about it as the listener?

Mike: Of course they are when they're doing it.

Geoffrey: I'm doing some writing about the Beatles and I was thinking, "What am I going to say about the future of it all?" And I suddenly got this feeling it's probably not really going to last that long. I used to think it was going to be like Mozart or something and last forever, but. . . .

Mike: You're wrong. Remember we now have a new communications era.

Geoffrey: I sometimes make it a point to ask little children what they think about the Beatles, and lately they've been saying, "Well, ah. . . ."

Mike: They're bored by it now because of the inevitable cycle, but the next cycle will be like, "Wow! What did we miss?" That's it, you know, they're up there forever, mate.

Mike: Hey, is George a Hare Krishna these days?

Geoffrey: He's not really, no. He actually told me, "I was never really into it that much." And he said to me, "I was only into it for a few months really heavily." How come I'm telling *you* about the Beatles? What is this?

Mike: Anything you want to know, just ask yourself! I read he said he was worried about being shot recently.

Geoffrey: Not a smart move. It draws it to you, eh? I know some people who went to Cavendish Avenue the other day and Paul actually came out to see them. I mean, they didn't even have to ring the bell.

Mike: He gets lonely.

Geoffrey: He seems pretty cool about it all. Not at all paranoid.

Mike: Yeah. That's right.

Geoffrey: Did Stuart [Sutcliffe] die because someone kicked him in the head during a fight which later caused a brain hemorrhage?

Mike: So they say. I wouldn't be surprised. I saw him just before he died and I didn't lay a finger on him!

Geoffrey: They say he was even more intellectual and far out than Lennon. There was apparently a really tight relationship between Stu and John, wasn't there?

Mike: Oh, Stu was just an art school friend of his.

Geoffrey: Actually, the other rumor is that John was the center guy and Paul was a bit bitchy towards Stuart because he was stealing his scene with Lennon.

Mike: Stu was fine. Good man. Nice guy.

Geoffrey: Poor Astrid had a weird time, it seems. There's been a lot of weirdness all around the Beatles, it seems. Astrid certainly got ripped off for millions of dollars on those first photographs she took of the Fabs, didn't she?

Mike: Oh, did she? Her photographs are in the Walker Art Gallery, some of them anyway. Not the best ones, I must admit. Very talented. In my book *Thank You Very Much* is a bit where Paul writes from Germany saying, "Mike, take your photos like Astrid. The trick is to blow the pictures up. That's the trick. Really good." But what he forgot to say was that you've got to be a bloody good photographer as well.

Geoffrey: Your photos of the Beatles are pretty far-out. They have kind of a similar thing, some of them, as Astrid's.

Mike: Yes.

Geoffrey: Is it true Paul erased some of Ringo's drum tracks like a few people have said?

Mike: Who?

Geoffrey: Paul. They said Ringo would do his drum tracks, he'd split, and then Paul would redo them.

Mike: Rubbish! Actually, Ringo would split and then Paul would erase John's guitar tracks! And George's. You got it right now.

Geoffrey: That's the scoop I needed. How many times has your brother been busted for pot, seven or eight times now?

Mike: Oh, a lot.

Geoffrey: Why doesn't he let the roadies take it around for him if he has to have a smoke?

Mike: Yeah, he's a bugger for punishment, an old Liverpool joke, that.

Geoffrey: Isn't it going to screw up his immigration soon?

Mike: Might do, yeah.

Geoffrey: Just think of it.

Mike: Oh, I've thought about it—he was in a Japanese prison cell. We were worried about that Jap business, though, the family. We were very worried here in Liverpool. When one of your own is incarcerated in a Japanese prison cell, you worry, you know. We've only seen the war films. They may be little but they've got bloody big swords!

Geoffrey: Anyway, tell me more about the Maharishi? I've got a few snaps at home with you sitting at his feet. Linda says in the foreword of her photograph book she thinks very fondly of him and digs his philosophy even now.

Mike: He is very nice and so she should.

Geoffrey: So why was he so maligned by the Fabs?

Mike: Go ask the Fabs. You know, all of us that were around then have a very nice feeling towards him.

Geoffrey: So why's it taking Paul so long to do his Rupert cartoon? I noticed he had the Rupert scarf on in a recent picture.

Mike: We were brought up on Rupert. A lady who is now a Beatle Guide phoned me a while back and said, "I've got you and Paul's first Rupert annual I found in my attic." And I said, "That's nice." "What should we do with it, Mike?" You see, this girl's mum was a midwife as was me mum, so I said, "Well, I have no idea. You could sell it at Sotheby's and make a fortune. Or what would be a nice idea, why don't you give it to Paul from you as a Christmas present or something? It would be beautiful." I left it with her and the next thing I knew it was in the Walker Art Gallery.

Geoffrey: Did the Beatles ever put anything on their records backwards?

Mike: Only their clothes. No, they weren't into that. They used to walk backwards at Christmas or sometimes I would see 'em walking backwards down Oxford Street. "Oh, there's those bloody backward Beatles again!"

Geoffrey: What about pedaling bicycles backwards?

Mike: Only dope—they always peddled their dope backwards.

Geoffrey: John's mother was killed on that road by a car and you can see why. They really zip right along there.

Mike: It was—they say it was a policeman, too. Yeah, it was after me mum died. It wiped John out. I remember that. We got much closer, him and I, and of course Our Kid.

Geoffrey: The story goes John was sitting in the kitchen with Paul and he said, "I don't know how you can be so normal seeing your mother's dead." Let's change the subject for a moment. You know, the other day I happened to run into the Thompson Twins. . . . so I said, "Mind if I have a snap?" So the chick freaks. "Oh no, oh Lord, *no!*" But yet I met Paul and Linda on the street and they will spend twenty minutes talking to you. These are together people. The point is. . . .

Mike: It's Liverpool, mate.

Geoffrey: How can you just take a guy, give him everything that most men just get a taste of or never have at all in their lives, and have him end up so cool? I hear that he goes to the Rye barber and says, "Short back and sides" as opposed to having, you know, some flighty hairdresser come down with his caravan of lovely French maidens to do the latest things to his hair. How does he stay so normal?

Mike: Well, he'll have the flighty hairdresser the week after he's been to the Rye barber. Again, what I was trying to say just before was that can only come from your grounding, your upbringing, right? And that's why you don't get thrown when you're at the top, when the pressure's really on.

Rowena: I don't know the Thompson Twins, but I should imagine that they're quite far removed from their families. They've got their own scene, whereas people like Paul are always in contact with their families. . . .

Geoffrey: It's strange because there was a period when it wasn't cool to dig your family. Remember "kill your parents" and all that business during the sixties?

Mike: I didn't ever go through that myself. Perhaps it's because both of mine were already dead. No, I don't remember "kill your parents."

Geoffrey: You don't remember all that radical stuff? The Yippies? Maybe you didn't get that so much over here? Does "revolution" ring a bell?

Mike: Revolution?

Geoffrey: You remember the revolution, don't you, Bwana? What was all that about now? Don't trust anyone over thirty. Jesus, I'm thirty-one myself! The high post-psychedelic period when you weren't supposed to dig your family—*it wasn't cool, man.*

Mike: Well, I'm afraid Liverpool would have transcended that very easily.

FRIENDS

PART SEVEN

Only a Northern Song

TOP TO BOTTOM:

John and Yoko arrive at Gatwick Airport following a working holiday in Denmark. January 27, 1970.

The Lennons pose with charismatic Apple promo man Pete Bennett in New York following the release of Lennon's classic, Imagine, in the early 1970s.

CLOCKWISE FROM TOP:

At the press launch for Apple's Radha Krishna Temple LP: today a genuine classic to devotees of Krishna worldwide.

The McCartneys in the spacious back garden of their sprawling St. John's Wood home.

Mrs. McCartney, the ever-lovin' cook of the house. Peasmarsh, Sussex.

*Macca at his father-in-law
Lee Eastman's Long Island estate.*

Denny Laine's birthday party, 1978.

Julian Lennon home alone shortly after learning of his father's tragic death. December 9, 1980.

Julian at the height of his unexpected, albeit very brief, pop stardom. June 12, 1984.

FACING PAGE, COUNTERCLOCKWISE FROM TOP:

Denny and Jo Jo Laine: happy together in London. February 25, 1974.

At home with son Laine during Wings wild heyday.

Denny and his parents at the Wings guitarist's wedding. November 5, 1978.

Sexy Jo Jo Laine, a troubled young woman caught up in the turbulent, often bitchy world of Wings.

THIS PAGE, LEFT TO RIGHT:

Lovely Apple girl Mary Hopkin. Shiplake, Oxfordshire, 1982.

The ever dapper Ringo arrives at a posh New York party.

FACING PAGE,
COUNTERCLOCKWISE FROM TOP:

Nature boy George says, "Hello."

Giuliano and Mike McCartney during a relaxing weekend at Mike's Heswall home on the Wirral just outside Liverpool, 1985.

Vrnda and former Beatle Pete Best backstage at The Joan River's Show, New York.

Julia and Geoffrey meet the press to promote their book, John Lennon: My Brother, *for which Paul McCartney penned a forward.*

Inside the Dakota with Sean and best friend, Max Leroy. 1983.

STUART SUTCLIFFE
Selected Quotations on John Lennon
HAMBURG, 1961

"With John it was different, because as I said, he was unlucky. Given the breaks other people had, he would have been alright. As it was, he brooded trying to find the answer. He was born old. He'd dried up before his time. He wilted, because he knew that someday he would wilt anyhow . . .

"He was obviously suffering from nervous tension and probably high blood pressure. This left him suffering from dizziness and headaches . . . when he stood up he complained of a black-out and tremendous headaches . . . I decided it was perhaps safer if I studied John more closely, in order that the plan I had in mind would work more thoroughly . . . Looking back, I can see that a terrible change came over John in the nine or ten months I knew him."

ALLAN WILLIAMS*
Interview
PHILADELPHIA, 1993

Allan Williams: In the early sixties, and in Hamburg, they all wore leather trousers. When Brian took the group over he didn't want them to look like four Gene Vincents on stage. On the last night they wore the trousers they went to an all-night place in Liverpool, Joe's Cafe. The Beatles were there with another group, Faron and the Flamingoes. You know that trick when you're all in a taxi and the last one out pays? They did something like that. They all ran out and left Faron to pay the bill, even Faron's band. But Paul had run out and left his leather trousers behind in the cafe. I don't want you to think he'd run out with no trousers—they were his stage trousers. So Faron picked them up and said, "I'm going to keep these because I paid for the food." Paul wasn't worried because it was the last time he was going to use those trousers.

*Allan Williams was the Beatles' Liverpool manager.

It was definitely John's group, he was the leader, but by then Paul was jockeying for power. So, towards the end of the Hamburg era, and when they got back to Liverpool, Paul and John were equally as powerful. It was Paul who got rid of Stuart Sutcliffe and he also, I believe, got rid of Pete Best.

BRIAN EPSTEIN
Selected Quotations on the Beatles
NOVEMBER 1964

"Ringo, the last to become a Beatle, came into the group not because I wanted him, but because the boys did. To be completely honest, I was not at all keen to have him. I thought his drumming rather loud, his appearance unimpressive, and I could not see why he was important to the Beatles. But again, I trusted their instincts and I am grateful now. He has become an excellent Beatle and a devoted friend. Ringo is warm and wry-witted, a good drummer, and I like him enormously. He is a very uncomplicated, very nice young man.

We rarely fall out because he, probably more than the others, is amenable to most of my suggestions."

"Paul is temperamental and moody and difficult to deal with, but I know him very well and he me. This means we compromise on a clash of personalities. He is a great one for not wishing to hear about things, and if he doesn't want to know, he switches himself off, settles down in a chair, puts one booted foot across his knee and pretends to read a newspaper, having consciously made his face an impassive mask.

"But he has enormous talent and inside a great tenderness and feeling which are concealed by an angry exterior. He is the most obviously charming with strangers, autograph hunters, fans, and other artists. He has a magnificent smile and an eagerness, both of which he uses not for effect, but because he knows they are assets which will bring happiness to those around him.

"Paul is very much a star, very musical, with a voice more melodic than John's and therefore more commercially acceptable. Also, and this is vital to me, he has great loyalty to the other Beatles and the organization around him. Therefore I ignore his moods and hold him in high esteem."

"John Lennon, Paul's friend from boyhood, his co-writer of so many songs, the dominant figure in a group which is, visually, without a leader, is in my opinion a most exceptional man. Had there been no Beatles and no Epstein participation, John would have emerged from the mass of the population as a man to reckon with. He may not have been a singer or a guitarist, a writer or a painter. But he would most certainly have been a *something*. You cannot contain a talent like this. There is in him a controlled aggression which demands respect."

"George, too, has his moods, though I cannot recall any particular now. I don't enjoy arguments, nor do the Beatles, so we avoid anything too contentious. George is remarkably easy to be with. He, like the others, has expanded as a person. Though collectively, on first sight, they appear to behave alike, they have specific characteristics.

"George is the business Beatle. He is curious about money and wants to know how much is coming in and what is best to do with it to make it work. He enjoys spending, but would always remain in credit. He likes cars, big and fast, but is careful to secure a good trade-in price for his old one.

"Strangers find him an easy conversationalist because he is a good listener and shows a genuine interest in the outside world. He wants to know, and I find this an endearing trait in a young man who is so successful and so rich that if he never learned anything new he would not suffer any loss. And, in addition to all these characteristics, he is, though not one of the prolific composers, very musicianly.

"George takes enormous care with tuning before a show. He has a very fine ear for sound and for a delicate half-tone and the others respect him for it. On stage he is the one who twiddles the tuning instruments and you can almost see his ears twitching to detect a faint discord."

"They were very fine, extraordinary young men. I don't believe anything like them will happen again and I believe 'happen' is the word, since no one could *create* anything in show business with such appeal and magnetism."

PADDY DELANEY*
Interview
LIVERPOOL, 1984

Geoffrey: You were the bouncer at the Cavern Club when the Beatles were around, correct?

Paddy Delaney: I was.

Geoffrey: What is your first remembrance of the Beatles?

Paddy: Their first appearance on the scene occurred on March 21, 1961. The first one I ever saw was George Harrison. In those days hairstyles were very strict and tidy, but George's was down to his collar. He was very scruffy and hungry-looking. I remember him ambling down the middle of the street and, for a minute, I didn't think he was coming into the Cavern. I stopped him at the door and asked if he was a member. Of course I knew he wasn't, and he said, "No," he was with the Beatles. Now we'd heard a lot about the Beatles over the previous weeks and I knew they were on that particular night, so I let him in even though he was wearing blue jeans. About fifteen minutes later, Paul McCartney tumbled down the street with John Lennon in close pursuit. Paul was carrying his bass and John had his hands dug deep into his pockets. I had an idea they were with George because they all had the same sort of hairstyle. It wasn't quite a Beatle cut then, but was still well past their collar. A little while after they strolled in, a taxi pulled up in front of the club and out came Pete Best. He was carrying the Beatles' first sound system, which consisted of two cheap chipboard speakers and a beat-up-looking amp. He also had a set of drums which he unloaded and took downstairs.

Geoffrey: What was their attitude in those days?

*Paddy Delaney worked as the Cavern's bouncer when the Beatles first appeared on February 21, 1961.

Paddy: They had a certain animal magnetism and a raw vibrancy to their music. There was an air about them that seemed to say, if you didn't like them, too bad, they couldn't care less.

Geoffrey: The Beatles ultimately became one of Liverpool's top groups. How affected were they by their early success?

Paddy: Shortly after they recorded "Please Please Me," Brian Epstein was giving them a weekly salary of only eight pounds. One night, Paul went over to the snack bar to buy himself a Coke and a cheese sandwich. He had enough for the Coke, but not the sandwich, so he asked me for a loan, and I said, "Yeah, sure, but don't forget me when you're at the top." He winked at me and said, "Don't worry, Pat, I won't."

Geoffrey: What about George—how was he holding up to the Beatles sudden hometown success?

Paddy: George was always a big-hearted lad. I remember him coming down Matthew Street driving a spanking new, second-hand car he had just bought with the first money he'd made from the Beatles. As he stepped out of his car and locked it up, I happened to be arguing with two girls who didn't have quite enough money to get in. This was a big night at the Cavern, the place was packed, and these poor girls were just standing outside in the street in tears. Well, George pushed past the two and into the club, but paused at the top of the stairs and motioned for me to come over. "What's the matter with those two, Pat?" "Look, George, I'm sorry, but they haven't got enough money to get in." Chuckling, he pulled a pound out of his pocket and told me to give it to them, but make sure they don't find out who it was from. "That's fine, George, but what excuse can I make for letting them in after arguing with them for the last half hour?" "You can do it, Pat," and, shrugging his shoulders, he disappeared down the stairs. I had to make up a story quickly so I went outside into the street and told them, "Look, there's nothing I can do about it girls. If you haven't got the money, how can you expect to get in? Oh, for Christ's sake, I'll tell you what, I've got a pound here, you go ahead and take it."

Geoffrey: Did they really fall for that?

Paddy: Not a bit. They said, "George gave you that, didn't he?" "No," I said. "What makes you think he would do a thing like that?" Well, the next thing I knew they both started sobbing their hearts out crying for George. "Take it or leave it," I said. "We'll pay him back," they screamed. "You'll pay *me* back on Friday." That is what I had to put up with for the Beatles and their girls. Now there's a story that's never been told before. It happened during their last gig at the Cavern. We were almost filled to capacity but there were still dozens of people lined up outside hoping to get in. Of course I knew it was my sad duty to be the one to turn most of them away, but as I walked outside to tell everybody we could only let in just a few more, a group of teenage girls handed me a toilet roll! "What the bloody hell is this all about?" I said. "Unroll it, Paddy," the crowd was all shouting. So I did, and my God, the kids had very carefully unrolled the damn thing, signed it and then rolled it back up again. They just passed it from one end of the line to the other. "Would you mind giving it to the Beatles, Pat? And tell them we love them." They knew they could never all get in, so I guess this "love letter" they wrote to the Beatles was the only way to let the boys know how they felt. That spelled out very clearly the real success of the Beatles to me, mate.

PATRICIA DANIELS*
Interview
LIVERPOOL, 1983

Geoffrey: Tell me about seeing the Beatles play the Cavern.

Patricia Daniels: I was about fifteen, still in school, and had a good friend who used to go down and see them perform all the time. One day she said to me, "You've got to come down and see this new group," and that was it. It was a long time ago now.

Geoffrey: They had leather clothes on?

---

*Patricia Daniels was an original fan of the Beatles back in Liverpool.

Patricia: They wore blue jeans or rock jumpers as we called them. They'd always say "Hello luv" when they went out to the bus stop, the snack bar, to get some ciggies. John was always the hard one—he'd say, "Come on, you've got a shilling for my bus fare, don't you, luv?" or something like that. And, of course, I'd always give it to him.

Geoffrey: Anything in particular you can remember about their gigs?

Patricia: We had only fifty pence once between me and three friends and had to hitch a ride to see them play. We'd missed the train as usual and ended up getting a taxi only halfway back. That's all we could afford.

Geoffrey: How about when the Beatles changed drummers—were you around then?

Patricia: There was a lot of opposition to that because Pete Best was definitely the handsomest one in the group. When Ringo came along, it was like it was suddenly a different band. A lot of girls had the hots for Pete Best and that was it. Once he went, they didn't like the Beatles any more!

Geoffrey: Which one did you like?

Patricia: All of them, really. In the Cavern you'd sit in the front if you liked Paul the best and sit on the opposite side of the stage if you liked John better.

Geoffrey: Where did you sit?

Patricia: Whenever I found a seat, it was usually in the middle!

Geoffrey: Did you like Ringo when he came in?

Patricia: You just had to get used to him, because there was no way that it was ever going to change.

Geoffrey: Do you remember seeing Brian Epstein?

Patricia: Yes, when we were kids we used to get sweets from the Epsteins. Mr. Brian used to be in the shop all the time.

Geoffrey: They called him "Mr. Brian"?

Patricia: Yes, I was about seven and I remember my dad would go to their store to make payments on our furniture, and we'd all be jumping from chair to chair and Mr. Brian used to come out and say, "Kindly remove that child from the furniture, sir. Don't you realize it costs good money?" But his father used to give us all the sweets we wanted.

Geoffrey: Did everyone know he was gay?

Patricia: That had nothing to do with anything. To us he was just a very influential, nice person around Liverpool.

Geoffrey: When the Beatles became famous and returned to Liverpool, did you see them?

Patricia: The last time they played the Cavern, yes. Actually, you had to be a part of it to know what was really going on. That was the last chance for all the people who had been coming along to see them play for years, to say goodbye. We just had to accept the fact that when they finally hit the big time, there was no way we could ever get them back again for a lunchtime session. Whenever we saw them on television, we'd all feel very proud we'd known them long before any of you lot had.

HORST FASCHER*
Selected Quotations
DATES UNKNOWN

"Every day they'd come to me and say, 'Horst, can we have the keys to the club so we can rehearse?' Even when they were drunk to nine or ten in the morning, at two or three in the afternoon you could see them on stage rehearsing."

---

*Horst Fascher was the Beatles bodyguard and friend while playing in Germany in the early sixties.

"We had fights every night at the club because, as you can imagine, people were buying booze all night long. The music was hot and so tourists came from all over. Drunken sailors jumped on stage and tried to sing with the band. I'd try to get them off and tell them not to disturb the performances. It came down to some little fights. I remember one time I didn't protect one of the Beatles, but rather Cynthia. Cynthia had come to Hamburg as a guest—John brought her over. He told me that if anybody bothered Cynthia in the audience I should take care of it. I promised I'd keep an eye on her. One night someone tried to pull her out of her seat. I went up to him and said. 'What are you doing? This is one of the musicians' girlfriends, so leave her alone. Also, she doesn't speak German, so why are you talking to her if she doesn't understand?' I thought it was over and turned away when I heard John shout through the microphone, 'Horst, please! Don't you see this idiot is still pulling Cynthia!' So I ran back and we started fighting. But that was the only time where I protected someone like a bodyguard."

"I couldn't say who was my favorite Beatle because when I met them the first time we all became friendly. Later on I had a lot of contact with Pete because we did many things together. Pete was my first real friend in the group I became close to. Later on it was Ringo—that's because I like drummers."

"It was New Year's Eve, '62–'63, the last time the Beatles played Hamburg. In the morning, when the club was empty, I would sometimes ask them if I could join in and sing a little bit because I've always loved to sing. I was always shy to sing on stage when people were there. That night they forced me to come on stage in front of the crowd. It was close to midnight and I was a little bit tipsy. I went on stage and did two songs with them. I didn't know that it had been recorded, and later on I found there was even a record of it on the market. It was a big mistake."

"One night there was [sic] only three Beatles on stage. So I went backstage to see where the fourth one was. It was John who wasn't on stage. So I went backstage behind the curtains and asked Paul, who was nearest to me, 'Where's John?' I ended up looking backstage and went to the toilet and there was one door closed. I said, 'John! Are you in there?' But there was no answer. I went next door to the shower room. I climbed up to the shower and looked over the wall. John was sitting on the toilet, pants down to his knees. A little girl was sitting in front of him doing it to him. I laughed a little, but I was angry because the others had to go on stage while he had his enjoyment. So I opened the shower really strong and turned the waste on them. Then I heard him yelling, 'You bastard! You Nazi bastard!'

"I turned away laughing and left them alone. Then there was laughing coming from the club. John had gone on stage with just his underwear, his Beatle boots, and a toilet seat around his neck. Everyone assumed Lennon had gone backstage to put on this silly outfit. No one knew what was really going on."

GEORGE MARTIN*
Interview
LONDON, 1990

Question: I understand that there were things that were picked up on the original Beatle recordings, like cars going by and planes flying over the studio. Is that true?

George Martin: Well, I don't know about cars and planes, but you certainly get squeaky drum pedals and that kind of thing. You hear warts and all, but I don't mind that. I think that's fine. They're pretty historic recordings. It was over twenty years ago now. It's a lifetime away and recording techniques were so different then that I think they stand up extraordinarily well. The only thing is, when I made those records the kind of record players people used, the kind of vinyl we used, and the kind of transfers we got demanded a certain kind of record be made because it had to break through the mush of the comparatively poor quality of those days. Everyone tends to forget that, in 1963, stereo

*George Martin was the Beatles' charismatic record producer. Today he runs AIR Studios, a successful recording facility in central London.

didn't exist in England at all for pop music. It existed for classical music. Multitrack recording didn't exist, so that we had mono machines or stereo machines. And stereo machines were mainly the domain of the classical people, but I managed to acquire a stereo machine for my recording and converted it to twin-track. The reason for that was, I didn't want to make stereo records. I wanted to have more than one track available, so I would have latitude in my recordings. Recording was done live in those days. You spent an afternoon and did all your work in the studio telling the boys not to be quite so close or bring the amp up or whatever. It was actually acoustic changes rather than electronic changes on the board. Because there wasn't a great deal of time, I found it convenient to use twin-track, putting all the instruments on one track and putting all the vocals and any lead solos (like guitars or piano) on that track as well and then compressing the two together, which gave a much punchier, bitier sound than if I'd just done mono in the first place. But that backfired because, many years later, some idiot at EMI took these and assumed they were stereo and put them out. This was the grandson of those terrible stereo records they were proposing to put out on compact disc. So I shouted and said, "Look, you're making a dreadful mistake. These were mono records, for God's sake, don't put them out in this fake stereo."

Question: That's interesting because, for years now, a lot of my friends who are musicians have been singing the praises of the mono versions of Beatle albums as opposed to the stereo version.

George: Well, we gradually got into stereo, of course, but it was a transitional thing. The earliest stereo records that were issued weren't very good. The first two albums should always be in mono, in my opinion. Numbers three and four I think that's a case of us looking at again and maybe doing a stereo version of those two, because I think we could do a better job now than we did then. As I got better in my stereo handling, in those new days in '65 and '66, the stereo improved. But I went through a few aberrations. I've kept those. For example, when I was remixing *Help!*, most of the voice is in the center and it's okay. But on *Rubber Soul,* almost all of the voices are on the right-hand channel and I thought, "Well, why the hell did I do that?" Looking back on it, I know that I was conscious of listening to stereo in mono form and everything in the middle comes out louder. So that was probably my early attempt to try and make it compatible. As we got into that, *Revolver* was very much better and, of course, *Sgt. Pepper* was okay all around.

Question: What was the first Beatle album recorded in stereo for stereo?

George: Well, we never, ever recorded in stereo. By that, I mean the classical people would record in stereo, putting it straight down to two-track which then became a master. We always recorded in multitrack form, even though we didn't have multitrack. So my initial pioneering attempts to get multitrack by using a stereo machine in twin-track led, after the first two albums, to our getting a Studer one-inch wide tape four-track machine. And what I used to do on the four-track was, I used to go from one four-track to another. In the early days, I just did the straight four-track and perhaps put bass and drums on one track and guitars on a second track and lead vocal on a third and maybe backing voices on a fourth. But, obviously, I used to mix things in with that, so you'd have things like tambourine on a backing voices track or even an extra guitar on a vocal track. But it did enable me afterwards to make some kind of stereo out of those four. As we got into projects like *Sgt. Pepper,* I began thinking more in stereo terms and I would even use two of the tracks as a stereo basis. And then I would dub from one four-track to another, always working out in advance what kind of losses I'm going to get in dubbing, so I would tend to put on a bit more bass and a bit of that when I went from one four-track to another. So it was a creative process where you ended up with a four-track master which had a couple of tracks in genuine stereo. In other words, there were things in between the tracks apart from stuff discretely in the tracks themselves.

Question: So it's not necessarily true to say that *Sgt. Pepper* was the first stereo Beatles album.

George: I think it was the first really good stereo album we made. I mean, *Revolver* wasn't bad, but *Revolver* led into *Pepper.* The last track of *Revolver* was "Tomorrow Never Knows," and it will be impossible to mix that again because, again, although we only had a four-track master, the actual mix itself was a performance. Into the four-track master, I mixed lots of tape loops. I remember I'd just taken over Abbey Road Studios at the time and I had different control rooms and had eight tape machines, mono tape machines, dotted all over the place, with people holding the tapes with pencils and feeding them into the mixer together with my four-track master and going straight onto the twin-track eventual master. So there's no way I could re-create all those random loops going onto that two-track. So that one I would definitely, severely leave alone. That was a true stereo mix.

Question: I loved all of the backwards guitar stuff.

George: Yes. I'd introduced John to backwards music on "Rain" when I took his voice and turned it 'round when he was out on a coffee break. When I played it for him, he flipped. They went through a helluva phase then of trying all sorts of backwards things. As you know, we had backward cymbals on "Strawberry Fields" and George would like to do backwards guitar solos. It was fun for awhile, but then, like everything else, it got a bit boring.

Question: But it was an exciting time for music with all of this experimentation going on and they had the technology to do those kinds of things.

George: Yeah. Well, I've always been intrigued by that. I mean, even before the Beatles came along. I was experimenting with tapes and doing my own kind of "musique concrete" before we had synthesizers. I loved looping things and putting things backwards, and speeding them up, then slowing them down, and dropping bricks onto piano strings. It was a lot of fun. It was all a part of growing up in the recording world.

Question: What would you say was the greatest technological advance made between "Please Please Me" and *Sgt. Pepper?*

George: Well, technologically, there wasn't really a great stride. There wasn't a tremendous breakthrough, because we still had only four-tracks on *Pepper* when I was yearning to have more tracks. The great stride we made was learning to cope with the deficiencies we had to put up with and develop a technique of making good sounds even on four-track. Technologically, there was no great advancement. The breakthroughs came even after the Beatles. The real revolution has come now with digital recording and so on.

Question: In your 1979 autobiography, *All You Need Is Ears,* you cited "Yesterday" as being a turning point in your relationship with the Beatles. You wrote: "That was when I started to leave my hallmark on the music. It was on 'Yesterday' that I started to score their music."

George: Well, it changed in the respect that that was the first time that a Beatles record was issued with only one of them on it. In fact, when we made it, I was talking to Brian Epstein about it saying, "You know, this is really Paul's song. He sang on it, there's no other Beatle on it. It's just him and my strings. What should we do about it?" "Well," he said, "Well, if you're thinking of Paul McCartney solo, that would be wrong. That would break up the Beatles. It's got to be the Beatles." And that's what it was. The fact that we did that opened up the way for the world being our oyster and turned the boys on to realizing that they weren't limited to three guitars and a drum kit, and that they could pluck from the palette of colors any one they wanted. That led us on to other things like orchestrations and weird sounds.

Question: So you're not out there looking for another group to work with, like you worked with the Beatles?

George: No, sir! I've done my apprenticeship long ago. No, I couldn't possibly. I'm too old anyway to look for new talent. There are plenty of good, young producers who are doing a fine job and I leave that to them. I don't think I would be capable now of recognizing what the young public wants. I know what I'd like. But once tastes change, you can't keep the mental age of twenty-five all your life.

Question: When you talked about double-tracking the first Beatle albums, was that an attempt at capturing their early live sound that you witnessed when you went up to Liverpool?

George: Well, yes, because I was very conscious that they exuded a tremendous field of magnetism. They had great charisma. When I first signed them, it wasn't because they could write great songs, because they couldn't. Nor was it because they had beautiful voices, because they didn't. It was because they had that wonderful, electric vibrancy which made me happy, and I knew it would make everyone else happy, too.

GEORGE MARTIN
Interview
LONDON, DATE UNKNOWN

Question: What was your initial impression of the Beatles' sound?

George Martin: It really wasn't very good, but it was raucous and had vitality. We at Parlophone were Brian Epstein's last desperate try. He had already been 'round every label in the business, including EMI. I invited the boys down to London for a recording test and they played things like "Your Feets Too Big" and "Over the Rainbow." Awful! But I liked them immensely as people.

Question: What was it like to be "the Fifth Beatle"?

George: I don't like the term. It sounds like I'm living on the fading glory of a previous success. I still relish the excitement and immediacy of making records. I've produced for Jeff Beck, John Williams, Neil Sedaka, and the Mahavishnu Orchestra, amongst others. Concerning the Beatles, there have been all sorts of innuendoes. that I was the musical guru behind them; that they were puppets hanging on my string. It was unfair to them and it's unfair to me. We were a team of five. We all put our oar in, but I didn't control them creatively. I was an old man to them. They knew I was a square, I didn't see why I had to be like the rest of the bloody sycophants, hanging around trying to get into the scene. I wasn't privy to their most intimate moments, but we lasted a long time. And that's why! We respected each other and joked with each other. "Success hasn't changed you," I used to tell them. "You're still the arrogant, self-opinionated bastards that you always were!"

Question: Can you tell me about AIR?

George: Well, in 1963 I had a record at number one for thirty-seven of the fifty-two weeks. I had Cilla, Billy J., Gerry, and, of course, the boys. EMI, who were so conservative they considered me a maverick, made profits of £2,200,000 in twelve months on my records, and I got my salary of £3,000. No car, no Christmas bonus. So, by 1965, I decided to leave to form Associated Independent Recording (AIR). The Beatles came with me and it was a great relief to be able to choose for myself what to do.

Question: You produced all of the Beatles' records?

George: From "Love Me Do" through to the final album, which is my favorite, *Abbey Road*. The Beatles thing didn't end, it just sort of evaporated. *The Hollywood Bowl* album was a labor of love.

PETER BROWN*
Interview
TORONTO, 1983

Question: To your knowledge, did any of the Beatles ever consciously put backwards messages in their music?

Peter Brown: Never.

Question: Do you think the breakup of the Beatles could have been avoided or at least postponed for a few years?

Peter: If Brian hadn't died, you mean?

Question: If any number of things hadn't happened—if Paul had been a little cooler and dug Yoko a bit more. . . .

Peter: Paul *tried* to dig Yoko, but it wasn't really possible to dig her at the time. She was just thrust at us, and there was no way you could take to Yoko much in those days.

Question: Is it true that in 1969, when Paul left the group, the Beatles

*Peter Brown was the Beatles' personal assistant throughout their heady Apple days in Liverpool and London.

considered replacing him with Klaus Voorman on bass and Billy Preston on keyboards?

Peter: No.

Question: I wonder if you could say anything about John and Yoko's wedding in Gibraltar?

Peter: The thing people don't realize is that John and Yoko were very hurt at that time, largely through their own fault. They'd made themselves the center of a media circus, and whatever they did was causing them derision in many ways. The romance relationship and love between them was *very* sincere, and they wanted to get married in a special way. John, particularly, had wanted to get married for quite a long time. I'd been in Holland one weekend when he called me up and said, "Hey, that's a great idea, you stay in Holland, and we'll come over and get married there," but I said, "No, you can't do that, John." And then when Paul tried to get married secretly, it became a media circus, so John and Yoko were all the more determined not to have to go through that. That's when he insisted to me, "Find somewhere fast that I can get married without any problems." Well, I tried *everywhere,* but then I discovered that Gibraltar was in the peculiar situation of being part of the British setup and remote enough that there wasn't any press corps.

Question: How did the 1977 death of Mal Evans affect the Beatles?

Peter: The only knowledge I have of Mal's death is what John Lennon told me. I went by for tea one day at the Dakota, and he said to me, "Did you know that Mal has been killed?" All Neil Aspinall did was to confirm John's story. Apparently Mal was getting into very bad shape and was shot by the Los Angeles Police Department, and his ashes were lost in the mail.

Question: Was John upset about it? Was Mal a very close buddy of his?

Peter: Yes, he was very upset about it. But he also thought it was ironic that the ashes should be lost. He couldn't help but think that was funny. Poor Mal.

Question: Was he at all like the image we've been given to understand over the years?

Peter: Oh yes, he was a lovely great bear of a man. He went from fixing phone transformer boxes to Shea Stadium—that's what Neil always said.

Question: President of Apple Records for a time, wasn't he?

Peter: I don't remember that. Not while I was there!

BILLY PRESTON*
Selected Quotations on The Beatles
1992

"It was heartbreaking to see [the Beatles] going through [the break up]. But they realized they had been messed over as far as business goes. What happened was, John had run into Allen Klein, and he was convinced Klein could pull everything together. And Paul said, 'Well, let's check him out first.' John was sure of Allen, and Paul said he wasn't coming back to the studio any more."

"They asked me would I like to be on Apple Records. I was with Capitol at the time. The next day I went to the studio and they said, 'You're on Apple.' Which was great as it gave me a chance to produce for the first time and also be able to sing, because most of my albums before that were just instrumental. George Harrison did most of the coproducing with me. Originally, it was supposed to have been all four Beatles producing a couple of songs for me, but that's when all the disturbances came up. So everybody kind of split up. But me and George hung in there."

"I remember working on Ringo's album [*Ringo*] and John and George being there. It was the first time in a long time they had been in the

---

*Keyboardist Billy Preston played extensively with the Beatles during their final days together. Recently, he has successfully overcome a serious drug dependency, but still faces a problematic future due to his years of abuse.

studio together. So they were all sitting around saying, 'It would be great to go out on the road, but also have other musicians in the band.' Ironically, John said it would be too much like starting over. That's long before he wrote the song."

"John used to always crack me up. The funny thing about John, he would just do anything he felt like, you know? He'd be playing and then he'd go sit on the piano. Yoko would follow him. Wherever he went, Yoko was right up under him. It was kind of funny to see that. We did a show once with the Plastic Ono Band and Yoko was in a black bag. We were all jamming for about ten minutes and she was rolling around on the stage."

"George is wonderful. Well, they're all really good people. George is very spiritual. He's a very loving and humble person. He's a very good friend and like a brother to me. I've spent a lot of time with him. We had a good time at his house, just playing and going out in the garden.

"I haven't seen him very much. I saw him when I was doing the Ringo tour. He came to a press conference. In fact, he thought I was still living in New York. But I still love him. We're so close, we think about each other and know that we both still care. We don't have to see each other every day to feel that."

DAVID PEEL*
Selected Quotations on John Lennon
New York, 1990

"I used to go over to Bank Street a lot to jam, especially to eat dinner. I knew a good free meal when I saw one. Yoko was a terrific cook of macrobiotic food. Nobody would bother him when he was with us. Allen Klein said to Lennon the reason he liked hanging around me was because Peel did everything Lennon was afraid to do himself. That's what

---

*David Peel is the eccentric street performer who captured the attention of John and Yoko in the early seventies. He recorded one album on the Apple label, *The Pope Smokes Dope*. David Peel was an Apple Recording artist and occasional friend of John Lennon.

I did. I brought out the side of John that just wanted to go crazy and party all night. But the bodyguards . . . he was cynical and mistrustful. A lot of people wanted handouts. He was paranoid about it."

"When you are close to John Lennon, the guy's so powerful and aware of world events you start losing your own identity. Being so close to him for a year or so was good and bad, you know. As soon as the carriage turned back into a pumpkin, Cinderella was a housemaid. When you're with John Lennon, you're a prince. When this trendy thing is over, you go home a pumpkin. Twelve midnight and you're back in your rags doing what you did before. Like me."

DAVID PEEL
Interview
NEW YORK, NOVEMBER 17, 1996

Question: Where were you when you first heard the Beatles?

David Peel: I was in the United States Army in Anchorage, Alaska. I was vaguely aware of the Beatles, but I'd heard "I Want to Hold Your Hand" on the radio and didn't know who the Beatles were, being seven thousand miles away in the middle of Nowhere, Alaska, in the tundra. I heard "I Want to Hold Your Hand" and it struck me like lightning. I thought they were an American band. I didn't know they had long hair, because I was in the military and long hair was totally out. The sons turned me on—it ripped away the boredom of the routine of serving my country. It energized me to the point my curiosity overwhelmed me, and I had to find out who they were. They were from England, where I'd never heard rock'n'roll from before. My naiveté allowed me to accept the Beatles from what I had heard, rather than the stereotypes laid out by their promotion.

Question: What do you believe to be their most important work?

David: Without a doubt, *Sgt. Pepper.* You've got to give credit to Paul McCartney for initiating the idea. I don't care how great Frank Lloyd

Wright is—if he doesn't have builders to create his architecture, he has nothing. It has to be *Sgt. Pepper* for a few reasons: (a) They were able to promote a concept outside of the Beatles; (b) the grand design of the cover, even the jacket was outside themselves and a complete work of art; (c) it was the first album I'd ever seen where the lyrics were actually printed. It's amazing George Martin was able to record the thing on four tracks. You can't do a decent record with four tracks at home, and to this day it holds its own technically. Remember, when Michelangelo and da Vinci painted, they didn't have the high-tech materials we have today. It is the Beatles' greatest work and will hold its own forever. Up there with Beethoven's "Fifth Symphony" will be *Sgt. Pepper's Lonely Hearts Club Band!* We waited months for it to come out. When it did, it was more than I ever expected. I came away thinking of the Beatles as masters of their art and intellectuals amongst the greatest of all geniuses.

Question: You later sang with Lennon on stage and produced some of John and Yoko's work.

David: I played in the Plastic Ono Band with John and Yoko at the One-to-One benefit in December of 1971. I was also on the *David Frost Show* in January 1972, where the Lennons were in my backup band, the Lower East Side. It was David Peel and the Lower East Side Super Apple Band and the Plastic Ono Band with John and Yoko. I also played with them in Andover, Michigan, in December 1971, and John played in my band in January 1972. He also did the soundtrack to my movie *Please Stand By*. John gave me two songs, including "Sometime in New York City" and "America," which Yoko sang with me.

Question: What is your overall impression of the Beatles' *Anthology*, especially the two new songs "Free as a Bird" and "Real Love"?

David: The *Anthology* is history. The *Anthology* is very good in that it gives you insight into how the Beatles worked and how great they were without the makeup of publicity. I have *The White Album* all done acoustically, it's excellent. Now "Real Love" and "Free as a Bird" use technology to keep it authentic without John, and I appreciate that. *The Anthology* gave the world a legacy that won't soon be washed away.

What you saw of John Lennon on *The Lost Lennon Tapes,* you now see for all four.

Question: Which do you like better, "Free as a Bird" or "Real Love"?

David: "Free as a Bird" I enjoyed very much.

Question: What did you think of the television series?

David: I've always loved history. Unfortunately, Generation X has no real leaders at all. They have no one to follow, no one to emulate. The Beatles' series shows what we did before, so that people can say, "There was something positive in the world!"

RITCHIE YORK*
Interview
Toronto, 1982

Geoffrey: How did you first become associated with John?

Ritchie York: Well, in 1968 he was starting to move away from the Beatles and doing things by himself, like the Plastic Ono Band. I was working for the *Globe and Mail* in Toronto, so I wanted to interview John and find out about his various activities.

Geoffrey: Let me ask you about Apple. What kind of place was it?

Ritchie: It was chaos. It was a great *idea,* very groovy, but in a practical sense it was absurd. A lot of the employees were milking it dry. It was a giant game. Swinging London was at its height and the ultimate thing to do was to work at Apple.

Geoffrey: You were around the Beatles when they were beginning to realize that Apple was never going to work, is that right?

Ritchie: Yeah, it was starting to go a bit sour. There were some very unpleasant meetings with everyone shouting and screaming at each

*Ritchie York was the Lennons' one-time personal assistant and a journalist of note.

other. John was trying to get Allen Klein in as their manager, but Paul wanted his father-in-law, Lee Eastman, running things. It was a very dodgy scene.

Geoffrey: How did John relate to you his feelings about the Beatles?

Ritchie: The Beatles were over as far as John was concerned. Phil Spector was remixing *Let It Be*, and none of them even showed up at any of the sessions, because no one really liked the album. John simply didn't want to be a part of it anymore. And of course they couldn't be bothered doing the sort of thing he wanted to do. They were always off on holiday somewhere, it seemed. The drive of the group had almost completely gone by late 1968. *Abbey Road* was basically done with each of the guys in the studio separately. It wasn't a group effort anymore. As a matter of fact, Paul put together that whole medley on side two almost entirely on his own.

Geoffrey: How were John and Paul interacting at this point?

Ritchie: It was very bitter. John wouldn't go near Paul. John always sent Ringo to do any dirty work with Paul.

Geoffrey: Surely Yoko was a catalyst in the breakup, wasn't she?

Ritchie: Not really. That's not to say, however, that John didn't impose her presence on them. He certainly did. During the filming of *Let It Be*, for instance, John would never have been there if Yoko wasn't included, and that, of course, helped build the Beatles' resentment against her. It wasn't Yoko's idea to try and snuggle up to the Beatles. John wanted to demonstrate his independence from the Beatles in a very practical way. He was basically saying, "Hey, I do what I like boys, and you do what you like." That was his attitude.

Geoffrey: How did you go from simply interviewing a guy to becoming one of his closest associates?

Ritchie: We just happened to hit it off, I guess. Actually, I realized that John wanted to make some serious statements with his music in the face of everything that was happening in the late sixties, and I wanted to lend a hand if I could.

Geoffrey: So give me a typical day in the life of John Lennon during the final days of the Apple kingdom.

Ritchie: Well, they'd drive in from Tittenhurst Park and arrive at the office at around eleven o'clock in the morning. Then they'd usually just stay for the afternoon and see people they felt were important to the youth movement. For example, Tom Donahue, the guy who started underground radio, came by a few times, as did Ken Kesey and the poet Richard Brautigan. Everyone would be trying to hit on them in those days. Remember, John and Yoko were the world's most famous couple. They also had a few friends from the media who dropped in occasionally, like Ray Connolly from the *Evening Standard.* It was a real zoo. Very often some kid with an idea would get John's ear (if he happened to be there when the phones had stopped ringing), and John would invariably give him his shot.

Geoffrey: John and Yoko traveled to Denmark in 1970. Did you accompany them?

Ritchie: They went to Denmark to meet with Yoko's ex-husband, Anthony Cox, and see Yoko's daughter, Kyoko. We all stayed at his farmhouse in the middle of this great snowy expanse in the Jutland region of Denmark. Cox made the two of them go through a kind of purification process before he'd allow them to see Kyoko. So they fasted for a few days, meditated, and some guy named Dr. Don Hamrik, who fancied himself a warlock, tried to hypnotize them into giving up smoking. John and I had to sneak outside whenever he wanted a smoke! Last, but not least, Cox somehow managed to talk them into getting their hair chopped off in celebration of the new decade. So I arranged for this lady barber called Aasse Hankrogh to come out from the hotel in Aalborg and do the job. The next morning every paper in the world carried the story in banner headlines!

Geoffrey: What were John's spiritual beliefs at that time?

Ritchie: He was into peace and human beings. A very intense humanist.

Geoffrey: Tell me about the Bed-In in Montreal. What did they hope to accomplish with that?

Ritchie: Publicity for peace. Remember, they couldn't get into the States, but they wanted to get their message across to the nerve centers of the world. In England they were considered a bad joke by the media, so they couldn't very well do it there. They did a Bed-In in Amsterdam originally, but the idea was always to get the attention of America. They flew down to the Bahamas, but it was too hot there to stay in bed for a week and a bit too far removed from the American press corps, so they settled for Montreal. It was about as close as they could get.

Geoffrey: You traveled on your own quite a bit for John during the campaign, right?

Ritchie: Ronnie Hawkins and I both went around the world spreading John's peace message. The idea was to try and set up John and Yoko centers everywhere so that we could produce their events internationally. We planned on using Telstar at one point in order to syndicate things like the peace festival. Anyway, in Hong Kong, someone at a press conference said, "Okay, it's fine telling us all this, we think peace is great, but why don't you go and tell the Red Chinese!" So we said, "Sure," and had one of the locals paint up a couple of "WAR IS OVER" signs for us. We climbed into an old beat-up Volkswagen with a local reporter named Sybil Wong and a couple of photographers and drove down to the first border checkpoint at Lockmachau. Somehow or other, we managed to convince the guards to let us pass, and we just drove right up to the top of this hill, which was the Chinese no-man's-land. Anyway, we held up the signs facing China, and, of course, immediately all the guards rushed out and were going to arrest us. We talked our way out of that one, but the strange thing was, the next day the CIA confiscated all our film, as they somehow thought that this little peace protest might escalate into an international incident. Incidentally, a week later someone was shot simply for standing in the same area!

Geoffrey: Were you aware of that possibility before you went in?

Ritchie: Oh, yes. I didn't care, but Ronnie Hawkins was a little worried about it. Remember, this was long before anyone from the West had gone into China, not even the ping pong players!

Geoffrey: How did John react?

Ritchie: He thought it was the greatest thing that happened on the entire trip!

Geoffrey: Tell me about the infamous Mosport Park John and Yoko Peace Festival.

Ritchie: Well, the original idea was to hold the biggest music festival of all time.

Geoffrey: Of course all the Beatles were going to be there.

Ritchie: Yes, George had agreed, Ringo certainly would have done it, and Paul was yet to be confirmed, but John was very hopeful. The intention was to get every major rock star in the world there. Even Elvis was going to do it!

Geoffrey: Was it to be a free festival or were people expecting to be paid?

Ritchie: John wanted everyone to get some money. He figured that no one should be working for nothing, but they were certainly free to donate some of it back into a big peace fund if they wanted to. The main problem with the festival was the total lack of any real organization. It was such a mammoth undertaking that eventually it was buried under the strain of its own weight.

Geoffrey: Whose idea was it to hold the festival?

Ritchie: Mainly mine, but the whole thing was being handled by the Brower and Walker Agency out of Toronto. I went for the idea because, after the incredible success of Woodstock, a beautiful sequel devoted to world peace was absolutely the right thing to be doing. Eventually, I took off with Ronnie on this global peace tour and by the time we got back, John and Yoko were becoming pretty disenchanted with the whole thing.

Geoffrey: Tell me about John and Yoko's meeting with Canadian Prime Minster Pierre Trudeau. Did you arrange it?

Ritchie: Yes, we talked to Ottawa from the Bag office quite a few times in order to sound them out.

Geoffrey: Could John get through to anyone in the world he wanted to?

Ritchie: Yes, but until that time no political leader had ever met with him. In England, John and Yoko were generally regarded as a big joke. Somehow they managed to antagonize the old establishment something terrible. He had to get through to a prominent politician to lend credibility to his movement and, of course, we were hoping to try and wrangle an endorsement. Trudeau was willing to meet them as long as there was no advance publicity, so we did it and then announced it afterwards.

Geoffrey: Beyond the publicity, what was the meeting all about?

Ritchie: Just to talk about peace and music.

Geoffrey: How was Trudeau disposed towards John and Yoko?

Ritchie: Very friendly. He thought the whole thing was great and even offered the use of the Canadian army for security! John was extremely nervous, having never actually met a world leader on a one-to-one basis before. But afterwards he felt fantastic.

Geoffrey: What do you think John would have to say about the nature of his death?

Ritchie: I think he expected it in a way. There was always the chance it would happen. John was a very misunderstood guy and a sincere, dedicated man, as well as a great humanitarian. He believed things didn't really have to be the way they are. Things could be different if people really set their minds to it. All any of us can do now is to try and keep John's spirit alive.

COLONEL TOM PARKER*
Telegram to Brian Epstein
LOS ANGELES, AUGUST 17, 1964

Brian Epstein
Hilton Hotel, San Francisco

Dear Mr. Epstein,
On behalf of Elvis and myself, welcome to the USA. Our sincere good wishes for a successful tour and a wonderful trip to all your engagements. If there is anything I can be of service with as a friend, do not hesitate to call on me. There isn't much I can do as I have been laid up for several weeks with a back ailment. But my efforts will be to be of some help if need be. Give my best to Chris Hutchins and if you have time, give me a call when you come to town.

Sincerely,
The Colonel

ELVIS PRESLEY
Bad-mouthing the Beatles
DECEMBER 21, 1970

Memorandum for: The President's file, Richard M. Nixon
Subject: Meeting with Elvis Presley, Monday, 12:30 P.M.

The meeting opened with pictures taken of the President and Elvis Presley.

Presley immediately began showing the President his law enforcement paraphernalia, including badges from police departments in California, Colorado, and Tennessee. Presley indicated he had been playing Las Vegas, and the President indicated he was aware of how difficult it is to perform in Vegas.

*Colonel Tom Parker was Elvis Presley's longtime manager.

The President mentioned he thought Presley could reach young people, and that it was important for Presley to retain his credibility. Presley responded that he did his thing by "just singing." He said that he could not get to the kids if he made a speech on the stage, that he had to reach them his own way. The President nodded in agreement.

Presley indicated he thought the Beatles had been a real force for anti-American spirit. The President nodded in agreement and expressed some surprise. The President then indicated that those who use drugs are also those in the vanguard of anti-American protest. Violence, drug usage, dissent, protest all seem to merge in generally the same group of young people.

Presley indicated to the President in a very emotional manner that he was "on your side." Presley kept repeating that he wanted to be helpful and wanted to restore some respect for the flag which was being lost. He mentioned he was just a poor boy from Tennessee who had gotten a lot from his country, which in some way he wanted to repay. He also mentioned he has been studying Communist brainwashing and the drug culture for over ten years. He mentioned that he knew a lot about this and was accepted by the hippies. He said he could go right into a group of young people (or hippies) and be accepted, which he felt could be helpful to the war on drugs. The President indicated again his concern that Presley retain his crediblity.

ELVIS PRESLEY
FBI Memo
January 4, 1971

From: M. A. Jones
Subject: Elvis Presley
         William N. Morris
         Former Sheriff, Shelby County, Tennessee
         Bureau tour 31-12-70

Presley indicated he is of the opinion that the Beatles laid the groundwork for many of the problems we are having with young people by their filthy unkempt appearance and suggestive music while entertaining in his country during the early and middle 1960s. He advised that the Smothers Brothers, Jane Fonda, and other persons in the entertainment industry of their ilk have a lot to answer for in the hereafter for the way they have poisoned young minds by disparaging the United States in their public statements and unsavory activities.

ROGER RUSKIN SPEAR*
Interview
LONDON, 1984

Roger Ruskin Spear: You've heard of Bruce Lacey?

Geoffrey: No.

Roger: You've heard of Ivor Cutler, but not Bruce Lacey, that's interesting.

Geoffrey: The only reason I've heard of Ivor is because of the *Magical Mystery Tour*. [Ivor Cutler played the part of Buster Bloodvessel.]

Roger: Ah, yes. But Bruce Lacey was the gardener in the Beatles' house in *Help*.

Geoffrey: That's right, he mowed the carpet with those little clattering teeth, didn't he?

Roger: Right. You've hear of the Alberts? Well, Ivor used to play with the Alberts.

Question: How did your band, the Bonzos, come to know the Beatles?

Roger: At the time Lennon had seen the New Vaudeville Band and they wanted a funny band for *Magical Mystery Tour,* in the nightclub scene. Now we knew Mike McCartney and the Scaffold from doing university shows. The Scaffold were sort of bubbling under and bands that bubble under tend to meet at universities. So we were always doing the

---

*Roger Ruskin Spear was formally a member of the Bonzo Dog Do Dah Band. He owes this author twenty quid.

same venues. Anyway, Mike said to his brother, "You want the Bonzos, not the Vaudeville Band." They said, "Who are these Bonzos? We've never heard of them." So anyway, we got the job on *Magical Mystery Tour* and that's how we met. We were asked to play at the wrap party — John Lennon personally invited us. We were up north doing some wretched gig when our management rang up and said we'd been invited to the Beatles' party and "by the way they want you to perform. Unfortunately, you can't go because you're due in Worthington"! So complete explosions went on and Brian Somerville, our publicist said, "Oh, you guys have got to do it. I could never get together a publicity party like this." So we moved heaven and earth and it cost us a fortune. We went down and did it, but in the end it didn't really do us any good at all. It was just a big booze up with John Lennon throwing up in the loo and all that sort of thing. But from then on I suppose, we knew the Beatles.

Geoffrey: There was, I believe, a big jam at the end of that do with the Beatles and Bonzos.

Roger: It wasn't so much the Beatles . . . .

Geoffrey: Lennon?

Roger: He may have done. I think his main contribution was that he decided we'd better do our act. The Beatles said, "Would you like to play? You can play for a bit." Of course, at any binge like that, full of show-biz people no one really wants to know. So we started doing our act and Larry ['Legs' Larry Smith] came on with these plastic boobs and John yelled out, "Put 'em away, Larry, we've all seen them!" From that point on we all thought "forget it!" Then one of the Beach Boys got up with Lulu so we just sashayed into a Beach Boys tune. Yes, I think the stage eventually filled with people, Lennon could have gotten up. I remember Carl Wilson and the Bee Gees, a lot of people were there. But I don't remember Ringo, I think John Lennon was mainly shouting. It's all he was capable of.

Geoffrey: Do you think the Fabs were a cut above their peers?

Roger: No, they were just regular blokes who happened to make it.

They really didn't know what they were doing at all. It's just that everything they touched turned to gold for some reason. This particular party was dreadful. At that stage it was terribly boring.

Geoffrey: What did you go as?

Roger: Ourselves.

Geoffrey: But everyone wore a costume.

Roger: *They* did, but we were the Bonzos! Everyone was so trying to be mad and outrageous. It was a thing to drag the wife along to—a must-see. Later, when Paul came along to produce our record, "I'm the Urban Spaceman," he knew exactly what he wanted. He was talking to the engineer saying, "Well, when we did such and such, we were in the red, pushing this and doing so and so. Can you do that?" And the engineer said, "No." He seemed to know the sound he wanted, though. The Bonzos were six artists working together, all wanting to do our own thing. Just imagine telling six artists to paint the same picture in red. The good thing about Paul doing the record was that everyone naturally listened to him.

Geoffrey: I believe you didn't want it known that Paul had anything to do with it, so you listed the producer as one Apollo C. Vermouth.

Roger: Yes, but Paul didn't really want it known either. He certainly did have the golden touch alright. I don't know what he did, but suddenly it sounded more like a proper record. He was playing the ukulele. At the time we had an American playing bass, Joel, he was trying his best, but McCartney went out, and said, "You do this." Of course all the engineers were bored, reading their papers, after hearing the same thing over and over again. He wouldn't actually play it himself though. Viv, Paul, and another ukulele player played in a corridor, but I think they turned Paul's up a bit louder. After the session Larry wanted badly to be seen next to Paul McCartney and I remember Paul saying, "Cheerio, lads, it was great. Thanks very much." Our manager was saying, "Can we have a meal, Paul?" He said, "No, I've really got to go." There he was, strolling down the road with Larry still walking beside him, not really thinking about anything, but trying desperately to be noticed. "Hey, it's Paul McCartney and I'm walking next to him!" He carried on walking all the way down Bond Street, the rest of us just fell about in a heap laughing at Larry trying to be seen next to Beatle Paul McCartney. I mean, if Larry had had a photographer he would have paid him a thousand pounds to take some pictures. And that was it. Paul went off and I never saw him again.

Geoffrey: That's Larry, I guess, with his "I'm a great big showbiz star!"

Roger: Yes, that was his act. That was all he ever really did in the band, and obviously it worked well. A lot of people, however, quickly saw through that. When I used to say I was in the Bonzos, they'd say, "What a load of shit, that. Bloody Larry Smith, God, and all that rubbish!"

MAHARISHI MAHESH YOGI*
Interview
THE NETHERLANDS, DECEMBER 24, 1992

Geoffrey: Many of us first heard of you back in the late sixties. To what do you attribute the renaissance of desire for a spiritually more profound way of life we experienced back then? Do you see that as a special time in any way?

Maharishi Mahesh Yogi: That was the time that this complete knowledge [Transcendental Meditation] started to be found in the market. Before it was in the Himalayas or was difficult to be found here and there, but then it started to float in the market. That was the sixties and seventies and, since then, now it's almost a household word.

Geoffrey: Recently in London there was a benefit for your Natural Law Party, which was headlined by your old friend George Harrison.

Maharishi: Yes, I heard about it.

Geoffrey: Could you tell me how George came to be involved?

*His Holiness The Maharishi Mahesh Yogi was the Beatles' first and most controversial teacher. He continues to head a worldwide spiritual movement based in Switzerland.

Maharishi: Performers always look to opportunity. This was the first onset of a new field of politics, so he thought he would do it.

Geoffrey: Do you have special affection for George Harrison? He's certainly meant a lot to people for many years now. How do you see Mr. Harrison?

Maharishi: I see him as an exceptional musician in his own talent, whatever the effect. He has become popular, and I attribute this to his talent and also to the British press in telling us [about him]. The British press is very intelligent to promote their national values.

Geoffrey: But Mr. Harrison has used popular music to promote the tenets and philosophy of Transcendental Meditation and spirituality. Surely you must applaud him for properly using the medium to help enlighten the world?

Maharishi: I was happy when he started to meditate. I knew he would make a big impression in the world as soon as he started to meditate. That's how the talents grow with this program. All the world of artists and all the different values, the whole society has taken a good turn.

SHAMBU DAS*
Interview
TORONTO, 1982

Geoffrey: Shambu, how did you meet George Harrison?

Shambu Das: I first met him in Bombay in 1966. He came around with Ravi Shankar. All the Beatles were great admirers of Ravi from listening to his records. The Beatles met Ravi at a party at Peter Sellers' home. After that evening, George wanted to learn to play sitar. At the time, I was looking after some of Ravi's business affairs, so I advised George to come along and learn if he wanted to. I was teaching regularly at Ravi's school, and Ravi suggested I personally look after

*Shambu Das was George Harrison's day-to-day sitar instructor in India during the mid-sixties. He lives today in Toronto, where he teaches sitar and performs widely.

George's progress. Once in a while Ravi would come in and see how the lessons were going. He used to sit in and teach George occasionally.

Geoffrey: What about the young Indian fans—were they just as enthusiastic as the reports you'd received on Beatlemania?

Shambu: Oh, they wanted to see him, all right. But he wanted privacy to study his music, and they soon began to hassle him. First we were staying at the Taj Mahal Hall Hotel. We kept changing his room, but people were still bothering him. Finally, we decided to leave the city and find a really isolated place to practice. So I said, "Let's go to Kashmir—there is this nice lake I know surrounded by hills, and there's some fancy houseboats available." So George rented a very luxurious houseboat—it had a lovely living room, dining room, master bedroom, and, of course, was very nicely decorated. We lived there almost seven weeks.

Geoffrey: He was just beginning to learn to play the sitar. Was this his first real exposure?

Shambu: Yes, he loved it. Earlier he put some of the Beatles' music to the sitar. Later, when he started learning to play, he became much more serious. He knew what the technique involved and he became very sober about it. Ravi Shankar used to come by once in a while. We would all sit and practice together. We had a fantastic time. Pattie, his first wife, was there—she was very friendly to everyone. We used to visit some Hindu temples in the area, then we'd come back home and practice.

Geoffrey: Was he a good student?

Shambu: He was *very* intelligent. He used to put in seven or eight hours a day of practice. Later, after he left, he started writing to me about how much he'd really enjoyed his visit to India. He wanted to do this *Wonderwall* album and needed help from me. He wanted to record it in India. When George came around, that meant all the big shots were always popping up. I was taking care of all the musical elements— that's what I was mainly responsible for. I played sitar and several of my friends played other Indian instruments. George and I were consulting on a lot of things. How he should do this or that, throwing things back and forth. We recorded for almost a week, and while he was there he started to use his hands to eat. The first time he did it was in my house—we'd sit on the floor and eat Indian-style together. He loved it—he was a good friend. Anyway, that was his second visit. The third time, all the Beatles came to the Maharishi for training in Transcendental Meditation. At that time I was busy with Ravi Shankar's movie, *Raga*. I was assigned to do some work on that, and there was a whole crew from New York that came over. I think it was Columbia Pictures and Apple Films doing it. At the same time, George wanted me to visit him in Rishikesh. I went, but couldn't stay for long. I was only there four days, but the Maharishi was very interested in me, and one day as he was sitting and talking to the Beatles he said, "We would like you to come work for us." But I knew that Ravi was in another pot philosophically and he had a different opinion on these matters.

Geoffrey: How did George feel about that? He has said he always felt that Ravi was like a father to him, and yet he went to study with the Maharishi?

Shambu: That is what I'm trying to say. They both had a very different view of life in those days, but I still stayed for awhile.

Geoffrey: Why did the Beatles come to the Maharishi—what was their interest?

Shambu: The Maharishi made a lovely space for them in his ashram on top of a very beautiful hill. I don't know how he ever arranged to get all of this together. Even the bungalow I was given was fully outfitted by American standards. A lot of reporters were there because of the Beatles as well. There were dozens of press people around. I stayed about three nights, but I had to get back for the filming of *Raga* with Ravi. I met the Beatles there and they were all very intelligent. One night I played a private concert for the Beatles, their girlfriends, and the Maharishi in a lovely room reserved for the Beatles' personal use. The next day I wanted to leave, but the Maharishi was so impressed with me he started saying I should try and stay on a bit longer. He wanted to get some newspaper men to sit down and talk Indian philosophy with me. That evening as I was leaving he said, "Please, Shambu, come back again," and George seemed very happy. The Beatles were completely devoted to the Maharishi back then. On the plane home, I met this big industrialist from Bombay, and he asked me if I saw that morning's paper. There was a headline that one of Ravi Shankar's very close associates had bowed down to the Maharishi as if he had become his disciple. "Well," I said, "this is the Indian custom. When you meet a religious person you should always touch their feet, and that's what I did." Anyway, I flew on to Calcutta to join some people from Columbia Pictures. Ravi was coming home from Japan that day, and all the crew were at the airport waiting to take some footage of his arrival. After we finished shooting, Shankar, his lawyer, and myself were in the car driving to the hotel when I noticed he was acting a bit stiff. I didn't realize he had already seen something in the Japanese newspapers about me visiting the Maharishi. I said, "Why are you so upset?" and he said, "How was your ashram visit?" In a very funny way, you know, so I said, "It was very good," and he said, "I saw the item in the paper—so what is your plan now, Shambu?" "There was no plan, Ravi—I just visited the Beatles, that's all."

Geoffrey: Were they writing any songs while they were there?

Shambu: They were certainly meditating and learning the Maharishi's philosophy, but I didn't hear any songs, no.

Geoffrey: How long did they stay?

Shambu: They stayed, I think, for three or four weeks. All the while we were shooting *Raga* in different cities for ten days. Then, all of a sudden, we got a cable that George was coming down to see us in Southern India. He was apparently disturbed for some reason, but I still don't know exactly what happened. He just wanted to talk with Ravi Shankar alone. So Shankar took him to some very isolated place and they spent a couple of days together, and then George started feeling better. Then everyone ran away from us and I didn't know why. I was there at the ashram only two weeks before and they were very happy, but in just a few days' time everything had changed completely.

Geoffrey: Why did the Beatles come to India? What were they looking for?

Shambu: I felt they were looking for something in their life beyond reputation and money. They were looking for some kind of peace of mind.

Geoffrey: Were you ever in England with George?

Shambu: I was with George in his castle once in Henley-on-Thames during the late sixties. He had just bought it only a month before, so he and Pattie hadn't settled in very well. He picked me up from Heathrow Airport and we went to see his castle. He told me his plans to build a recording studio and generally fix up the house. I was there for just two days. After that, most of the time we talked on the telephone.

Geoffrey: You played on *Wonderwall*—did you record on any other projects with George?

Shambu: No, after that he didn't use the sitar, because he became so involved with guitar and he understood the seriousness of playing sitar. He's still a great admirer of Indian music, though. He likes to listen to it, but after the lessons he wanted to play it only as it should be played. But he was doing some very good sitar-playing himself, the way we play it in India.

Geoffrey: Did he progress to a very high level of excellence?

Shambu: Yes, to quite a fine level. You could see he was advancing very quickly. But later he wanted to come back to his other music. He just couldn't give enough time to sit down and practice properly everyday. I think that bothered him.

Geoffrey: Maybe you can talk about the "Concert for Bangladesh." I know you were involved in that.

Shambu: I was in Montreal at the time, and I got a call that George wanted me in New York to help with the concert. He was going to perform a benefit for the various war-relief programs aiding the refugees from Pakistan and Bangladesh. Ravi and George planned the shows to raise some money to try and help them. The day before the concert, I arrived in New York and a big limousine was waiting to pick me up. I said to the driver, "Where am I going?" No answer—everything was very top secret! At the hotel where I was staying, the Central Park Plaza, I eventually met up with George's road manager, Mal Evans. Anyway, he comes to my room and says, "Shambu, you have to come quickly." "Great," I said. "Why?" "We have to change the atmosphere in George's room because everyone is very nervous about the show." Now I was always laughing and joking around with everyone in India. So I went up to George's room, and quite a few people were there—Bob Dylan, George, his father, sister, and Pattie, among others. George didn't see me come in, so I sneaked up behind him, put my hands over his eyes, and said, "Come on, tell me who it is!" And George says, "Hey, Shambu!" and everyone began to laugh. He was going to the final rehearsal and sound test at Madison Square Garden later that afternoon, so we had a quick lunch together and joked around a bit. His father was so happy, I remember—I'm sure I helped to break the tension. Then George says, "You're going to ride in my car, Shambu!" I said, "Sure, George," so I went along to the Garden and sat near the stage with his father and sister, Louise, listening to his music in the empty house.

Geoffrey: What did George confide to you about his involvement with the Hare Krishna Movement? Did you see any change in his life after he became friends with its founder, Srila Prabhupada?

Shambu: He changed, I think. He certainly stopped smoking quite a bit. George really like Prabhupada's philosophy. He was always talking about his spiritual life. He was definitely going in that direction. I guess of all the Beatles, he was probably the most serious about the spiritual side of things.

FRANCIE SCHWARTZ*
Quotation
APRIL 1974

"John obviously loved Paul enough to let him run wild if it would help ease the tension Paul was creating in the studio and at home. Yoko could see it, too.

*Francie Schwartz was Paul McCartney's live-in girlfriend in the late sixties. Today, she is a successful author and businesswoman.

"But Paul was treating them like shit, too. He even sent them a hate letter once, unsigned, typed. I brought it in with the morning mail. Paul put most of the fan mail in a big basket, and let it sit for weeks, but John and Yoko opened every piece. When they got to the anonymous note, they sat puzzled, looking at each other with genuine pain in their eyes.

"'You and your jap tart think you're hot shit,' it said. John put it on the mantel, and in the afternoon, Paul bopped in, prancing much the same self-conscious way he did when we met.

"'Oh I just did that for a lark . . .' he said, in his most sugarcoated accent.

"It was embarrassing. The three of us swiveled around, staring at him. You could see the pain in John. Yoko simply rose above it, feeling only empathy for John.

"I was sad to see the Lennons go, even though it took pressure off Paul."

BOB DYLAN ON JOHN LENNON
Selected Quotations
NEW YORK, 1967-1976

"The last time I went to London, I stayed at John Lennon's house. You should see all the stuff Lennon bought: big cars, a stuffed gorilla, and thousands of things in every room in his house, which obviously cost a fortune. When I got home I wondered what it would be like to have all those material things. I figured I had the money and I could do it, and I wondered if it would feel like anything real. So I bought all this stuff, filled my house with it and sat around in the middle of it all. I felt nothing."

1967

"John and Yoko add a great voice and drive to this country's so-called "art institution." They inspire, transcend, and stimulate, and by doing so, only help others to see pure light, and in doing that, put an end to this mild dull taste of petty commercialism which is being passed off as art by the overpowering mass media. Hurray for John and Yoko! Let them stay and live here and breathe."

1976

DENNY LAINE*
Interview
LONDON, 1977

Question: Whose idea was it to do an album of Buddy Holly songs?

Denny Laine: Originally, it was Linda's father, Lee Eastman, who suggested it, but I had the idea a long time ago to do something like that. I did one solo album before I joined the band, and if I was going to do something solo I wanted it to be a Buddy Holly album, or a folk album—something a bit different. But obviously it's not me leaving Wings to do a solo album—you don't get that feeling about it. It was Lee's original idea, but as I say, it's always been in the back of my mind. He just sparked it off.

Question: Why Holly?

Denny: Because I like his stuff. We were playing it back in the good old days—it was the first stuff I listened to.

Question: With respect, do you not think some of the more cynical journalists would question your motives, knowing that Paul owns the publishing to the Holly catalogue?

Denny: I'm sure they will. I mean, I could say I did a Buddy Holly album because we've got the copyright, but that's ridiculous—I wouldn't do it if I didn't like his stuff. It's as simple as that, so they can say what they like.

Question: Do you envisage doing an album of your own songs apart from Wings?

Denny: I did once, but I don't anymore. To explain that a bit, I'm writing with Paul now, all the time. I don't take my songs and finish them and give them to the group any more—I use a little bit of my songs and a little bit of Paul's ideas, and the same with his songs. If I did do a solo album it would first of all be holiday time, so I don't fancy it—I'm busy

*A founding member of The Moody Blues and Paul McCartney's copilot in the band Wings, Denny Laine has been a longtime associate of all the Beatles.

enough—but it would be a fun sort of thing at home really if I did it. This is how this Holly thing came about—it was just done in Scotland in a little shack, a place called Rude Studios.

Question: Why did you choose to do it in that form, rather than going into a studio with the musicians?

Denny: Because we were fed up with going into studios—that's all we ever do. This is just a little four-track studio—well, it wasn't really a studio. It was a shack which we hired stuff for and gave it a name.

Question: And it was only yourself and Paul that were actually involved?

Denny: Yes, Paul did the backing tracks, ninety percent of them, and then I just did my ten percent—little guitar and vocals.

Question: How long did it take?

Denny: It took about three weeks, I suppose—it was certainly no longer. Paul laid down all the backing tracks before I went in to do the vocals. In the morning he would be working on the backing, and I would go over in the afternoon and help him finish them off, and do vocals. Then we added more to the tracks, in a bigger studio. Not to add more ideas—just to make them a little more professional.

Question: How is it working with McCartney as a producer?

Denny: Well, I have worked with him for a long time. As a producer, he produces all the Wings stuff as well, so it's no problem.

Question: Is it any different with just yourself and Paul in the studio, compared with the whole group?

Denny: We get things done a lot quicker. Yes, of course, it means less people to be involved with.

Question: When do you think you will start doing another solo album, and what sort of project do you envisage?

Denny: Probably a folk album or something in that vein. Something like the Buddy Holly things, rough and ready. The same kind of thing, but a different style of music. That's what I want to do—something different. Different styles on each album I put out. But I haven't got any plans, really.

Question: And again, would you work with Paul as producer?

Denny: Oh, yes—I wouldn't dream of working with anybody else. No way. I can't see the point in that, you know. We have worked so long together, built up a very easy way of doing things and a very positive way of doing this, so if I worked with anybody else I would only be banging my head against a brick wall every night, saying how can I get across to these blokes.

Question: So you have a very easy communication with Paul?

Denny: Oh, yes. He knows what I want and knows what he is after. I know what he is capable of doing, and I wouldn't ask other people to do it, because not many people believe you can get certain sounds, or don't try, or don't have the experience or power to say, "This is what we want—let's get it!" He's got a lot of ideas a lot of producers don't have. Firstly, he knows my work, and secondly, I enjoy working with him.

Question: Can you encapsulate for me how you came to join forces with McCartney originally?

Denny: Oh, yes. I knew him from the Beatle days. After the Moodies and the String Band, trying to make it again, but not really going out of my way, as I was not getting the results, the kind that I wanted. I started to make this *Laine* album, but again, I wasn't being believed. Let's put it this way—I am the sort of person that if I am not believed, I'll become stubborn, to the point of being a maniac. It was just a mock-up to prove myself. Anyway, Paul happened to call me up, and it was the weekend that I had just finished some of the mixes from the album. So when he rang me up I just said, "Thank Christ for that—I have somebody to work with that I haven't got to explain everything to," so that was the decider, really. Just one of those things of fate.

Question: It has been a remarkable relationship, to say the least.

Denny: No problems, none whatsoever. I mean, we've probably had more problems with other people joining and leaving than I ever had with a band.

Question: Do you think people might misunderstand the motives for musicians within a group undertaking solo projects?

Denny: Lots of groups do it because there is an insecurity thing there. But I have never been like them. Say at the worst point, maybe things were difficult before we really established ourselves with the band. If I was going to leave at that time, which I wasn't, I am the type of person to leave and do something else. But stay is what I have done—but I would not have a group and give everything I've got and have something else waiting around in the background, because you can't do two things at once.

Question: Was it refreshing to do something on your own?

Denny: Yes, it was, but again it was within our involvement. Jimmy [McCulloch] has done some things outside the group, but I can't see the sense in that myself, because we have got a setup which is far superior to most. Business-wise included, and that is obviously the most important matter. I have never been insecure with this band, but obviously with the newer members there may be this problem, because it's not the easiest band in the world to stay with. That is because you've got a high standard that you want to be better each time, and a lot of people have got cold feet. In fact, they have regretted it, and I don't mind saying that, because I don't care what they have told the press. You might be able to buy yourself a new car, a new house, and then you would see how much work is involved, how much pressure there is, and you might start thinking, "I'd better put my money here and do this because I might not be around very long or make the album." Nobody really has another life within the group, because I just don't believe in it. To neglect Wings would be sacrilege.

JO JO LAINE
Letter to Lee Eastman
Written Near the End of Wings

London, December 6, 1979

Dear Lee,

Obviously, it doesn't seem to make the slightest bit of difference what people think of you or how much they respect you. I have nothing to gain (or lose) by letting you know my feelings about Denny's association with MPL. Not that you would care anyway! I may be married to the guy, but it certainly doesn't mean I have to be in the same trap (as he has) for the last eight years. Life goes on for me whether I get money telexed from the Eastmans, or not. It just really hurts to see Denny brainwashed into thinking he's a *star*, he's considered one of the Family, the money's coming in for him (as it has always been promised) . . . (bla bla bla), Denny will be payed *later* because it's all tied up with Apple etc. . . .

I've seen this going on around him since the day we met but, like Denny, I believed one day his loyalty to Wings would be rewarded. It seems very typical of you as a leader of the *pack* to lay down the law about certain advances. (As though Denny were a kid!)

I know myself what the "gentleman's agreement" was between Paul and Denny. I know that when Paul and Linda decide to pack it in with the group one day (which can't be too far off), they couldn't give a shit what happens to Denny. Paul was very crafty to marry into a family like yours. It's a perfect position to take people or leave 'em, whichever he chooses . . .

The times I've argued with Denny about this, and if ever I leave him it will be because of the respect I lose for him letting himself be used like this! You even try to bullshit *me!* You know damn well Denny has only been a highly payed musician with Wings. Nothing more, nothing less. Denny hasn't been looked upon as an individual artist or songwriter. Denny's very coyly reminded he wouldn't be anywhere, or making as much, if he wasn't playing with Paul McCartney. Big deal! "The money's good, so why complain?" It may be good, but it certainly is not what he deserves, and you know it. I honestly believe you never had any intention of changing Denny's role, contract or no contract (or any other member of Wings for that matter). It's really not too difficult to figure out why everyone has left the band. At the same time, neither is it such a bad job, playing for Wings and getting good money for it. That's if you don't have the confidence in yourself to move on to something more satisfying. Paul has certainly done a very good job in undermining Denny's confidence . . .

I always had an untrusting feeling about you when we met, remember? You never acknowledged me when I was standing beside Denny. Maybe I wasn't important enough for you?

I hate it when Denny's treated like a child who has to ask daddy for his allowance, not knowing if you'll say yes or no . . .

P.S. By the way, this letter may be used as evidence against me if you like, so I'll sign it Joanne Laine Hines Petrie.

STEVE HOLLY*
Interview
NEW YORK, 1984

Geoffrey: How did you come to join Wings?

Steve Holly: I was living in a village in England where I'd lived since I was about eight years old. Denny Laine moved into the same village and we became drinking buddies at the local pub. We had a few parties, and he didn't even know I played the drums until one evening, when there was nobody around that could play, so I sat in. He looked at me and said, "My God, I've known you all this time and didn't know you played." So then I did some solo work with him, but, more importantly, I did an album with Kiki Dee that Elton John produced. Later Elton asked me to play on the *Single Man* album, and, when I had done that, I think Denny realized I could hold down a professional gig, so he asked me to audition for Wings. When I was going to school, I used to get these little savings certificates for twenty-five cents and save them

*Steve Holly was Wings' final drummer, having joined in 1978.

up. I was saving for a drum kit of my own when I was only eight years old.

Geoffrey: Tell me about the audition. Did you feel apprehensive?

Steve: I was fine when I first got there. It was held in the basement of Paul's offices in Soho Square, and I was feeling great when I arrived with Denny. Laurence Juber and I were auditioning together, but I was a nervous wreck by the time he finally arrived, because I'd had hours of twitching in the cellar of this building just waiting for him. But after we got playing it was very comfortable, and he made me feel at ease, so we had a good time.

Geoffrey: What did you do, old rock numbers?

Steve: The usual kind of twelve-bar boogies and generally just bashed around a bit. We played some reggae tunes and a few little contrasting things just to give an overall picture of what I could do. I knew that if I was good enough I would probably get the gig, because they didn't want to go through a long, drawn-out audition, and Paul wanted to get things moving fairly quickly. I felt that as long as I was at least adequate, I would have a shot.

Geoffrey: How did you find out you got the job?

Steve: It was at the end of that afternoon. We played for about two or three hours and Paul suddenly said, "Fine. That's a good group, sounds great, let's go for it." He made his decision then and there, which is the fastest I've personally been through any audition! Denny and I went out afterwards, had a few drinks and celebrated. Then we flew out to America to meet with Lee Eastman and discuss the terms of our contracts and salaries.

Geoffrey: Was life with the McCartneys social, or mostly work?

Steve: There wasn't a tremendous amount of social activity. It was more of a working situation. I think Paul's opinion of it from the word go was at odds with mine. I felt as if I was in a group I wanted to be part of for a long time, and I was very upset when it fell apart. Of course, I was more specifically upset about Paul's pot bust in Japan and that tour not coming off, because I felt that, somehow, if that tour had gone on we would have become a very strong group. But, looking at the twenty-two shows we played in the U.K., there were obviously problems we had to iron out before we could take on the world, as it were.

Geoffrey: What about Linda's musical contributions to Wings?

Steve: Well, her thing is that she's so close to Paul he just wants her around.

Geoffrey: Does she actually play?

Steve: She can play single-note lines, and she plays pack chord stuff, but it's all pretty much programmed. She's the first person to admit she's no virtuoso keyboard player. I mean, she can't whiz around the board with lightning fingers or solo with the guys when they're just jamming, but she is certainly capable of learning parts and playing them.

Geoffrey: Were you still with Wings when John was assassinated?

Steve: No. But it was very close on the heels of the Japanese tour. It was a period in Paul's life when it was just one upset after another.

Geoffrey: Did Paul ever talk to you about it?

Steve: No. I mean, I felt I couldn't really speak to him. It was much too personal, and I wasn't the person to ring him up and say, "Hey, I'm very sorry about John." There were plenty of other people doing their best to console him, and plenty of press on his trail to get his comments, and I felt my calling him would just complicate matters, so I stayed completely out of the picture. For four or five months afterwards I didn't even see him. Then, of course, when we did see each other again, it was after they'd decided that the band was to be no more, so it was a fairly strained period of time.

Geoffrey: What is life around the McCartney farmyard like? Is it like Paul's song "Heart of the Country," with kids running around barefoot, Shetland ponies, and dogs chasing about everywhere?

Steve: You've just put it into a nutshell—that's exactly what it is! Of course, there's the corporate side to the man, but predominately he keeps that down-home flavor as firmly entrenched as he can. I'm a great admirer of his lifestyle and the way he runs his life. The kids are very unspoiled. They go to regular schools, and they've all got great attitudes.

Geoffrey: How does Paul handle the fans?

Steve: He's a perfect gentleman. He goes out of his way. It doesn't matter who it is—he'll take time and speak to people. He's amazing. He was always the one that kept the Beatles' image so clean. He always went out of his way to shake people's hands, to do this, to do that. John, I'm afraid, was far more critical of that situation altogether.

Geoffrey: Let me ask you about the infamous pot bust in Japan. Where were you when you first realized what was happening?

Steve: We were all there at the same time, and we were told at the airport that there was a minor complication, so we should go on to the hotel and that we'd be meeting later. I was very tired, as it was an eighteen-hour flight, so I checked into my room and went to sleep. Later, I was awakened by Linda at seven-thirty in the evening. She was laughing very nervously and said, "Hey, Paul's been busted." And because she was laughing, I thought she was kidding around, so I just said, "Yeah, great, Linda, I'll see you downstairs for dinner." I left it at that and got up, had a shower, got dressed, went down to the bar, and there were a lot of MPL staff sitting around with very forlorn faces and plainclothes police everywhere. The fans were going crazy, and I suddenly realized that she must be telling the truth. I hung out a couple of days, hoping they would find some way around it and the tour would pick up, but after three or four shows had been missed, I realized there was no way they were going to save the tour—or the band, for that matter.

TINY TIM*
Interview
NEW YORK, FEBRUARY 17, 1984

Geoffrey: Why are you here at this Beatle convention?

Tiny Tim: Well, I recorded a song with George Harrison way back in 1968 called "Nowhere Man," when I was invited to his suite in New York. I told him how I loved the melody and I went into the song. And he said, "Stop," put on his tape recorder and said, "Just say, 'Merry Christmas, Beatles,' and then go into 'Nowhere Man,'" which I did. He put it on every album from here to Australia!

Geoffrey: When did you first meet the Beatles?

Tiny: Well, I met George in '68 and then I did a show with Mr. Ringo on *Laugh-In* back in 1972 or '73.

Geoffrey: Have you ever met John Lennon?

Tiny: No, but he lived right near me at the Dakota, and I saw him in the street about a month before he died. He had dark glasses on and was walking with a girl. I know he wanted to say something, but it was the heat of the day, and I understood he wanted his privacy so I just kept walking.

Geoffrey: Are you a Beatles fan yourself?

Tiny: I wouldn't say I'm a fan, per se, of anybody. I like today's music no matter who it is, whether it's the Beatles, the Rolling Stones, or Jim Morrison and the Doors. Actually, the Beatles were very instrumental to me in learning a new type of music. Here's what the Beatles did that no one touches on: They brought to America the modern art of popular music. Before 1955, it was all straight melodic music. When the white man's rock'n'roll appeared in the fifties, it started to divert, and when the Beatles first happened in 1964, they initiated a new cult. It was something you just couldn't buy sheet music to and learn it like

*Outrageous crooner Tiny Tim first rose to prominence in the mid-sixties. It was around this time that he first met George Harrison. He passed away in 1996.

that. You had to *hear* the record as well, what the beat was saying. People like Dean Martin, Frank Sinatra, Bing Crosby, Tony Bennett, never succeeded after that because they all stayed back. They refused the challenge of that new sound. And basically, it's very hard to convert from conventional art to something really new. But the kids were able to adapt. And basically that's what the Beatles started. They began a whole new trend in music and the old-timers were afraid to take up the challenge. Personally, I *refuse* to lay back in that mold. I try to be "born again" with my music, like I'm sixteen years old again. And that's what the Beatles did—they brought modern art to popular music.

Geoffrey: Where do you live?

Tiny: About two doors down from the Dakota, where they shot John Lennon. It was a great tragedy for America that it happened in this country, but at the same time America also *made* the Beatles, so in a sense it's equalized—but it's still very unfortunate. I performed a number on a show once which I don't think went on the air. It went something like this:

Here lies John Lennon
In life sang many songs
He had his joy and sorrow
Was oft times sad at heart
May his sleep here be peaceful
Beneath God's clear blue skies
While passing drop a flower
Where John Lennon lies.

Geoffrey: Twenty years later, kids are still flipping out over the Beatles. What do you think about that?

Tiny: It's nothing shocking. Sixty years on I still remember Valentino when he passed away in 1926. People remember Elvis Presley, and thirty years from now they'll still be remembering Mr. Lennon. John was a very great artist and he was killed in such a shocking way—it's a tough way to go like that. Life is so short. "We come on the scene without asking, and we leave without wanting to go."

GINGER BAKER*
Interview
BUFFALO, 1991

Geoffrey: How did you feel about the Beatles when they first happened?

Ginger Baker: As regards their early stuff, frankly, I was totally unimpressed. I had the feeling they didn't know a hatchet from a crotchet. They were playing simple little ditties, total pop music, which to me was on the same level as Elvis Presley. Who, by the way, we all thought was a total wanker and I still do, for that matter.

Geoffrey: So do I.

Ginger: I've never been impressed with Elvis, though the whole world seems to think he was extraordinary. To me he was very like the Stones, a white guy trying to do black music and not succeeding very well. We [the Graham Bond Organization], on the other hand, weren't trying to play black or white music. We were just playing. We put the Beatles on the same level as them. To us they were not even considered anywhere near what we were.

Geoffrey: When did you first meet the Beatles?

Ginger: Not for a long time. Eric [Clapton] was much more the socialite than I. Eric was the guy who was out mixing with people like the Stones and the Beatles. George Harrison was, I think, the first Beatle he met. Later, I did some recording with George and played quite a few sessions with Billy Preston, at the time of Bangladesh. I played on most of the [Apple] Billy Preston albums. I'm actually playing on his single, "That's the Way God Planned It." It was during the period when Eric and George wrote "Badge." Lots of people ask me what it's about, but I haven't the faintest clue. It's a good song, though. It's got a great guitar riff, absolutely beautiful. It's pure Eric, the way he executes, that is absolutely amazing.

*Former Cream and Blind Faith drummer Ginger Baker has known and worked with the Beatles in various configurations over the past two decades. His unpublished autobiography was written by Geoffrey Giuliano.

Geoffrey: Didn't Paul McCartney and Wings record at your studio in Lagos?

Ginger: Yeah, they came to our studio and recorded some stuff for *Band on the Run.*

Geoffrey: Do you remember which songs?

Ginger: One of them was "Picasso's Last Words" and a couple of other tracks. We did get a credit, but we never got paid.

BO DIDDLEY*
Interview
Toronto, 1983

Geoffrey: Tell me about first meeting the Beatles.

Bo Diddley: I saw them being rushed into a bobby van in 1963 when I was in England. That was in London when they first started out, and later when they came to the United States I met John Lennon and George Harrison quite a few times. I spent a fantastic evening with Lennon once in New York City at Max's Kansas City.

Geoffrey: What year was that?

Bo: It was during the time that John was playing with the Elephant's Memory Band. I think the dude was great.

Geoffrey: Tell me about meeting George.

Bo: It was just, "Hey, man, how ya doin'?" He told me he admired my work and he was very glad to meet me and I said, "Likewise, man."

Geoffrey: What about John—anything you remember there?

Bo: Yeah, me, John, and Chuck Berry were up on stage once closing Max's.

Geoffrey: How did John seem to you?

*Fabled guitarist Bo Diddley was an acquaintance of all of the Beatles.

Bo: Well, the man was truly great and a neat fellow, too. He was very nice, and it's just a tragedy that we lost him. It's a damn shame.

Geoffrey: If you would have asked the Beatles who their early influences were, I'm sure you would have been one of the people they would have named.

Bo: Yeah, me, Chuck Berry, Fats Domino, Little Richard, and Ray Charles—they kind of mixed us all together and built their career around our stuff to get their sound. They were very different, but they wasn't really rock'n'roll. I don't know what you would call them really, but they *wasn't* rock'n'roll.

Geoffrey: Pop music, maybe?

Bo: Wasn't really pop, either. It was just something very *different,* and the songs were somehow so electrifying. The Rolling Stones became a part of the rock scene because they played the type of music that rock-'n'rollers could immediately identify with.

Geoffrey: Wait a minute—the Beatles used to do "Long Tall Sally," "Roll Over Beethoven," and a lot of the old tunes.

Bo: But it didn't have the same seasoning. You couldn't really call "It's Been a Hard Day's Night" rock'n'roll!

Geoffrey: Well, what was their magic?

Bo: I don't know, but they sure had it.

Geoffrey: Didn't you like them?

Bo: I liked them—if I didn't like them I'd tell you. A lot of cats would try to get you to say something dirty about them, but I ain't got nothing dirty to say about *anybody,* you know.

Geoffrey: What did you think in 1964, when they hit it so big in America?

Bo: It knocked us all off of our chairs, man! I just looked up and started seeing less and less Bo Diddley records in the stores and said, "Uh oh, something is going on here!" Then up popped acid rock. The

Beatles were hanging in on the outside of things, but you can't say they were really acid rock, either. I mean, we had the Grateful Dead, Jimi Hendrix, and many other acts coming into existence during that time, and the Beatles got a free ride along with everything that was going on then. You didn't catch anybody able to do what the Beatles were doing at the time, but there were thousands playing screaming guitar licks.

Geoffrey: No one could ever seem to beat them in terms of pure popularity, though.

Bo: That's right—we got cats right here in America that could play the Beatles under the table any time, but they wouldn't *ever* be accepted like the Beatles were.

Geoffrey: Maybe it was their personalities that got them so for.

Bo: It was something, man! Part of it was the long hair, the English accent, and their whole overall look, and it surely did make it, brother! They were great. I loved them, man—that's about all I can say.

JERRY RUBIN*
Selected Quotation on John Lennon
New York, 1984

"I felt the Yippies was Beatles music put to politics, and John was the most politically aware of the Beatles. On his *Working Class Hero*† album, John was singing to my soul. I found him to be a good friend, honest, loving, and brilliant.

"I came often to visit them at their bed. In those days John and Yoko slept, ate, wrote, and conducted business from an enormous king-sized bed in their apartment in the West Village. With them I discovered the utter absurdity of fame; they could not go anywhere for fear of being mobbed. Crowds huddled around John as he walked down the street

---

*Well-known sixties political radical Jerry Rubin befriended John and Yoko when they first moved to New York in the early seventies. He was killed in a freak car accident while crossing the road several years ago.

†Actually, *John Lennon/Plastic Ono Band*, Apple Records.

and he had to brush people away. Waitresses got so nervous they would drop all of their dishes.

"All the potential paranoids of human interaction are exaggerated by fame. Sometimes I looked at them and all I could see was the myth. I would think to myself: 'Oh, wow, how exciting, I'm with John Lennon, I want to hold your hand!' Then I would look at him again and see a scared, bright, working-class kid with granny glasses. I could see the person behind the image and I would feel genuine love for him.

"John was very interested in politics, and for months I brought scores of revolutionary political figures of the sixties to their bedside for animated discussion: Abbie Hoffman, Dave Dellinger, Huey Newton, Bobby Seale, and Rennie Davis. One night, four of us, Abbie, myself, John, and Yoko, took a knife and cut our fingers and smeared the blood together in a blood oath 'for the hell of it' on the front page of Ram Dass' book, *Be Here Now*.

"John and Yoko suggested I join their fledgling band (even though I could neither carry a tune nor play an instrument) to break my isolation as a politico out of touch with music. So John handed me a drum and asked me to play back-up on 'Imagine.' The next week the band played the Apollo Theater at an Attica benefit and I was there with a tambourine. When John and Yoko hosted *The Mike Douglas Show* I helped them back up Chuck Berry doing 'School Days.' This, the culmination of every musical fantasy I'd ever had, was possible only because every musician had amplification but me.

"As the government closed in on John, he got paranoid; for a time he even considered the possibility I was a CIA agent who had snuggled close, seduced them into a rock tour, and then nabbed them. He didn't really mean it, but the hot breath of the U.S. government complicated our friendship.

"I learned a lot from John. As an ex-Beatle he received as much pressure as an ego can sustain in money and mass love. Yet he was unsatisfied. Backslapping from the outside was not what counted. What counted was how John felt about himself. His post-Beatles music and private life exemplified this desire to know himself from the inside out.

"John eased me over my age hurdle by telling me how proud he was to be thirty-one, 'the best age of all.'"

TONY MANSFIELD*
Interview
TORONTO, 1983

Geoffrey: Where did the "J" in Billy J. Kramer come from?

Tony Mansfield: John Lennon suggested we put in the "J" for Billy *Jesus* Kramer. We started working with the Beatles a lot becasue Eppy wanted the boys on the road with some solid backup. Eppy also had Gerry and the Pacemakers, the Dakotas, the Big Three, Tommy Quickly, Johnny Sanders, the Remo Four, and Cilla Black. We used to meet the boys on the road for a meal in a restaurant somewhere. They had a black Austin Princess. Eppy often used to go around with the Beatles. We had polite escorts bring us to the theater and take us out again. The Beatles kept to themselves a great deal—they *had* to. They started moving further away from people the more famous they became. We did an awful lot of shows with the Beatles. 1963 was the last time we worked with them—it was "The Beatles' Christmas Show." Ritchie and I used to be quite friendly. I used to watch him play a lot, and John sometimes used to stand at the side of the stage and watch me play.

Geoffrey: Before they were really famous, was there any inkling of their incredible charisma?

Tony: When I first worked the Cavern, something hit me about them, you know. First of all, Paul was playing a very deep, driving bass. They were doing things like "Some Other Guy." They were really rocking even though Pete wasn't a particularly good drummer. A very good-looking boy, but he just didn't fit in physically or even mentally with the boys' sense of humor. I'm talking now as a drummer about another drummer. He really was a real gentleman, but that goes for all the boys. They were nice to work with.

Geoffrey: Wasn't John very caustic and cynical in his own way?

---

*Tony Mansfield, a founding member of the Dakotas, played drums for Billy J. Kramer throughout the sixties and was friendly with all four Fabs.

Tony: Not to us, never. He was never once rude to me.

Geoffrey: How did he get that reputation, do you think?

Tony: Oh, I think people gave it to him. People started treating him like he was higher than God. Everyone was capitalizing on the Beatles, trying to make some money, including our band. With the greatest respect to Mr. Kramer, he had no real talent or charisma. He had no confidence because he was always so goddamned worried he was going to fuck the show up, and invariably he would! Our second record was written by John and Paul, who came down to Abbey Road with the lyrics writen on the back of a Senior Service packet. The only record I'd ever done with Kramer which I'd learned *before* I went into the studio was "Do You Want to Know a Secret." In fact, Mike Maxfield has the original demo of that. EMI offered him £15,000 for the tape, but I don't think he's sold it to them. It was given to us to learn, and Michael must have kept his copy.

Geoffrey: Did John or Paul ever rehearse with you?

Tony: They always showed us the chord structures on acoustic guitar.

Geoffrey: What tune was this?

Tony: "Bad to Me," our second hit with Billy J. Kramer. All together we had six records written for us by John and Paul. The first was "Do You Want to Know a Secret," with the B side being a Lennon and McCartney tune entitled "I'll Be on My Way." Then, of course, "Bad to Me" was a monstrous hit for Billy, and the B side off that was "I Call Your Name." The Beatles later recorded that one themselves. And "From a Window" was the final one. When we were recording "From a Window" I'll always remember John singing, "Yesterday I shit out of a window."

Geoffrey: What did you think of George Martin?

Tony: Well, George was the fifth Dakota just like he was the fifth Beatle. Norman Smith was our recording engineer, who also happened to be a drummer, by the way. Martin was an extremely interesting person to work with, a great musician and arranger. We used to hang on his every word to do things properly.

Geoffrey: The Beatles have said he had a kind of schoolmaster toughness. They used to call him *Mr.* Martin. And if they wanted to smoke a joint they'd have to go up on the roof, I've been told.

Tony: It was the same with Brian. He had that same flair of authority as George. I remember that Eppy used to get very annoyed at Billy occasionally. We were doing "Thank Your Lucky Stars" once and he came running in after the show and glared at Billy and said, "The Dakotas were lovely . . . but you, Billy, *ha!*" and steamed out of the room like a little boy. We were all dying to crack up, but we couldn't. Sure, Brian was gay, but we never really thought of him that way—it just never came up.

Geoffrey: What did you think when the Beatles were giving you their tunes to record?

Tony: Nothing very much—we were all just working together. We were just glad to have a job. It was like living on a balloon and we were all just waiting for it to burst. Brian worked us all an awful lot.

Geoffrey: There was never any animosity then between the other NEMS groups and the Fabs?

Tony: I know the Beatles had a lot of respect for the Dakotas because we were very professional. First of all, they copied us by getting their amplifiers covered in black like we did. We have Vox 30s and were trying to model ourselves on Cliff Richard and the Shadows. I remember watching the Shadows and they had their amps covered exactly the same. They looked dead smart, you know, so that's what we tried to do, and John said to me, "Well, that's good. Where did you get your amps done?" I said, "Barrets in Manchester, John." I also bought a Ludwig kit in 1961 and Ritchie played on it a few times (especially when we toured together), and the next thing I know, Ritchie's got his own Ludwig set!

Geoffrey: How did Brian's interest in the Beatles manifest itself on a day-to-day basis? I suppose he always made sure that everything was absolutely perfect for them?

Tony: No, they worked very hard! I remember doing a week in London with them once and they would rehearse all day at the theater because we were doing a "Royal Variety Show," which was a very important gig. We didn't party because we were always too damn tired. When we did do a week in one place, it gave us some time to catch up on our sleep.

Geoffrey: When you did make merry with the Fabs, what were the parties like?

Tony: Well, I went to Paul's twenty-first birthday party at his auntie's in Liverpool. Bob Wooler and John Lennon had a punch-up. We were just enjoying ourselves, you know. I don't think anybody was too drunk and disorderly, except maybe John.

Geoffrey: Was John with Cynthia that night?

Tony: No, John was always very quiet about Cynthia—no one was supposed to even know about her. I never dared talk to John about anything other than music when we first met the Beatles. We were talking about Paul earlier, and I remember him playing us an acetate of "I Saw Her Standing There" in Dick James' office in London. Then he sat down at the piano and banged out "From Me to You," which was also written on the back of a Senior Service pack. He was reading the lyrics off the back and playing on this very old piano. "What do you think of this, boys?" he said. Paul was always very interesting. He used my electric razor when we were on the road together. He called it "the Rabbi" because it made such an incredible noise, it sounded like an old rabbi praying. He'd say, "Can I use the Rabbi, Tony?" He always made such a row over that damn electric razor—man, what a character! All of them used to continually borrow stage makeup off us. Remember, these are the days when we were wearing smart suits and the kids were all screaming for the Beatles wherever we played.

Geoffrey: Did the Beatles use your sound system, or did they bring out their own?

Tony: They had their own amplifiers, Vox 30s and Vox 100s, but usually they used the house system. Neil would generally set the lights for the boys.

Geoffrey: Did the Beatles ever moan to you that they couldn't hear themselves play?

Tony: There were times when George's amps would go off or John would break a guitar string. Ritchie's *still* got a pair of my timpani sticks and a pair of brushes as well. Ritchie was a good solid drummer, man, he never used to gaff up on stage, you know.

Geoffrey: A lot of people say he wasn't that hot, you know.

Tony: He was absolutely rock steady, my friend. The Dakotas stood in for the Beatles at a rehearsal for *Thank Your Lucky Stars* TV show. They were late for the camera shots, so I sat in on Ritchie's drums, Rob was on Paul's Hofner, etc.

Geoffrey: Did you guys ever get together and jam?

Tony: Well, Paul used to play my drums. He's left-handed so I had to change them over for him. I don't think we ever jammed, though.

Geoffrey: Was Paul a good drummer?

Tony: O aye—he's a bit better these days, actually.

Geoffrey: Did you ever see the Beatles recording at Abbey Road?

Tony: Yeah, I saw them finishing off "You Can't Do That," and of course, we've done many radio shows together.

Geoffrey: What shows?

Tony: *Thank Your Lucky Stars, Saturday Club, Easy Beat,* and we did another one with the Stones, actually. I remember they were doing the song "Bo Diddley" and trying to figure out the drumming on it. We also worked with the Stones in the States, as well.

Geoffrey: What were the recording sessions with the Beatles like?

Tony: They always had loads of instruments coming in and out. Actually, on that particular session when the boys were leaving, George Martin said to me, "Your session isn't until seven o'clock—what are you doing for the next hour? Do you want to make seven pound ten shillings?" I said, "What for?" He said, "I want you to put some drums on a Matt Monroe record I'm doing."

Geoffrey: When was the last time you saw Ringo?

Tony: It was about seven years ago at the Royal York Hotel in Toronto. Actually, my ex-wife Brenda told me that Ringo was in town and was staying at the Royal York, so I just phoned up and asked to speak to Richard Starkey. His personal assistant Hillary Gerard came on the phone. I told him who I was and he said, "Well, with a story like that, I suppose it has to be true." So I said, "I hope so," and Ritchie came on the phone and the first thing he said to me was, "Seems like fifty years since I spoke to you, Tony." He invited me over the next day. He threw his arms around me, actually, which was very nice, and gave me a great big hug. Don't forget, I knew Ritchie when he was playing at Butlins in North Wales. We spent about three hours together talking about our families and things. He told me about his children and the split with his wife Maureen.

Geoffrey: How about some quick memories of the following: Pete Best.

Tony: A beautiful guy who couldn't really play the drums very well. As a drummer he never really played *enough*, and what he did do just wasn't that tasteful. Basically, I don't really think he did the job properly.

Geoffrey: George Harrison.

Tony: He *was* always the "quiet one." Very polite and funny at times. When we used to go in the Beatles' dressing room after a show, they had their own silly little words they used all the time, their own personal Beatles terminology. They made us all feel very comfortable. I remember listening to Paul once when I was in the band room after the Finsbury Park Empire show. They were watching an old film and Paul was going, "Look, there's my uncle, the second guy on the left; he was an extra."

Geoffrey: Ringo.

Tony: He has a very good way about him, and he's a very solid drummer as well. He always had a nice word to say to everybody, and he was so funny. I remember using his Premier kit at the Cavern and knocking his bass drum off the end of the stage.

Geoffrey: Paul McCartney?

Tony: A good musician, lots of energy. He always listened to you when you were talking—or he *seemed to,* anyway.

Geoffrey: He was a diplomat, wasn't he?

Tony: Yes, very much so. He was a good businessman. Whenever we were in the studio with John and Paul, we always did our jobs properly, and of course we generally had to learn their tunes on the spot. So it was certainly never boring, I will say that!

Geoffrey: Norman Smith.

Tony: Fabulous, great. I'll always remember Norman with his little cigarettes—he used to roll his own. He'd always smoke them right up to the bitter end. He was always worrying about how the drums were going to sound. He was very concerned with doing a good recording and, of course, it was the same thing with George Martin. We worked very hard in the studio doing records like "Bad to Me," "From a Window," and "I'll Keep You Satisfied." We learned them all in the studio. We'd put the bed tracks on first and Billy's marvelous voice on afterwards.

TONY MANERO*
Interview
NEW YORK, SUMMER 1992

Question: Tell me your story about meeting John Lennon.

Tony Manero: It was back in May of 1974. I saw three guys walking down the block. John was always my idol. I went up to him and said, "I know a lot of people hassle you, but I just want to thank you for your music. I've enjoyed you and you've helped me through a lot of emotional times." Outside Jimmy's Bar in Greenwich Village he said, "Why don't you come inside for a drink?"

---

*Tony Manero was the inspiration behind the seventies film *Saturday Night Fever* and a successful New York businessman.

Question: Who else was with him?

Tony: Harry Nilsson was also there. After we ordered drinks, John switched seats to be next to me. He said to me, "Are you gay?" When I told him I wasn't, he looked really disappointed. He could have been joking, but he wasn't. My initial reaction was fear. And yet I wouldn't leave because it was John Lennon. I said to him, "No, man, I don't go that way." "Are you sure?" he said, "Look, I'll take you to Hollywood." John was calling me "the pretty one." He told me, "You're the prettiest chick I've seen all day." He said, "You look like a pretty little Indian or Arab chick," because of my color skin. I remember Harry was borrowing one hundred bills from him.

Question: Then what happened?

Tony: At one stage I went out, and when I came back he was talking to this woman and he said, "She said, 'I thought he was Paul, meaning McCartney.'" So John turns around and says, "No, he's prettier than Pauly. He's got a nicer mouth than Pauly. Pauly's got a small mouth." Then he turned to me and said, "Let's go get some chicks." This man was giving me a dream to pay millions for. I hung out with him. John almost admitted his gay tendencies. He put his arm around me. He said, "It feels good to hold someone. You know what I mean?" Prior to that he said, "There is nothing wrong in being gay. Two people exchanging feelings is not wrong. Did you ever try it?" People were following us. We were wasted and he put his arm around one girl and said, "Suck my cock." He stuck his tongue down her throat. We were loaded. Somebody stole the hat right off his head! He was so nice. I remember we had a hamburger. Later we went back to his hotel rooms, 1608, -9, and -10. There was Harry's bedroom, John's, and a living room with a keyboard. He gave me a guitar, but it was later stolen. He propositioned me in the street. Hassled me if I'd ever made love to a male. "Will you give me head, man?" he asked. But I wouldn't do it. "Come on, Tony, why don't you give me head?" We went back to his hotel and he propositioned me again. After John died I wished I'd done it. He tried to kiss me. He put his arm around me. He was making moves on me like a guy would make on a woman. We were on the couch and we lay down. I said, "Wow, maybe I should have." I never asked him if he'd had sex with a man, but it was obvious to me he had. I was at the hotel for a few days. But he never bothered me in the middle of the night. He never attempted it again. There were feelings and looks. He was very loving, like when a guy is very lonely. The man was bisexual—there is no two ways about it. He was feeling me out.

Question: What do you say to people who might not believe your story?

Tony: John did come on to me. He did try to make love to me. He asked me to perform a lewd act—that's the truth. The man was bisexual—there was no two ways about it. Any of his fans who can't dig that, I'm sorry, because if you listen to his music, sensitivity and experiencing is what it's all about.

HOLLEY JOHNSON*
Interview
TORONTO, 1984

Geoffrey: Looking back at your own musical roots, and given that you are from Liverpool, did you feel any influence from the Beatles' work?

Holley Johnson: The Beatles were good when they came back from India and were dropping acid every day!

Geoffrey: Do you feel that the success of bands like the Beatles helped to open up the scene for other music makers from England to hit a wider audience?

Holley: I think England has always set the pace for the rest of the world anyway. To me, Lennon was a true original. Perhaps the last of the great two originals. As far as I'm concerned, John was the Beatles full stop!

*Holley Johnson was lead singer for Frankie Goes To Hollywood.

KIRSTEN GREPNE*
Interview
HENLEY-ON-THAMES, OXFORDSHIRE, 1983

Geoffrey: When did you first visit George Harrison's home, Friar Park?

Kirsten Grepne: I moved to Henley-on-Thames when I was about sixteen. I went to school at Friar Park. It was run by an order of Selesian nuns. I spent four years up there and had many happy times. We had a particular nun, I think her name was Sister Ella, who would not allow us to wear patent-leather shoes because our knickers might shine in our shoes, so that was out! We weren't allowed to wear trousers or go out with non-Catholic boys, as that would be a mortal sin and we'd go straight to Hell! There was a great fear of this sort of thing. The house was originally designed and built by Sir Frank and Lady Crisp and apparently had fantastic gardens, which have now been fully restored by George. At the time they were a little run-down, but the nuns took us on nature rambles through the caves, tadpole hunting, and rolly polly down the hill. We had a lovely time amidst all the carved gnomes and things. The light-switch plates were in the shape of friar's noses with big grins on their faces. There were loads of gargoyles, particularly in the chapel. There were, however, certain things about the gargoyles which the nuns didn't like.

Geoffrey: You mean genitals?

Kirsten: Yes. They did little paintings to disguise the gargoyles' private parts.

Geoffrey: You mean underwear?

Kirsten: That's right—no genitals to be shown! Nevertheless, they were very nice nuns. We had to be guarded to preserve our future.

Geoffrey: When did you first hear the nuns were leaving the Park?

---

*Former model Kirsten Grepne is a longtime close personal friend of George and Olivia Harrison. She resides in Henley-on-Thames, Oxfordshire.

Kirsten: In fact they wanted to keep it or turn it into a senior school, but it closed down.

Geoffrey: When did you meet the newest owner, Mr. Harrison?

Kirsten: It's a story I have since told George. It was during my hippy days when I was just sixteen and I was standing at the bottom of the gates of Friar Park waiting to be picked up by my father. There was this person rustling around in the bushes dressed in Wellington boots with very long hair. He was in the trees and he peeped through. I did, in fact, recognize him, as everybody in town knew one of the Beatles had bought Friar Park. He had a brown felt hat on and he said, "Are you waiting for a bus, luv?" I said, "No, it's okay, I'm quite fine." He said, "Would you like to come up for a cup of tea?" I said, "No, it's quite all right." That was the first time I met him. George has pretty much always stayed to himself. He's not seen. It's not that he fears going into a place, but it doesn't happen often. My next meeting with George I was in the company of a very interesting and outrageous gentleman by the name of Magnet. He's very well known in the rock scene around Henley. We went up for tea and a boat ride on the lake in 1981. We just popped in briefly for dinner and God knows what.

Geoffrey: How did George seem?

Kirsten: Fine—he's always very friendly.

Geoffrey: What is Friar Park like now that George has taken over?

Kirsten: It's absolutely lovely. It's pretty much the way it used to look when Sir Frank and Lady Crisp were up there. The buildings are all washed down. It looks like a fairy castle made of pink and white stone.

Geoffrey: Obviously George made some changes—he put in a swimming pool.

Kirsten: Yes, he has, exactly where our old grass tennis court used to be.

Geoffrey: There's not many people invited into George's home, is there?

Kirsten: No. I went up there through the introduction of friends, and I have since been there on several occasions with Mr. "Legs" Larry Smith, a friend of mine, a swine and *idiot*! We've had some very happy times there—they are very nice people. I suppose as you know they are vegetarians?

Geoffrey: Does Olivia do the cooking?

Kirsten: On occasion, yes. When I go up there, we just talk. It's a laid-back, normal evening, if one likes laid-back evenings. George is into car racing and has numerous videos of different rallies. He loves it. George is interesting, very unaffected and genuine. He has a great sense of humor and he's very calm. Occasionally he has on the odd expensive jacket, but in general he could be anybody.

Geoffrey: What about Olivia—what is she like?

Kirsten: I first met her at Jon Lord's house at a fireworks party. She brought Dhani. I find them a very nice couple.

Geoffrey: What kind of boy is Dhani?

Kirsten: He's sweet—very nice. Good-looking, interesting, and chatty.

Geoffrey: How do you think he feels about being a Beatle's son?

Kirsten: I don't think he fully understands. He goes to a local primary school—that's their choice. They obviously feel they would like him to go to a normal school and be brought up as normal as possible.

Geoffrey: Give me a rundown of some of the people who come to the Park.

Kirsten: Well, there's always "Legs" Larry, who may or may not do a tap dance! Jon and Vicki Lord, Joe Brown and his wife are very much favorites. Also, Ian Pace is another chum, as well as his wife, who is the twin sister of Jon Lord's wife, Vicki. There is a set of people who've been around for the last few years.

Geoffrey: You've also been with Ringo on a social level, right?

Kirsten: Yes, I first met him at a party at Jon and Vicki's.

Geoffrey: Did you meet his wife Barbara?

Kirsten: We had a very nice chat about horse riding.

Geoffrey: What did you think of Ringo?

Kirsten: He's very much the comedian.

Geoffrey: How did George and Ringo interact with each other?

Kirsten: Fine—they played pool.

Geoffrey: Is there any sign in George's house of him once being a Beatle?

Kirsten: Not exactly, but there is a juke box in the massive front hall, where we used to have assemblies as schoolgirls. There are several old Beatle records in it. There are also several gold records in the video room.

Geoffrey: Anything else you'd like to say about George and Olivia?

Kirsten: I'm very happy they came to Friar Park, because the way things are in Britain at the moment, all these nice large homes like the Park could very well have been taken over by the National Trust, or even knocked down. I'm very happy they are there to see that Friar Park will be properly preserved.

CHRIS CHARLESWORTH*
Selected Quotation on John Lennon
London, February 1997

"I remember back in the mid-seventies John was in L.A. living with Lou Adler. I was at the private bar upstairs at the Rainbow Room, and Tony Kino (from Apple) mentioned he was there with John Lennon. I told him I'd always wanted to meet him, so Tony very kindly introduced me. I asked for an interview, which we did the next day around Lou's

*Chris Charlesworth is a respected author and prominent London publisher. In the seventies he acted as the U.S. correspondent for *Melody Maker* magazine.

pool. John asked a lot of questions about the royal family and Britain and talked about it quite a bit. It was fairly obvious he was quite homesick.

"Another time I was at Ashley's in New York and John was there with Peter Boyle and his columnist wife Lorraine, and, of course, Yoko. After a while the wives left and John said, 'You know, only men with mustaches and beards ask for my autograph. When I was in the Beatles men came up to me and George asking the meaning of life, but Paul and Ringo always got the girls!' Then, a half hour or so later, a pretty young girl came up and he pulled her on his lap, squeezed her tits and said, 'McCartney, you bastard, I finally got one!'

"On another occasion I was with Keith Moon and his bodyguard, Dougal Butler, when we stopped by Pierre's to call up to the suite John shared with May Pang. He told us to come on up. When we got there he said, 'What can I offer you to drink? All I've got is this bottle of wine (Rothschild 1845 or something) that [Allen] Klein sent me for my birthday. However, as I'm in a lawsuit with him at the moment it might not be safe to drink! It could be poisoned! I certainly don't want to drink it because I'm a world-famous millionaire Beatle, and I don't want May to drink it because I'm in love with her at the moment. And Keith, I don't really think you should drink it because you're famous as well and you obviously need your bodyguard, so Chris, it looks like you're the most expendable!' I said, 'Well, thanks a lot, John,' and I drank a glass as they waited to see if I'd drop dead or not. Then I said, 'I better try some more (only because it was absolutely the best wine I'd ever had).' It was the most incredible wine! It had to have cost about $1,000. I drank about a third of the bottle before I told them I thought it was okay!"

HELEN SIMPSON*
Interview
LIVERPOOL, JUNE 1984

Geoffrey: What is your job here at Beatle City?

Helen Simpson: I'm curator.

Geoffrey: What exactly does that involve?

Helen: As curator, I'm responsible for the whole of the exhibition. Responsible for all the Beatles' items we have here, as well as their guitars and other instruments, etc. We're very much involved with their long-term care and, as curator, my particular job is making sure all these items are going to be around five hundred to one thousand years from now.

Geoffrey: How did Beatle City get started?

Helen: It was an idea of Terry Smith's, who runs the local independent radio station. He said to us, "Why don't we expand into the media business, but keep it within Liverpool so we can do something for the city." Before this, there was no place for those who associated Liverpool with the Beatles to come, and this is why we began Beatle City. To begin the collection, Terry started with purchases from Sotheby's Rock Auction, which can't continue because we simply don't have the money to. But it did provide a nucleus from which people have come forward to donate other Beatles items and loan us things.

Geoffrey: So you were getting your material at Sotheby's? How long have you been collecting?

Helen: Yes, but not constantly collecting so it's very young, in fact, probably only about nine months old to be exact.

Geoffrey: So you're interested in getting together with people who would like to donate things for the exhibit?

Helen: We're very much interested in that, of course. If people would

*Helen Simpson was the curator for the now defunct Beatle City museum.

like to share what they own with the rest of the world, I think that would be marvelous. Say if someone came along and had something that is special to them, a particular album cover, original signatures or perhaps something that was very much related to the Beatles (and their instruments in particular). We would be delighted to be able to put them on show here. They could still own them, of course. They could be put on loan or they could donate them to us as a gift, any sort of arrangement people might like, even just a short-term one.

Geoffrey: Is this considered a permanent exhibit?

Helen: Oh, this *is* a permanent exhibition. It changes in the sense that we have more items coming in and we can certainly expand, but it is permanent, will be here for evermore. The only time it may move is to a larger premises. But, at present, we are happy here, and we've got a lot more space and certainly can take in a lot more items.

Geoffrey: So this building was designed and built specifically for this exhibit?

Helen: Yes, basically all it was were four walls and a roof. That's all we started with, but the whole structure within it has all been designed specifically for Beatle City. The concept of this museum is to expand and become a second home for those people who are fond of the Beatles.

Geoffrey: Who designed the exhibition?

Helen: It was Colin Milnes, who is very well known in the museum world. He's worked on the *Queen Elizabeth II*. He's a very good designer. He arranged the basic layout, but all the objects and the items were down to the curator.

Geoffrey: It doesn't seem like you have a resident Beatle expert or consultant. How do you deal with that?

Helen: Not a resident on the premises, but it depends what sort of information you're being brought. If someone said to me, "What happened on May 4, 1965?" I would have to say, "I can't tell you, you'd have to go and look it up." I'm not a Beatle brain, but one thing that we do have is expertise on is how to find information by going to the original sources and understanding how to verify things. We've got a wonderful set of personal contacts, and we're going all the time to people who can help verify detail.

Geoffrey: How would you answer the criticism that this place is nothing more than simply another cash-in on the Beatles?

Helen: The way I see it is that the Beatles are a part of Liverpool history, just as the football team is, just as much as its Maritime Museum, and if you ever want to truly reflect the history of the city, you've got to have the Beatles as well. Whether you like their music or not—I mean, some people would say, "I prefer Jerry and the Pacemakers." But in fact the music of Liverpool *has* to be shown, which we do in its early stages, and we would like to expand on to the Beatles. I mean, that is why Liverpool is famous at the moment.

Geoffrey: Is this a commercial museum?

Helen: Yes, this particular one is a commercial museum, but remember Radio City is an independent radio station. It's got a lot of backing from the English Tourist Board and the Merseyside County Council; all in all we'd like to make Liverpool more of a tourist center. It's always been a heavy industrial place, but the docks have shrunk, the heavy industry has mostly gone away, and shipbuilding is no longer needed. Still, it's a beautiful city. It's got some magnificent buildings, it's got a wonderful art gallery, a very well-known county museum, and a maritime museum that's just being developed which will be second to none. Likewise, we wanted to expand into the other aspect of its history, which is its musical history. In particular, the Beatles.

Geoffrey: Apart from the obvious fact, why is it more relevant to have the Beatles museum here than in Los Angeles or New York?

Helen: Because, as we began, we made a point of introducing it to Liverpool and pointing out the fact that the Beatles didn't emerge from a background of no competition, as it were. In fact, there were many marvelous other groups. Rory Storm and the Hurricanes were probably much better performers in their early days, for instance. You've got such a strong music sense, it's the same even today. If a group gets to the top in Liverpool, they've reached a very high standard—much higher than from any other city.

Geoffrey: This is a monumental exhibition to the Beatles, which was comprised of four, now three, living human beings and relatively young people. So how do you deal with the Beatles as people? What do you think their reaction would be about what you've done here? Because it's a very rare thing that people have had museums dedicated to them when they're only about forty years old.

Helen: It's a very unusual situation to be in. Actually it's probably closer to an art gallery which displays works by living artists. In a way it's nice that it's still going on and people can see the process that actually brought the Beatles together. You know, a whole party of Russians came in recently from the Moscow Classical Ballet and, while they vaguely knew some of the music, they knew absolutely nothing of the individuals in the group. It was very interesting for them, I think, to see their background, the houses they lived in, and how they met up, you know. It made an impact on them, I'm certain.

Geoffrey: Have you had any reaction from the Beatles themselves or their family on this museum?

Helen: Yes, but not from the Beatles directly. Initially, we began by informing them of what we were doing, but not asking them for things. I'm sure it must be very strange to have your past on public view. We've kept them informed, of course, but its so much easier, now that we've actually got an exhibition here, to point out to people what we're doing.

NEWSPAPER REPORTAGE

PART EIGHT

Though the News Was Rather Sad

Those Hippie Drugs Are Killers

1967

NEW YORK—When the Beatles sang "I'd love to turn you on," the British Broadcasting Corp. turned them off.

Their hit record "A Day in the Life" was banned by the BBC because of the offending line. The government-owned radio-TV network pointed out that "turn on" is a slang expression for the use of LSD, marijuana, and other drugs.

"Nonsense," replied Beatle leader John Lennon.

With a look of wide-eyed innocence, Lennon said he couldn't understand how the BBC got the ridiculous notion the hairy howlers were singing a dope commercial.

Then Paul McCartney, the last bachelor Beatle, revealed he had been taking LSD "just to see what it was like." A few days after his startling statement hit the front pages, prompting the *London Mirror* to call him an "irresponsible idiot," Lennon and George Harrison also admitted they had flown on LSD trips.

Such candid confessions from the world's most popular rock'n'roll group were enough to shatter their "good guy" image and drive any normal manager wild. But Brian Epstein, the Beatles' indefatigable discoverer, promoter, and manager, was not a bit disturbed by all the unfavorable publicity.

In fact, he appeared to enjoy it. Epstein, thirty-two, a gay British bachelor whose Beatle-masterminding has made him a multimillionaire, said he knew all about the group flights.

And he admitted having done some high flying himself!

"I have used marijuana and have tried LSD five times," Epstein told an interviewer. "One trip was terrific; another was terrifying.

"My opinion is that pot [marijuana] is definitely less harmful than drinking alcohol. I am not addicted to either, but I have been very drunk and very high.

"Besides pot and LSD, I have experimented with other drugs," he added.

His experiments killed him.

Frail, effeminate Epstein was often known as the Fifth Beatle or the

Beautiful Beatle. He was better mannered, better educated, and better looking than the singers. But though he may have longed to be "one of the boys," the Beatles never fully accepted him as part of their close-knit group.

As John Lennon once observed: "He's got no use for women."

One Saturday night last August, while the Beatles were at a "meditation retreat" in Wales with Indian mystic Maharishi Mahesh Yogi, Epstein threw a party at his country estate fifty miles south of London. As the guests danced to blaring Beatle records, Brian suddenly walked out, jumped into his car, and drove away.

He returned to his townhouse in London's swank Belgravia section near Buckingham Palace. The next morning, his Spanish butler entered his bedroom and found him dead. The Beatles expressed their sorrow, but did not attend his funeral.

Police found seventeen pill bottles, most of them empty, in Epstein's bedroom and bathroom. The coroner ruled he died of an accidental overdose of barbiturates (sleeping pills) and antidepressant drugs (pep pills).

Medical evidence indicated he was killed by an accumulation of drugs over a period of weeks, instead of a single massive overdose. He had gulped pills, tablets, and capsules to make him sleep and wake him up, to send him soaring and bring him back down.

Epstein felt he could handle drugs, but a few weeks before they killed him he said: "I would warn everyone not to take LSD or other drugs unless they had a full, comprehensive understanding of what they are doing."

Obviously, Brian Epstein did not.

And neither do the Beatles, who have quit bragging about their dope flights since Epstein's one-way trip. And neither do the Rolling Stones, three of whom have drug convictions. Nor do any of the other loud-mouthed travel agents, from psychedelic priest Timothy Leary, who are all encouraging millions of kids to turn on and take off with drugs.

Psychedelic Pied Pipers like acid-addled Tim Leary are luring hundreds of thousands of youngsters into the nightmare world of drugs. What they don't realize, or don't tell their converts, is that mind-twisting drugs like LSD, DMT, and STP can be more dangerous than the narcotics: opium, morphine, and heroin.

In Oregon recently, a young mother discovered that her baby, which appeared normal at birth, was turning into a grotesque freak. One side of the infant's head was growing much faster than the other. The child also had an intestinal defect.

The mother was an LSD user. Doctors have uncovered several other cases in which LSD-taking parents produced children with serious mental or physical defects . . .

"LSD is a dangerous form of drug roulette . . . in which users run a clear risk of psychotic breakdown and long-run physiological danger," says a Harvard University pamphlet on the A (for acid) bomb Dr. Leary tested at Harvard.

"We now know that long-term psychological damage can result from LSD, which is far more dangerous than marijuana. Numerous cases have been reported of prolonged psychotic reactions lasting from a few months to two years."

A Brooklyn medical student dropped out of college and broke up with his wife because of LSD. Then, during a three-day binge, he stabbed his mother-in-law to death.

A California student, convinced LSD had made him immune to death, stepped in front of a speeding car and was killed instantly.

A five-year-old Brooklyn girl, who swallowed an LSD-saturated sugar cube, became temporarily insane and suffered psychological after-effects—including a lowered IQ, nightmares, and panic—for nine months!

For a prank, an amorous young man spiked his date's drink with a drop of acid. She had horrible hallucinations, thought she was going crazy, and killed herself.

Another girl, a New York college student, saw a yacht waiting for her in an LSD dream. She stepped aboard and plunged to her death out the window of a seventh floor apartment.

At this very moment, there are thousands of "LSD psychos" in hospitals and mental institutions all over the country. From ten to fifteen percent of all patients admitted to the Neuropsychotic Insititute at UCLA are acidheads. According to resident Dr. Duke Fisher, they suffer "florid psychoses with terrifying visual and auditory hallucinations, marked depression, and anxiety bordering on panic, and many suicide attempts."

When Britain's pop music king died from his dope experiments, few people recalled another August Sunday, five years before, when another member of entertainment royalty was found dead among her empty pill bottles.

Marilyn Monroe was a secret drug addict and the habit killed her. But unlike the turned-on celebrities of today, she didn't brag about her fatal weakness.

Beatle Paul
MBE, LSD, and BF
1967

Beatle Paul McCartney, twenty-five yesterday, is one of the oldest teenagers on record. At the moment, he is not behaving like a teenager—even an elderly one. He is behaving like an irresponsible idiot!

He confesses publicly to having taken the hallucination drug LSD. He says "maybe" he might even take it again. He talks about this dangerous drug in such glowing terms that, despite his statements to the contrary, you might well think he was recommending LSD to his many teenage fans!

Perhaps millionaire McCartney ought to see a psychiatrist who will explain just why LSD is regarded as a dangerous drug. Perhaps he ought to see a psychiatrist anyway. Perhaps Mr. McCartney ought also to consult a lawyer who will tell him it is an offence to be in unauthorized possession of LSD.

INFLUENCE
This mixed-up Beatle may protest that he doesn't advocate LSD for anybody else, and that he doesn't want his fans to take it. But he must certainly know his own influence. By talking so enthusiastically about LSD, isn't he encouraging his fans to break the law by being in posses-

sion of the drug? Isn't he encouraging them to try the devilish drug themselves? Most teenagers, fortunately, have more sense than to mess about with dangerous drugs. Most teenagers will continue to regard LSD as a menace. But it will be no thanks to Mr. Paul McCartney, MBE, LSD, and BF!

The New Beatle: John, George, Ringo . . . Now Comes Klaus

LONDON, MARCH 20, 1971

The Beatles are back. But from now on it's John, George, Ringo . . . and Klaus! The new Beatle, in place of Paul McCartney, is twenty-year-old German-born guitarist Klaus Voorman. The surprise move comes in the middle of a court fight by Paul to have the group broken up.

Last night, for the first time in a year, John, George, and Ringo were back together at their Apple offices discussing future recordings. And with them was Klaus. The new Beatle has always been close to the group. He was once a member of a trio known as Paddy, Klaus, and Gibson, which was also under the management of the late Brian Epstein, manager of the Beatles.

Later, he joined Manfred Mann as bass guitarist. Recently, he has played as a session guitarist on George Harrison's albums and with John Lennon and the Plastic Ono band. He is also a close friend of Ringo Starr. Klaus is married to actress Christine Hargreaves of *Coronation Street* fame and lives in Hampstead. He is a fine artist as well as musician and designed the cover of the Beatles' album *Revolver*.

An associate said: "Paul refuses to return to the group and so what are they to do? . . . When Ringo was ill once in the Beatlemania days they took on Jimmy Nichol. It worked then, why shouldn't it work now?" Paul McCartney and his wife Linda are in America. He could not be contacted last night for an opinion on the new line-up. The other Beatles refused comment.

But the move and the copyright of the Beatles name with a new face in the line-up may well lead to further legal action. Solicitors for John, George, and Ringo said yesterday that they would appeal against last week's High Court decision in Paul's favor appointing a receiver and manager to look after their affairs in place of Allen Klein.

Beatle's Tittenhurst Park in Dreadful State of Disrepair
1973

Council officials are ready to inspect Ringo Starr's English country mansion—whether he likes it or not. They are worried that the house, set in seventy-nine acres at Tittenhurst Park, near Ascot, is in dire need of repair. The two-hundred-year-old mansion, officially listed as historically important, has been empty and unused for more than a year since Ringo left Britain to live in America. He wants to sell it, but so far the only person who offered to buy it disagreed about the price. He offered £250,000. Ringo hopes to drum up £600,000.

People who own listed buildings are required by law to maintain them properly and allow officials "reasonable access." If the property is not up to standard the council can order the owner to repair it. If he refuses, the council can do the work itself and send the owner the bill.

The estate agents who are trying to sell Ringo's old home admit it's over-priced and that it needed work the last time they saw it. Estate agent Frank Bowyer of Chancellors and Co. said: "It was not derelict or anything like that. But there are a lot of flat roofs and gullies and there was rather a lot of water penetration." Now Windsor and Maldenhead council has formally asked for permission to inspect the building. The main house has seven bedrooms, two dressing rooms, three bathrooms, a sauna, offices, three reception rooms, a kitchen-cum-breakfast room, a utility room, and a recording studio, formerly utilized by John Lennon.

Lennon in Legal Limbo
1976

The immigration service reserves a special bureaucratic hell for aliens who have the slightest taint of narcotics in their past. Thieves, rapists, and even murderers have less trouble gaining admission to the United States than someone convicted of even the most minor drug charge. Six years ago, John Lennon came close to being deported because of a 1968 marijuana charge in England. The deportation move was really a political vendetta against Lennon, who had been outspoken in his opposition to the Vietnam War. Lennon was able to beat the trumped up deportation order because of the superb legal work of his attorney, Leon Wildes. Since that time, the public attitude has changed towards both the Vietnam War and the drug habits it spawned. Most Americans now agree with Lennon that the war was a tragic mistake and his arrest for possessing a small amount of marijuana for personal use is no longer really a crime.

Beatle Lennon a "Headache" to Feds

1972

According to the documents which Mr. Lennon's lawyer Leon Wildes obtained from the government under court orders, Senator Strom Thurmond, Republican, of South Carolina, wrote a personal and confidential letter to then Attorney General, John N. Mitchell, on February 4, 1972 suggesting that action against Mr. Lennon could avoid "many headaches." Attached to the Thurmond letter was a memorandum from the files of the Senate Internal Security Sub-Committee, asserting that a communist group was preparing to go to California to disrupt the 1972 Republican National Convention, and that a confidential source had learned "that the activities of this group are being financed by John Lennon." A second memo from the same files contended that "radical New Left leaders plan to use Mr. Lennon as a drawing card to promote the success of rock festivals to obtain funds for a 'dump Nixon' program."

My Sweet Lad!
George Is a Dad

Former Beatle George Harrison has become a dad at last. And he's voted his little son a smash hit. "I'm absolutely delighted at being a father," he said last night. "I'm overjoyed it is a boy." His Mexican girlfriend, Olivia Arias, gave birth to the five pound baby at Windsor.

George, thirty-four, is the last Beatle to produce an heir to his millions. The other three musicians have nine children between them. George was married to model Patti Boyd for eleven years, then lost her to his close friend, rock guitarist Eric Clapton. He met Olivia in Los Angeles when she worked for his company, Dark Horse Records.

She and George, who live in a £500,000 mansion in Oxfordshire, have named their baby Dahni. But the proud parents have no immediate plans to wed.

Lennon Wins a Skirmish in Battle
to Remain in U.S.
MAY 13, 1972

John Lennon, the former Beatle, and his wife, Yoko Ono, won a preliminary skirmish yesterday in their fight to remain in the United States, when the Immigration and Naturalization Service ruled yesterday they were "outstanding artists," a possible ground for granting permanent residence.

They still face a deportation hearing next Tuesday to determine whether they can, in fact, stay. A major barrier is a 1968 conviction against Lennon in Britain for possession of marijuana.

"If There's Mercy, I'd Like It, Please"
MAY 21, 1972

The scene: The hearing room in the Immigration and Naturalization Service building in lower Manhattan. Yoko Ono, sitting in the witness chair in a denim pants suit, wringing a handkerchief, whispers in a choked voice: "You're asking me to choose between my child and my husband. I don't think you can ask any human being to do that." John Lennon, in the witness chair in a nearly identical suit, wringing a handkerchief, tells the inquiry officer: "I don't know if there's any mercy to plead for because this isn't a Federal court, but if there is, I'd like it, please."

Strange words, indeed, coming from the world's best known pop couple. But last week, as the hearing phase of the Government's effort to deport John and Yoko from the United States closed, the Lennons remained enmeshed in a legal, ethical, bureaucratic, and artistic controversy that some friends liken to a soap opera and others to the McCarthy era travails of Charlie Chaplin.

Even if they weren't John and Yoko, their case might warrant considerable attention as a challenge of American immigration laws. John, the former Beatle, is British; Yoko, although she has lived in New York for most of her life, is Japanese. When their visas ran out early this year, they made known their intention to apply for permanent residence here, mainly so that they might continue to search for Yoko's eight-year-old daughter, Kyoko, whom her former husband, Anthony Cox, spirited away two years ago.

A Texas court granted Mrs. Lennon custody of the child recently, but only on the grounds that she be raised in the United States. Thus, the Lennons feel they would be sacrificing the child if either or both of them were to be deported.

But that's only what Norman Seaman, a concert producer and close friend of the Lennons' called the "Stella Dass" side of the story. The Government immediately moved to deport Mr. Lennon on the grounds that his conviction in England in 1968 for possession of "cannabis resin" automatically makes him ineligible for permanent residency. "The law is not discretionary," explained Vincent Schiano, the Government's prosecuting attorney, whose flamboyantly patterned Hong Kong suits make him look more like a member of the rock underground than the conservatively dressed Mr. Lennon. "Even if we loved the Lennons, it wouldn't make any difference."

But supporters of John and Yoko, suspecting they are being persecuted for their nonconformity and antiwar efforts, contend that it should make a difference. During the two months of hearings they sought to show that the Lennons are an invaluable gift to this country, to be cherished as great artists rather than banished like Mafia chieftains.

Mr. Lennon's lawyer also sought to prove that the intent of the residency law was to exclude narcotics traffickers, not a rock musician allegedly pressured into pleading guilty for having a small amount of hashish in his home he now says was planted there.

A stellar cast of establishmentarians: Mayor John V. Lindsay; Metropolitan Museum of Art Chief Thomas Hoving; talk show host Dick Cavett; the Rt. Rev. Paul Moore Jr., Episcopal Bishop of New York; former British Ambassador to the United States, Lord Harlech all came forward to attest to the moral and musical worth of Mr. Lennon, whom many consider as siginificant an artist in 1972 as Mr. Chaplin was when he was kept out of the United States two decades ago. Mr. Hoving told the court, "If John Lennon were a painter, he would be hanging in the Metropolitan Museum."

The inquiry officer will hand down a decision sometime after July 1st, when the defense is scheduled to submit a brief arguing the inapplicability of the English pot bust. If the decision goes against Mr. Lennon, appeals could prolong the case for months, perhaps years, in which case the Lennons would ironically be forced to remain within the borders of the United States.

Lennon Stays in the Shadows

JANUARY 6, 1973

Apple are promising an all-out promotional campaign for the new Yoko Ono album, *Approximately Infinite Universe*, to be released in America on January 8th. Yoko will be doing interviews, however, on her own. Lennon will not participate, as he has in the past, because it's said he doesn't want to take any of her limelight.

In fact, Lennon hasn't been seen around for some considerable time. He hasn't been leaving his home in the Village, a situation which is currently fuelling the speculations of New York tastemakers. It's understood, however, that John is highly conscious of the treacherous path he's forced to tread with U.S. immigration authorities, and he doesn't want to court any more adverse publicity. Whatever the reasons—and the rumors are various—it seems that John Lennon is alive, but not feeling particularly prosperous, in New York.

Beatle Lennon Gains in Fight to Stay in U.S.
1975

Deportation proceedings against ex-Beatle John Lennon were formally set back in a 2–1 decision by the Federal Court of Appeals, NY, yesterday (Tuesday). The case was referred back to the Immigration Department with a recommendation that Lennon be allowed to stay in the U.S. The court vacated the refusal by immigration authorities to grant Lennon permanent residency. Chief Judge Irving R. Kaufman wrote the decision for the majority, in which he was joined by Judge Murray Gurfein, with Judge William Mulligan dissenting.

On September 23, Lennon had received a temporary delay in the Government's efforts to deport him on an old marijuana charge. The Immigration and Naturalization Service granted the delay on "humanitarian grounds," because wife Yoko Ono is expecting.

Harrison Plays Japan
NEW YORK

"I knew that eventually I'd have to try it again, and I thought I'd better do it soon before I got too old to take the trouble. Besides, I wanted to stop smoking and having to sing every night was the best motivation I could think of."

It was 1974 when Harrison last braved the limelight on a North American tour, but during that time this particular quarter of the Fab Four has been anything but resting on his laurels. The formation of Dark Horse Records and his movie company, Handmade Films, are only two of the milestones along the way. A fistful of solo albums, including *Dark Horse, Thirty Three and a Third,* and *Somewhere in England* yielded to a well-deserved respite from the music business in the mid-eighties. 1989 marked a spectacular return to form with *Cloud 9,* his aptly titled ninth solo album, spotlighting the smash hit (and Live in Japan showstopper) "Got My Mind Set on You." The Traveling Wilburys rounded out one decade and launched him into a new one. "It was Eric who encouraged me to give performing a go again," Harrison explains. "He made it very easy by offering to let me step into the band he'd been working with."

The band in question, featured in various combinations on a number of Clapton's recent releases, includes drummer Steve Ferrone, percussionist Ray Cooper, keyboard wizards Greg Phillinganes and Chuck Leavell, bassist Nathan East, backing vocalists Tessa Niles and Katie Kasson, along with guitarist/vocalist Andy Fairweather-Low and, of course, Clapton himself on guitar and backing vocals. "It was a great line-up," enthuses Harrison, and, again, very encouraging for me to discover how much we all enjoyed working together.

"Eric also thought Japan would be a good place to play," Harrison continues. "The audiences there are generally very nice, very polite, which would give us the opportunity to concentrate on the show without worrying about being staged off by the audience."

Harrison also admits to another reason for choosing Japan for his return to live performing. "I have a lot of fans there," he explains. "They'd been asking me for twenty years to come and play and when I finally decided to go ahead, I felt like I really owed it to them."

With a superb concert document under his belt, Harrison is currently pondering his next project. "It might be fun to tour with the Wilburys," he allows, "or go out again with this show and a new band. I did a benefit concert recently at the Royal Albert Hall and the reception was tremendous. Maybe it's time to do some playing in England and Europe, maybe eventually even America."

Macca's Perfect Prize

1990s

Paul McCartney broke off from rehearsals for his *Oratorio* at Liverpool Cathedral to accept a top award from the people of his city. He was voted "Scouse Personality of the Year" in the Whitbread Scouseology Awards, run in conjunction with the *Echo* at the end of last year.

When he finally received the award he said: "I'm chuffed. This means more to me than all these music paper awards. This is the people of Liverpool voting for me. This is Scousers saying: 'You're okay, Macca.'

"It is great to be back home and what a fantastic place the Cathedral is.

"To think I was nearly a choirboy here myself, but they turned me down.

"Please say thanks to the readers who voted for me."

The award was handed over by *Echo* marketing editor Phil Young, joint founder of Scouse Promotions, who was in the same class as Paul at Joseph Williams County Primary School, Childwall. Profits from phone votes for the Scouseology awards last year went to the Alder Hey 75th Birthday Appeal. And McCartney said, "I was glad Linda and I were asked to be joint presidents of the appeal. I couldn't believe it when I heard they had raised £1.7million."

I Did It My Way, Says Macca

1990s

Paul McCartney still defends his decision not to have studied music the "right way." The composer of the world's most played popular song, "Yesterday," said that to have learned to read and write down a musical score in orthodox fashion would have cramped his style. People who had followed the formal path often ended up imitating Schubert or Beethoven.

"It's good that I'm not too familiar with all that. I think it would have spoiled me if I had done it the right way. And I think that if I start doing it the proper way now, I would lose a lot of my freedom." The ex-

Beatle, who has actually composed more than four hundred songs by ear, has left the writing down and arranging to others.

In the case of the semi-autobiographical *Oratorio,* his collaborator was the film composer, Carl Davis. McCartney worked on the *Oratorio* ideas during his world tour. But he insisted that he sat with Davis during every single minute of the subsequent orchestration. That way, he retained personal control over the concept of the piece. He had worked in a similar way with the musician George Martin when he was in the Beatles.

"The orchestra is the ultimate synthesizer, and that's the way I approached it. You can do anything with it." McCartney, looking realized enough in a dark blue three-piece suit, although privately admitting to being somewhat nervous, said that people would have to judge his *Oratorio* for themselves.

As regards the *Oratorio* format, he enthused: "Although at first I wasn't quite sure what we were writing when we were writing it, the form is very long and flexible. You don't have to stick to any structure. You have more freedom."

And yes, he had played a rehearsal tape through for George Harrison, who had popped around to his house and he had been quite impressed. "But he's into George Formby now," added the composer of the hour.

The McCartney Millions

MARCH 11, 1997

Paul McCartney has never opted for tax exile. But it helps to own a $100 million art collection and properties that have considerably appreciated in value over the thirty years he has been accumulating real estate.

He paid $150,000 in 1975 for the 160-acre estate in Peasmarsh in Sussex: his house there alone is now worth more than that. He still owns Rembrandt, the five-bedroom house in the Wirral near Liverpool that he bought for his father for $8,750 after the Beatles' barnstorming tour of America in 1964.

After the Beatles stopped touring in 1966, Paul bought a substantial

Regency house in North London at Cavendish Avenue, St. John's Wood, still a base in the capital for the McCartney family.

Their 1,500-acre hill farm in Kintyre near Campbeltown is still a favorite summer refuge, and McCartney recently spent $360,000 buying a farm to the east, extending the family's privacy. Locals complain that he has cast beady eyes on two more farms to the south. In effect, he is surrounding his property with a no-go area. His policy is to let farm animals on his land die a natural death where possible, not a policy to endear him to a farming community. The McCartneys also own a sanctuary on Exmoor, bought to protect deer from the surrounding hunts.

Money can't buy you love, however, and if the bottom ever dropped out of the market for a McCartney song, the bottom would drop out of his world, too. Since McCartney's company, MPL, has not gone public, the pattern of his income can only be an informed guess, including that much-quoted figure of an overall worth of $420 million. MPL handles all his and Linda's business. It incorporates the largest independent music publishing firm in the world, and the U.K. end operates from his handsome Regency office overlooking London's Soho Square, with a replica in the basement of Studio 2 at Abbey Road, where the Beatles recorded for EMI's Parlophone label.

Paul now records for MPL under licence to EMI. In December 1992 he signed a $100 million deal with Capitol-EMI covering the rest of his recording career, a life contract.

But his business brain has not always served his cause. At a lunch party marking Adam Faith's entry into music publishing, McCartney made the mistake of encouraging Michael Jackson to jump on the publishing gravy train. Unfortunately, Jacko outbid him for Northern Songs, which was by then part of Lew Grade's ATV empire (now Sony-ATV). Northern Songs, otherwise known as the Lennon–McCartney songbook, was bought by Jackson for $53 million on August 10, 1985.

In 1994 he exhibited a piece of carved wood in aid of Bosnia. He accepts commissions; he does not crudely flog his artworks in the marketplace. Meanwhile, the money rolls in as well as out. The Beatles' *Anthology* videos in their boxed set notched up 350,000 advance sales in America, so Britain's richest pop star is heading for another record-breaking year.

What continues to motivate him? Derek Taylor was one of the first journalists to review a Beatles concert. Born in Liverpool, he is one of Paul McCartney's most cherished links with the past and works part-time on publicity for Apple Corps, which acts for the Beatles and coordinated the *Anthology* on CD and video. He saw Paul's growing disenchantment with the original Apple setup and noted with some pleasure how Paul set up his own company, MPL (McCartney Productions Ltd.). "Paul pays enormous attention to detail. All perfectionists can be exacting at times and Paul doesn't like short cuts," says Taylor.

Paul never regained control over the early songs he wrote under the Lennon–McCartney credit. Nor did he persuade Jackson to increase his royalties. Thus, John Lennon's widow, Yoko Ono, who was able to renegotiate her assassinated husband's share, earns more money from "Yesterday" than McCartney (who actually composed it without Lennon's aid.) His compensation was the acquisition of an enormous song-publishing empire, including the rights to all Buddy Holly's songs and musicals including *"A Chorus Line," "Hello, Dolly!," "Annie," "Guys and Dolls,"* and *"Grease."*

McCartney's old band Wings actually gave him a bigger personal income than the Beatles, but now income from the Fab Four backlog is catching up, with the *Anthology* in its various forms being a huge and deserved success. It was produced with great tenderness and a genuine desire to be even-handed with history. Television sales alone of the six-hour *Anthology* to 40 countries could gross $50 million, and the extended boxed video version has sold well. Sales of the double album, *Beatles at the BBC,* may have brought in $3 on every set. Then there is the recording income from the three *Anthology* double albums which will probably realize sales of 20 million copies worldwide. Another $8.5 million could be heading into the McCartney coffers.

Even before this Beatles' relaunch, McCartney was still earning $20 million a year in royalties from the Beatles, split between his share of record sales and songwriting royalties. Apple Corps, founded in 1963 as the Beatles Ltd., still handles Beatles business, including royalties and merchandising, plus revenue from TV, films, and photos. It had a turnover of $17 million in the year to January 1995.

Up to December 1995, the last recorded figures, MPL Communications, founded in 1968, disclosed a turnover of $11.9 million, with pretax profits of $3.5 million and net assets up from $5.9 million to $8.2 million. There is a sister company in America. In 1996, Paul McCartney's 25 percent share of Apple Corps and his 40 percent share of Maclen Music and its subsidiaries were worth an estimated $150 million.

Despite some massive hits, he has struggled to produce songs of the same wistful, classic quality. Maybe the mood of the times has changed. But sitting on his laurels is not what Paul McCartney is all about. The best may be yet to come.

"Paul likes to keep his office as orderly as possible, a quality he shares with George Harrison. They are tidy people. Apple was messy. All sorts of people wandered in and out.

"When Paul set up MPL I went to see what he'd made of it. It was on three or four floors and it was exactly what he'd wanted Apple to be. It was beautiful, orderly, nice carpets, plenty of hush, nice modern paintings on the walls.

"He puts in a five-day week. This is a man who could be sitting on an island in the sun, but he loves hard work."

What makes Paul tick? "He's a man of very high intelligence," says Taylor. "He's a born impersonator. He used to infuriate me by imitating other people on the phone.

"What is obvious is his enormous personal charm. Behind all that, where nobody sees it, he's extremely generous. He can be sensitive to criticism like anyone else. We had some very bad rows over a book I wrote, but he bore no malice because it was not a disloyal book. He's nice with the little people."

Beatle Paul's Boyhood Home Goes Public
1990s

"My mum would have been dead chuffed to think that our little council house would end up with the National Trust," said Paul. "It's a fantastic honor for me and our family.

"This house was the scene of many formative Beatles years, such as leaving for Hamburg and rehearsing our act and writing songs. Sometimes we made a bit of a row; I hope it will be quieter now the National Trust has got it."

By the time the Liverpool Fame School, as it was dubbed, opened last summer, McCartney's MBE was an inadequate expression of the public's regard. Knighthoods had already been awarded to Beatles recording manager George Martin and pop contemporary Cliff Richard.

Then, in mid-December, Paul McCartney breezed into LIPA, rounded up some students to dance behind him, and stood on the balcony of a rehearsal room with a film crew, delivering what appeared to be his acceptance speech for yet another show business award. On December 31, that secret piece of film was shown on all the major TV networks. Paul McCartney was graciously accepting the award of a knighthood for services to the pop industry.

He has become a sort of living hologram. For a multimillionaire with nothing left to prove, there are more important things in life than trundling around appearing in person, even if he occasionally travels by private jet or chauffeur-driven Mercedes to shrink the distances and avoid over-eager public contact, so now he sends a film of himself.

Linda's on the Mend after Breast Cancer Surgery

MARCH 12, 1997

In December 1995, the shocking news was revealed that at the age of 53, Linda McCartney was suffering from cancer—the same disease that killed McCartney's mother Mary when he was only 14—and had undergone a lumpectomy to remove a malignant tumor from her breast, revealed during a routine scan at the Princess Grace Hospital in London.

On their silver wedding anniversary, McCartney claimed he and Linda had spent only nine out of their 9,000 nights apart. Six days after her operation, he stood sadly in the drive of their farmhouse at Peasmarsh, East Sussex, where Linda was already back and resting, and appealed to the media to allow her the peace and quiet she needed.

"The operation was 100 percent successful, thank God," he said. "We're very optimistic about the future and, for the moment, everything goes on as normal. The doctors have said she will need a couple of months to recuperate."

His brother Mike, a father of six, who had suffered skin cancer two years earlier, commented, "Thank God for the wonders of modern science. Things have changed a lot since our Mum died. Thank goodness we've got the facilities to arrest this thing early on."

Oh No, Poor Yoko
LONDON, 1997

When Yoko Ono heard that diaries kept by John Lennon in his last five years had surfaced, her reaction was seriously uncool. She will be even more enraged to hear that a book based on them, by prolific pop chronicler Geoffrey Giuliano, will come out in the autumn.

Ono wanted to publish the diaries herself and suggested strongly to American publishers they should not take Giuliano's book. But the author circumvented this problem by getting up his own imprint, Indigo Editions.

His account should prove interesting reading. "By the time he died, Lennon's life revolved around drugs, television, and day dreams," Giuliano tells me. "It's left to people like me to sort out the facts from the myths when the publishing houses are too frightened."

Sounds groovy.

Yoko Says "Oh No" to John's Diaries
SHE'S TRYING TO STOP PUBLICATION OF SECRET ENTRIES
1998

John Lennon's widow Yoko Ono will do anything necessary to block the publication of her late husband's diaries, which she claims have recently been shopped around to a number of London publishers.

The diaries, written in five leather-bound *New Yorker* notebooks, tell the story of the rock star's last five years in New York, prior to his murder by obsessed fan Mark David Chapman in 1980.

Little is known about this period of Lennon's life because he lived as a recluse in the massive Dakota apartment building on Central Park West. Some biographers claim he was addicted to heroin and may have been insane during the period.

Ono says the diaries are so personal she will go to any lengths to keep them under wraps. "It is known the last entry was on the day he died," Ono said. "That was so personal and should be protected. I will take all measures to respect his privacy and name. I am getting advice from my lawyers and I will do my best for John."

Lennon's journals were stolen from the Dakota by the rock star's personal assistant, Fred Seaman, a few days after his death. Seaman was convicted of stealing the diaries in 1983 and received five years probation. He agreed in court never to reveal the contents of the diaries, but he subsequently wrote *The Last Days of John Lennon* and provided source material for Albert Goldman's warts-and-all biography of London in 1988.

After the theft, the diaries weren't returned to Ono for almost a year and she and her legal advisers believe that multiple copies were made and are now in the hands of Beatles' memorabilia collectors.

"All the dairies were returned, but that's not to say all the Xeroxed copies that were made at the time were returned," said Eliot Mintz, Ono's spokesman. "If there's just one copy out there it's very easy to clone it."

Since Beatles memorabilia is extremely valuable, Ono fears the temptation to cash in on what could be a multimillion-dollar book deal will lead to the publication of the diaries. Her worst fears were realized recently when London publishers told *The Mail On Sunday,* a London newspaper, that American writer, Geoffrey Giuliano, had approached them with a package that included photocopied excerpts from the diaries and some tapes of Lennon making audio journal entries.

Giuliano doesn't deny he's been talking to a number of British publishers about writing a new biography of Lennon, but says he knows nothing about the diaries. "My meetings in London have been misconstrued as an attempt to sell the diaries," he told *The Post.* "I have no ability, intention, or desire to be involved in any way in the publication of Mr. Lennon's diaries."

Mintz says there is nothing to prohibit Giuliano from writing a biography of Lennon, but added that, if they ever find he is using stolen property as source material, they will stop him.

Acknowledgments

Associate Researchers: Sesa Nichole Giuliano and Deborah Lynn Black
Intern: Devin Giuliano

The authors would like to thank the following people for their kindness in helping to realize this book: Stefano Castino, Avalon and India Giuliano, Devin Giuliano, Sesa Giuliano, Her Grace Nandini Devi Dasi, His Divine Grace A. C. Bhativedanta Swami Prabhupada, Kashi Nath Narayan Jones, Tyrone Jones, KRB Music, and SRI/The Spiritual Realization Institute of America.